The Acquisition and Retention of Knowledge: A Cognitive View

The Acquisition and Retention of Knowledge: A Cognitive View

by

David P. Ausubel
Distinguished Professor Emeritus,
Graduate School,
The City University of New York, U.S.A.

KLUWER ACADEMIC PUBLISHERS
DORDRECHT / BOSTON / LONDON

Library of Congress Cataloging-in-Publication Data

ISBN 0-7923-6505-4

Published by Kluwer Academic Publishers,
P.O. Box 17, 3300 AA Dordrecht, The Netherlands.

Sold and distributed in North, Central and South America
by Kluwer Academic Publishers,
101 Philip Drive, Norwell, MA 02061, U.S.A.

In all other countries, sold and distributed
by Kluwer Academic Publishers,
P.O. Box 322, 3300 AH Dordrecht, The Netherlands.

Printed on acid-free paper

Printed in the Netherlands.

To the memory of
George Richard Wendt
who first introduced me in 1938
to the intellectual excitement of
postulating explanatory mechanisms
for the psychological processes of human
learning and retention, which eventually
became assimilation theory.

Alphorism for Fly-Leaf

Knowledge is meaningful by definition. It is the meaningful product of a cognitive ("knowing") psychological process involving the interaction between "logically" (culturally) meaningful ideas, relevant background ("anchoring") ideas in the particular learner's cognitive structure (or structure of his knowledge), and his mental "set" to learn meaningfully or to acquire and retain knowledge.

The author

CONTENTS

PREFACE

In 1963 an initial attempt was made in my *The Psychology of Meaningful Verbal Learning* to present a *cognitive* theory of meaningful as opposed to rote verbal learning. It was based on the proposition that the acquisition and retention of knowledge (particularly of verbal knowledge as, for example, in school, or subject-matter learning) is the product of an active, integrative, interactional process between instructional material (subject matter) and relevant ideas in the learner's cognitive structure to which the new ideas are relatable in particular ways.

This book is a full-scale revision of my 1963 monograph, *The Psychology of Meaningful Verbal Learning,* in the sense that it addresses the major aforementioned and hitherto unmet goals by providing for an expansion, clarification, differentiation, and sharper focusing of the principal psychological variables and processes involved in meaningful learning and retention, i.e., for their interrelationships and interactions leading to the generation of new meanings in the individual learner. The preparation of this new monograph was largely necessitated by the virtual collapse of the neobehavioristic theoretical orientation to learning during the previous forty years; and by the meteoric rise in the seventies and beyond of constructivist approaches to learning theory.

It need not be thought, of course, that the acquisition and retention of knowledge are necessarily restricted to the formal instructional contexts of schools and universities, where designated teachers and pupils interact in stereotypical ways mostly for this purpose. Actually, the acquisition and retention of knowledge are pervasive and lifelong activities essential for the competent performance, efficient management, and improvement of daily work tasks.

The identical psychological processes underlying the formal acquisition and retention of knowledge can also take place informally through systematic and even unsystematic reading, educational television, intellectual conversational discourse, etc. Nevertheless it is undeniable that the greatest scope for the systematic use and improvement of meaningful reception learning and retention—for acquiring and retaining knowledge—lies in the formal instructional practices of elementary and secondary schools and of colleges and universities. Tulving (1972) refers to the latter more formal kind of memory as "semantic" and to the more informal, everyday, and transient kind as "episodic."

The reasons for this difference in the primary source of what is conventionally considered "knowledge" are fairly self-evident: *Semantic* memory is the ideational outcome of a meaningful (not rote) learning process as a result of which new *meaning(s)* emerge. These new meanings are the substantive products of the interaction between potential meanings in the instructional material and the relevant "anchoring" ideas in the learner's cognitive structure; eventually they become, sequentially and hierarchically, part of an organized system, related to other similar, topical organizations of ideas (knowledge) in cognitive structure. It is the eventual coalescence of many of these sub-systems that constitutes or gives rise to a subject-matter discipline or a field of knowledge.

Rote learnings, on the other hand, obviously do not add to the substance or fabric of knowledge inasmuch as their relation to existing knowledge in cognitive structure is arbitrary, non-substantive, verbatim, peripheral, and generally of transient duration, utility, and significance. Typically they (e.g., telephone numbers) have a limited, practical, and time- and energy-saving usefulness.

Characteristically, semantic memories tend to be both long-term and significant because they are typically intended by the learner to become part of an existing and growing body of knowledge, and also because the meaningful learning process itself is necessarily complex and, thus, requires an extended period of time for completion. They are also usually significant because utterly trivial or frivolous snippets of information would hardly be intentionally incorporated into existing serious bodies of knowledge. Although in this book the term *knowledge,* in accordance with traditional usage, will be reserved for significant, long-term, meaningfully learned, and organized (as opposed to isolated or randomly distributed) memories, it should be appreciated that the opposite characteristics may sometimes prevail under certain circumstances in one or all respects.

One possible but unlikely misinterpretation of this book's terminology, first appearing in the title itself, *The Acquisition and Retention of Knowledge,* and later throughout the text is the possible suggestion that the conventional dictionary definition of "acquisition" in a learning context implies a passive, sponge-like, mechanical, authoritarian, and uncritical ingestion of information, as an end in itself, rather than for the generation (production, construction) of viable (hierarchically-ordered and -organized subject matter) knowledge. However, in the context of this book, "acquisition" also has the more usual and *general* meaning (that also applies here) of "gaining possession" of new meanings (knowledge) that were not previously comprehended or were non-existent. That is, in this latter context, "acquisition" only basically implied the familiar educational furthering of the goal of "gaining possession" of new meanings as expeditiously as possible, without necessarily making any specification of whether this goal is to be accomplished by rote or by a meaningful or authoritarian, unintegrated, passive, mechanical, sponge-like learning process. However, from the context of my 1963 book, and what appears on almost every page of this current monograph, it seems very unlikely that any of the aforementioned, negative implications of the term "acquisition" for the *process* of learning, will not impress many readers as very credible. rather, they will probably regard assimilation theory as involving primarily one particular kind of interactional meaningful learning process, closely related to the major theses of the constructivist movement; and the term "acquisition" in the title as merely indicative of general concern with achieving and promoting the goal of enhancing meaningful learning in school and academic-like settings in assimilating subject matter. It will almost certainly not be justifiably related in any credible way to the dictionary definition of "acquisition" as a theory of meaningful learning.

One possible weakness of the so-called "constructivist" position is that the learner's generation of new meanings which he purportedly "constructs" from the interaction between presented and related potential meanings in the latter's cognitive structure. This view seems to oversimplify and ignore somewhat the constraints and negative influences exerted by illusory relevances, misconceptions, subjective biases, motivational orientation to learning, cognitive style, and personality traits that enter involuntarily into the "constructive process."

In conclusion it can be said that the title of this current book refers primarily to the overriding and familiar educational goal and expected end-product of a consistent program of meaningful learning and master of hierarchically organized bodies of knowledge. There is little or no justification for the gratuitous assumption that the title refers to an outworn process of rote instruction and learning based on passive, authoritarian, sponge-like, and mechanical approaches to the learning of subject matter.

Various cognitive structure variables (the availability, specificity, clarity, stability, and discriminability of these relevant ideas), reflective of what learners already know, and of how well they know it, were considered in the 1963 volume to be the principal cognitive variables influencing the acquisition and retention of subject-matter knowledge.

Additionally, for the sake of completeness, such other cognitive variables as practice, review, instructional materials, motivational factors, and developmental changes in cognitive capacity to handle verbal abstractions were also considered. Further, a brief critique of the indications for, and limitations of, discovery learning was offered, and the role and mechanisms of influence of motivational *vis-à-vis* cognitive variables were evaluated.

In the present revised edition, however, it was deemed more important to focus almost exclusively on the underlying Assimilation Theory, i.e., on processes and mediating mechanisms of meaningful reception learning and retention and on the cognitive and motivational-affective variables that impinge on them positively and negatively. Cognitive structure variables, as indicated earlier (for example, the availability in cognitive structure of relevant anchoring ideas, their stability, clarity, and discriminability from related internalized ideas and from ideas in the instructional materials) were originally regarded as the most important proximate factors influencing the meaningful learnability and the degree of learning and retention of new, potentially meaningful instructional materials; hence, since they still are still largely so considered, they necessarily occupy a central place in the content of this book.

The chapter on instructional materials, however, was deleted because of its overly specialized and technical nature.

The chapters on developmental, practice, and motivational factors were nevertheless retained, because of their saliency as determinants of meaningful reception learning and retention and, thus, because of their obvious importance for the acquisition and retention of subject-matter knowledge that is gained in classrooms and similar learning environments.

Also eliminated from the present book was the chapter on discovery learning which is no longer the "hot issue" that it was in 1963. In the interim many teachers and educators have become disillusioned in regard to its potentiality for single-handedly rescuing education from most of its perennial problems. Thus, in addition to the fact that discovery learning *per se* is not basic to the theory of meaningful learning and retention, a thoroughgoing critique of its theoretical rationale and underlying assumptions is no longer needed or relevant.

Although glowing research reports and theoretical articles on discovery learning continue to appear from time to time in the educational psychology and instructional research journals, the frequency of this occurrence has been steadily decreasing. In addition, the rationale for the exaggerated interactional claims of the discovery researchers have become increasingly less polemical, tending to limit themselves more to the laboratory aspects of empirical psychological science and to experimental demonstrations of scientific method. This approach also tends to attract educational "rebels" to its banners.

On the other hand, Dewey's Learning by Doing reform movement in instructional methodology is still very much alive, but its theoretical rationale has very little in common with that of discovery learning. Doing is obviously not the same as independent discovery or even as assisted discovery, in the learning process, rote or meaningful, and also depends variably on mechanical intelligence and manual dexterity.

A chapter on cognitive development and readiness, included in the 1963 edition, was also not retained in the present edition because that chapter does not deal directly (or even indirectly) with the processes and mechanisms of meaningful learning and retention. It is concerned rather with a parallel examination of changes in developmental cognitive capacity, i.e., changes that exert a profound influence both on meaningful learning and retention and on a student's readiness at a given age or level of cognitive maturity for learning particular subject-matter material. Developmental readiness is often confused by teachers and students with the kinds of readiness that reflect the possession of that particular antecedent knowledge and/or subject-matter sophistication that is necessary for learning new sequentially-dependent instructional material.

During the intervening years since the appearance of the 1963 edition, the burgeoning of theoretical and research interest in cognitive approaches to learning and retention, in newly evolved elaborations and modifications of the author's original theoretical views, and in the availability of complete textbooks of educational psychology considering all significant variables affecting meaningful learning (including discovery learning); in the unprecedented attempt by Novak to ascertain an individual's organization of his cognitive structure by using his (Novak's) original technique of "cognitive mapping"; and the use of Assimilation Theory by several national departments of education in Latin America, as the theoretical basis for reforming both the curriculum and prevailing teaching methods, have all indicated the advisability of preparing a revised version of the 1963 monograph that would focus principally on the basic theory of meaningful reception learning and retention itself, i.e., on Assimilation Theory, including the nature of meaning; the conditions and processes of meaningful reception learning and retention; on cognitive structure and the developmental variables that influence it; on the relationships between the acquisition of knowledge (new meanings), on the one hand, and their retention, transfer, and forgetting, as well as the nature of and differences between the various kinds of meanings comprising subject-matter knowledge.

An entirely new feature of the present edition is the inclusion of an extended preview of the basic theoretical aspects the book as a whole that comprises all of the first chapter. It is intended as a general introduction and orientation to the interweaving theoretical views expressed in this edition, particularly Assimilation Theory and its various applications. It should not, however, be regarded as an advance organizer for which didactic device there are very definite criteria that are delineated and discussed in later chapters.

The reader will, therefore, hopefully focus in this orienting first chapter on the various more general aspects of the conditions, categories, and underlying processes of meaningful learning and retention, how they differ from their rote counterparts, and how they interact with cognitive structure, practice, motivational, developmental, and readiness variables, *before* he becomes too deeply immersed in the detailed functional aspects of these complex psychological processes. Thus, by mastering (or at least becoming thoroughly familiar with) this basic but telescoped previous of the whole before grappling with all of its complex and sometimes confusable separate parts, it is hoped that he can at least avoid some of the common learning experience of inability to see the forest for the trees, and that the overarching explanatory ideas of this book will maintain their continuity and theoretical thrust throughout. It is strongly recommended, therefore, that the reader first peruse the entire preview (all of Chapter 1), as quickly as he can do so with adequate understanding, in order to obtain a general impression of the book's subject matter as a whole, of its major theoretical thrusts and approach, and of the relationships between the separate parts of Assimilation Theory, both to each other and to the latter central theory itself. Then, before carefully and seriously reading each of the special chapters, it would probably be helpful if he read the corresponding abbreviated preview section in Chapter 1.

The promise of the cognitive approach to school (subject-matter) learning and to the acquisition, retention, and organization of knowledge in the learner's cognitive structure has been amply fulfilled since the publication of *The Psychology of Meaningful Verbal Learning* in 1963. Literally hundreds of research studies and dissertations on such related variables as advance organizers, integrative reconciliation, progressive differentiation, sequential organization of subject matter, review, overlearning, and the consolidation of learning, etc. have been conducted in a meaningful learning context (i.e., using potentially meaningful verbal learning material). What still remains to be done research-wise and educationally is (1) more long-term research on the acquisition and retention of entire courses of study and of sequentially-graded curricula over different age levels of students; and (2) the application of such findings to the curriculum and to instructional practices and materials. Some of the latter research is already under way in such countries as Mexico, Brazil, Venezuela, and The Netherlands.

It is now apparent to most students of the higher mental processes and of educational psychology that cognitive approaches (recognizing the role of the student's existing cognitive structure in acquiring, retaining, organizing, and transferring new meanings) are now being applied to such areas in school learning as mastery learning, concept acquisition, problem solving, creativity, thinking, and judgment. The rapid decline of neobehaviorism, first abroad (where it never took serious root in the first place) and somewhat later in the United States, where it first originated, is now an established fact of life both in American experimental psychology and in educational psychology. It has been accompanied by a corresponding diminution in the number of rote learning research studies and dissertations in school learning and related areas and in the virtual disappearance of teaching machines and operant reinforcement approaches to classroom teaching.

Another parallel trend alluded to earlier, reflecting the new interest in meaningful reception learning through appropriate expository teaching and instructional materials, has been the decline in "learning by discovery" approaches, "process learning," "inquiry learning," etc.

This latter trend has been accompanied by an upsurge of interest in epistemological factors in learning. For it is now generally appreciated that what is really knowable depends just as much on the nature, extensity, and limitations of human cognitive processes and capacities, and on their development over the life span, as on the objective nature of what humans seek to know, on its knowability, and on the methodology of acquiring such knowledge (epistemology, scientific method). Accordingly, in this book some consideration in a general sense is also given to (1) the relationship between bodies of knowledge, as represented by scholarly consensuses in a given discipline (e.g., textbooks, monographs, research studies) and how such knowledge is represented and organized in the cognitive structures of particular scholars and students, and (2) how this relationship changes as a function of intellectual maturity (age-level changes in information processing), and subject-matter sophistication.

The observant and discerning reader with a good memory may possibly be somewhat surprised by the degree of redundancy he encounters in this book. This redundancy, however, is more intentional than it is accidental. It largely reflects the author's strongly intuitive but empirically unconfirmed belief that the substance of a given idea is maximally strengthened in memory if it is discussed in whatever contexts for which it is relevant rather than receiving consideration only the first time and in the first place in which it appears in the text. Multi-contextual repetition of an idea, in other words, hypothetically consolidates it more in memory than does multiple repetitions within the same context. Multi-contextual redundancy is embraced so vigorously and unequivocally in this monograph partly because of Hull's* highly convincing experimental findings on concept formation and partly because American textbooks and university lecturers seem to avoid redundancy of any kind completely, and seemingly so compulsively, as if not doing so represented the violation of a sacred point of honor with them.

Redundancy is perhaps the earliest pedagogical and psychological device that teachers have used to facilitate meaningful (as well as rote) verbal learning. The rationale for this practice was simple but effective: Randomly- or even naturally- and meaningfully-arranged identical sequences are typically seldom repeated often enough, in uncontrived situations, and in close enough proximity, for students to appreciate that their components were related to each other in a particular way, and scored as "right" and "wrong" by the teacher. In time this device, known as "drill," although frequently derogated as rote an mechanical (mindless), became a standard and accepted instructional technique and part of every teacher's pedagogic armamentarium for enhancing learning.

The pedagogic practice of drill, however, came into general disrepute among many educators when "learning by doing" and discovery approaches were popularized. This early multi-contextual variant of simple redundancy, namely "drill," not only enhances learning the target task as a result of the learner's exposure to the multi-contextual trials, but also simultaneously differentiates this learning task from other similar and competing concept formation tasks.

Some readers might also be somewhat surprised by the preponderance of older references cited in the text of this monograph. This fact, however, reflects the much greater influence on the development and content of Assimilation Theory of such historical and current movements in psychology as Structuralism, Functionalism, Gestalt Psychology, and certain aspects of Schema Theory (Bartlett) and Cognitive Psychology, than of such other opposing psychological movements as Neobehaviorism, Information Processing, Cybernetics, Computer Models, and Associative and Semantic Network formulations.

The latter theoretical trends also dealt more in practice with rote rather than with the meaningful aspects of learning and retention and were generally more recent in origin than the former theories. It was considered, both historically and substantively, more abundantly relevant, therefore, to cite the theoretical ideas and research evidence of the former ideational movements because of their much closer theoretical relationship to meaningful reception learning and retention. It was regarded as more relevant and helpful to the historically-interested reader to possibly implement this above-described policy of citing references than to generate a spurious impression of up-to-dateness by citing many more recent and current references that actually have much less bearing on Assimilation Theory.

---

* Hull, C. L. *Principles of Behavior.* New York: Appleton-Century, 1943.

A note of caution is indicated in tracing and qualifying historically the theoretical trends delineated above. Much of the recent shift from neobehavioristic to cognitive approaches, both in experimental and educational psychology and in learning theory, is more apparent than real. A good deal of what passes these days as cognitive theory really deals more with perceptual phenomena, or is either neobehavioristic doctrine clothed in cognitive terminology or pseudocognitive theory couched in terms of underlying mechanistic (neobehavioristic) assumptions. The ineluctable American penchant for empiricism as an end in itself and for reductionistic, mechanistic, neurophysiological, and behavioristic approaches to psychological theory is much too strongly rooted in American academic psychology for neobehaviorism quietly to leave the field completely without first embracing some such transitionally reductionistic philosophy of science. It does this easily while rejecting truly cognitive versions of meaningful learning and retention processes for the acquisition and retention of knowledge.

I am indebted to Susan Davison for careful and accurate typing of the manuscript and preparation of the camera-ready copy of this book, and to my wife, Gloria, for imaginative coordination of its several parts and sources.

David P. Ausubel, M.D., Ph.D.
Port Ewen, N.Y.
January, 1999

CHAPTER 1

PREVIEW OF ASSIMILATION THEORY OF MEANINGFUL LEARNING AND RETENTION

MEANING AND MEANINGFUL LEARNING AND RETENTION

Meaningful reception learning primarily involves the acquisition of new meanings from presented learning material. It requires both a meaningful learning set and the presentation of *potentially* meaningful material to the learner. The latter condition, in turn, presupposes (1) that the learning material itself can be *nonarbitrarily* (plausibly, sensibly, and nonrandomly) and *nonverbatimly* related to *any* appropriate and relevant cognitive structure (i.e., possesses *"logical"* meaning) and (2) that the *particular* learner's cognitive structure contains relevant *anchoring* ideas to which the new material can be related. The interaction between potentially new meanings and relevant ideas in the learner's cognitive structure gives rise to actual or psychological meanings. Because each learner's cognitive structure is unique, all acquired new meanings are perforce themselves unique.

Meaningful learning is not synonymous with the learning of meaningful material. First, the learning material is only *potentially* meaningful. Second, a meaningful learning set must be present. Learning material may consist of already meaningful components (such as paired adjectives), but each component of the learning task as well as the learning task as a whole (learning a list of arbitrarily linked words) is not "logically" meaningful. And even logically meaningful material may be learned by rote if the learner's learning set is not meaningful.

Three kinds of meaningful reception learning may be distinguished:

KINDS OF MEANINGFUL RECEPTION LEARNING

Representational learning (such as naming) is closest to rote learning. It occurs when arbitrary symbols are equated in meaning with their referents (objects, events, concepts) and signify to the learner whatever meaning their referents do. Representational learning is meaningful because such propositions of representational equivalence can be nonarbitrarily related as exemplars to a generalization present in almost everyone's cognitive structure since about the first year of life—that everything has a name and that the name signifies whatever its referent means to the particular learner.

Concepts Defined and Kinds of Concept Learning

Concepts may be defined as objects, events, situations, or properties that possess common criterial attributes and are designated by the same sign or symbol. There are two general methods of concept learning: (1) concept formation, which takes place primarily in young children; and (2) concept assimilation, which is the dominant form of concept learning in school children and adults. In concept formation the criterial attributes of the concept are acquired through direct experience, i.e., through successive stages of hypothesis generation, testing and generalization. As a child's vocabulary increases, however, new concepts are acquired mostly through the process of concept assimilation since the criterial attributes of new concepts can be defined by use in new combinations of existing referents available in the child's cognitive structure.

Concepts constitute an important aspect of assimilation theory because comprehension and meaningful problem solving largely depend on the availability in the learner's cognitive structure of both superordinate concepts (in subsumptive concept acquisition) and subordinate concepts (in superordinate concept acquisition). It is also self-evident: (1) that human beings interpret "raw" perceptual experience in terms of particular concepts in their cognitive structures and (2) that concepts constitute the building blocks both for the meaningful reception learning of declarative propositions and for the generation of meaningful problem-solving propositions.

Concepts themselves consist of the abstracted criterial attributes that are common to a given category of objects, events, or phenomena, despite diversity along dimensions other than those characterizing the criterial attributes shared by all members of the category.

Concept Names

Because concepts have names, just like particular objects or events, named concepts can be manipulated, understood, and transferred more readily than unnamed concepts. These concept names are acquired through meaningful representational learning after concept meanings themselves are acquired. This latter process depends, of course, on the existence of a meaningful learning set and on relating the concept's potentially meaningful criterial attributes to relevant ideas in the learner's cognitive structure in a nonarbitrary, substantive fashion.

Meaningful Learning of Propositions

The meaningful learning of verbal propositions, though somewhat more complex than learning the meanings of words, is similar to representational learning in that new meanings emerge after a potentially meaningful learning task is related to, and interacts with, relevant ideas in cognitive structure. In this case, however, the learning task, or potentially meaningful proposition, consists of a composite idea that is expressed verbally in a sentence containing both denotative and connotative word meanings, and the syntactic functions of and relations between words. The differentiated cognitive content resulting from the meaningful learning process, and constituting its meaning, is an interactional product of the *particular* way in which the content of the new proposition is related to the content of relevant established ideas in cognitive structure. The relationship in question may be either subordinate, superordinate, or a combination of the two.

Types of Propositional Learning

Propositional learning can be either subordinate (subsumptive), superordinate, or combinatorial. Subsumptive learning occurs when a "logically" meaningful proposition in a particular discipline (plausible, but not necessarily logically or empirically valid in the philosophical sense) is related meaningfully to specific superordinate propositions in the pupil's cognitive structure. Such learning may be called derivative if the learning material simply exemplifies or supports an idea already existing in cognitive structure. It is called correlative if it is an extension, elaboration, modification, or qualification of previously learned propositions.

Superordinate propositional learning occurs when a new proposition is relatable either to specific subordinate ideas in existing cognitive structure or to a broad background of generally relevant ideas in cognitive structure that can be subsumed under it. Finally, combinational propositional learning refers to instances where a potentially meaningful proposition cannot be related to specific superordinate or subordinate ideas in the learner's cognitive structure but is relatable to a combination of generally relevant, as well as less relevant, content in such structure. Most propositional learning is obviously subsumptive or combinatorial.

It is important to recognize that meaningful learning does not imply that new information forms a kind of simple bond with preexisting elements of cognitive structure. On the contrary, only in rote learning does a simple arbitrary and nonsubstantive linkage occur with preexisting cognitive structure. In meaningful learning the very process of acquiring information results in a modification of both the newly acquired information and of the specifically relevant aspect of cognitive structure to which the new information is linked. In most instances new information is linked to a specific relevant concept or proposition. As a matter of convenience, we will refer to concepts or propositions as relevant *ideas* in cognitive structure. In order to indicate that meaningful learning involves a selective interaction between new learning material and preexisting ideas in cognitive structure, we will employ the term *anchorage* to suggest linkage over time to the preexisting ideas. For example, in subsumption, preexisting superordinate ideas provide anchorage for the meaningful learning of new information.

ROTE VERSUS MEANINGFUL LEARNING PROCESSES

Rote learning tasks, of course, are not mastered in a cognitive vacuum. They *are* relatable to cognitive structure but *only* in an arbitrary, verbatim fashion that does not result in the acquisition of any meanings. Since, for example, the particular stimulus and response members of a given pair of adjectives in paired-associate learning are linked together in purely arbitrary fashion, there is no possible basis for nonarbitrarily relating the learning task to anyone's cognitive structure, and the learner must also remember verbatim the response to each stimulus word (he cannot use synonyms).

This arbitrary and verbatim relatability of rote learning tasks to cognitive structure does, of course, have certain significant consequences for learning. First, since human cognitive equipment, unlike a computer, cannot handle information very efficiently that is related to it on an arbitrary and verbatim basis, only relatively short learning tasks can be internalized in this fashion, and these can be retained for only short periods of time unless greatly overlearned. Second, their arbitrary and verbatim relatability to cognitive structure makes rote learning tasks highly vulnerable to interference from previously learned and concurrently or retroactively encountered similar materials. As we shall see later, it is this basically different kind of relatability to cognitive structure (arbitrary and verbatim versus nonarbitrary and nonverbatim) that accounts for the fundamental difference between rote and meaningful learning processes.

Rote learning and forgetting, additionally, depend on the acquisition of discrete associative strength and its diminution through exposure to prior and/or subsequent interference by similar but confusable discrete elements already in storage or acquired subsequently (proactive and retroactive interference). Meaningful learning and forgetting, on the other hand, depend, first, on relating new, potentially meaningful material to relevant ideas in the learner's cognitive structure and, second, (in the absence of overlearning) on subsequent spontaneous and gradual loss of the dissociability of the new meanings, acquired through such interaction, from their anchoring ideas (obliterative subsumption). In both rote and meaningful learning the actual reproduction of retained material is also affected by such factors as cultural or attitudinal bias and by the specific situational demands of the reproduction setting itself. These differences between rote and meaningful learning processes account in large measure for the superiority of meaningful as opposed to rote learning and retention.

Reception versus Discovery Learning

Propositional learning, as described earlier, is typical of the situation prevailing in reception learning, when substantive propositions are *presented* to the learner, who is then required only to learn and remember their meaning. It is important to realize, however, that propositional learning is also a major type of verbal problem solving or discovery learning. The main difference between propositional learning as found in reception learning situations, on the one hand, and in discovery learning situations, on the other, inheres in whether the principal content of what is to be learned is discovered by, or is presented to, the learner. In reception learning this content is presented in the form of a substantive or non-problem-setting proposition that the learner need only understand and remember. In discovery learning, on the other hand, the learner must *first* discover this content by generating propositions that represent either solutions to the problems that are set or successive steps in their solution.

Actually, the reception and discovery varieties of propositional learning are involved successively at different stages in the problem-solving process.

Despite sharp differences between them, meaningful and rote learning are obviously not dichotomous in many practical learning situations and can easily be placed on a rote-meaningful continuum. Representational learning (e.g., learning concept names), for example, is much closer to the rote end of the continuum than either concept or propositional learning since its process embodies significant elements of arbitrary and verbatim relatedness to its referent in cognitive structure. It also happens sometimes that rote and meaningful learning follow each other successively in relation to the same learning material, as, for example, in the case of an actor who must first learn his lines meaningfully by himself and then memorize them verbatim for stage purposes.

Role of Language in Meaningful Learning

Language is an important facilitator of meaningful reception and discovery learning. By increasing the manipulability of concepts and propositions through the representational properties of words, and by refining emerging subverbal understandings in meaningful reception and discovery learning, it both clarifies such meanings and makes them more precise and transferable. Contrary to Piaget's position, language, therefore, plays an integral and operative (process) role in thinking rather than merely a communicative role. Without language meaningful learning would probably be only very rudimentary (e.g., as in animals).

MEANINGFUL LEARNING IS ACTIVE

Contrary also to beliefs expressed in many educational quarters, verbal reception learning need not necessarily be rote or passive (as it so often is in actual educational practice), provided that one uses expository teaching methods that are based on the nature, conditions, and developmental considerations characterizing meaningful reception learning. And, as we shall demonstrate in later chapters, discovery learning can also be, and in most classrooms typically is, rote in nature because it does not conform to the conditions of meaningful learning.

Meaningful reception learning is inherently an active process because it requires, at the very least (1) the kind of cognitive analysis necessary for ascertaining which aspects of existing cognitive structure are most relevant to the new potentially meaningful material; (2) some degree of reconciliation with existing ideas in cognitive structure—that is, apprehending similarities and differences, and resolving real or apparent contradictions, between new and already established concepts and propositions; and (3) reformulation of the learning material in terms of the idiosyncratic intellectual background and vocabulary of the particular learner.

The nature and conditions of active meaningful reception learning also demand a type of expository teaching that recognizes the principles of progressive differentiation and integrative reconciliation in instructional materials and also characterizes the learning, retention, and organization of subject-matter content in the learner's cognitive structure. The first principle acknowledges that most learning, and all retention and organization, of subject matter is hierarchical in nature, proceeding from the top downwards in terms of level of abstraction, generality, and inclusiveness. Integrative reconciliation is facilitated in expository teaching if the teacher and/or instructional materials explicitly anticipate and counteract the confusable similarities and differences between new ideas and established relevant existing ideas already present in learners' cognitive structures.

MEANINGFUL LEARNING IS MOSTLY RECEPTION LEARNING

We have already indicated that the acquisition of subject-matter knowledge in any culture is primarily a manifestation of reception learning. That is, the principal content of what is to be learned is typically presented to the learner in more or less final form through expository teaching. Under these circumstances the learner is simply required to comprehend the material and to incorporate it into his cognitive structure so that it is available for either reproduction, related learning, or problem solving at some future date.

Yet few pedagogic devices in our time have been repudiated more unequivocally by educational theorists than the method of expository verbal instruction. It is fashionable in many quarters to characterize verbal learning as parrot-like recitation and rote memorization of isolated facts and to dismiss it disdainfully as an archaic remnant of discredited educational tradition. Over the past five decades, activity programs, project methods, various ways of maximizing nonverbal experience in the classroom, emphasis on "self-discovery" and on learning for and by *problem-solving,* were introduced largely in response to widespread dissatisfaction with techniques of verbal instruction. Quite apart from whatever their intrinsic value is, these activities came into being primarily because of the general inadequacies of verbal instruction as practiced in schools. It has been commonly accepted, for example (at least in the realm of educational theory) that: (1) meaningful generalizations cannot be presented or "given" to the learner but can be acquired only as a product of problem-solving activity; and (2) all attempts to master verbal concepts and propositions are forms of empty verbalism unless the learner has recent prior experience with the concrete realities to which these verbal constructs refer.

INADEQUACIES OF EXPOSITORY TEACHING

Adequate reasons, of course, exist for some of the existing disenchantment with expository teaching and reception learning. The most obvious of these is that potentially meaningful subject matter is frequently presented to pupils in such as way that they can only learn it *rotely*. Another less obvious but equally important reason why meaning is perceived as an exclusive product of problem-solving and discovery techniques of learning stems from two serious shortcomings of prevailing learning theory. First, psychologists have tended to subsume many qualitatively different kinds of learning processes under a single explanatory model. As a result, widespread confusion exists regarding basic distinctions between reception and discovery learning and between rote and meaningful learning. It has not always been sufficiently clear, for example, that such basically different types of learning as problem solving and the understanding of presented verbal material have different objectives. Moreover, conditions and instructional techniques facilitating one of these learning processes are not necessarily relevant or maximally efficient for the other. Second, in the absence of an appropriate theory of meaningful verbal learning, many educational psychologists have tended to interpret long-term subject-matter learning and forgetting in terms of the same concepts (stimulus generalization, retroactive interference, and so on) used to explain laboratory forms of rote learning. It is hardly surprising, therefore, that reception learning has been widely perceived as a rote phenomenon.

Some of the more flagrantly inept and ill-conceived expository teaching-reception learning programs in the schools have resulted not surprisingly in unequivocal failure of pupil learning efforts, with consequent rejection of these practices by many teachers in favor of the newer discovery approaches. This outcome led in turn to the widely accepted view in educational circles that the expository-teaching reception-learning approach fosters the learning of empty verbalisms (instead of generalizations) devoid of all meaning and understanding. Characteristic of some of these unsuccessful expository practices were the following:

1. Premature use of pure verbal techniques with cognitively immature pupils.
2. Arbitrary presentation of unrelated facts without any organizing or explanatory principles.
3. Failure to integrate new learning tasks with previously presented materials.
4. The use of evaluation procedures that merely measure ability to recognize discrete facts or to reproduce ideas in the same words or in the identical context as originally encountered.

MEANINGFUL RETENTION AND FORGETTING

Assimilation Process in Meaningful Learning and Retention

Meaningful learning constitutes only the first phase of a larger and more inclusive assimilation process that also consists of its natural and inevitable sequential phase of retention and forgetting. Assimilation Theory explains how in the learning phase new potentially meaningful ideas in the instructional material are selectively related to relevant and also more general and inclusive (as well as more stable) existing (anchoring) ideas in cognitive structure. These latter new ideas interact with the relevant anchoring ideas; and the main product of this interaction becomes the meaning to the learner of the newly introduced instructional ideas. These emergent new meanings are then stored (linked) and organized in the retention (memory) interval with their corresponding anchoring ideas.

Assimilative Processes in Meaningful Learning

The assimilative processes in the meaningful learning phase, therefore, include: (1) selective anchorage of the learning material to relevant existing ideas in cognitive structure; (2) interaction between the newly introduced ideas and existing (anchoring) relevant ideas, with the meaning of the former emerging as the product of this interaction; and (3) linking in the memory (retention) interval of the emergent new meanings with their corresponding anchoring ideas. These new meanings naturally share in the increased stability and associated increased dissociability strength that follow from their linkage to their more stable anchoring ideas. In the interactional process, the anchoring ideas themselves are also obviously modified to a variable extent both by the new instructional ideas with which they interact, and later by the emergent new meanings to which they are linked in memory storage. This linkage and storage of the newly-learned ideas with the more stable anchoring ideas could, of course, also be considered part of the retention process once the linkage is established.

The natural history of meaningful learning self-evidently doesn't end with the acquisition of new meanings. Learning must always be succeeded by retention and/or forgetting which are its natural outcomes and sequelae. Whatever is learned must either be retained or forgotten. The assimilation process in retention-forgetting is admittedly somewhat different than in meaningful learning, but is comparable to it both in its overt psychological manifestations as well as in its underlying psychological mechanisms.

Assimilation Process in Retention and Forgetting

During the retention interval, newly emergent meanings are stored (linked) in relation to their corresponding anchoring ideas. However, only for a certain limited period of time (unless overlearned by repetition or rehearsal) are they dissociable and reproducible from their anchoring ideas as separately identifiable entities in their own right. When their dissociability strength falls below a certain critical point (the threshold of availability), forgetting or gradual reduction to the anchoring ideas in question (obliterative subsumption) occurs. Cognitive structure factors (variables) that enhance or detract from the initial acquisition of new meanings (i.e., availability of relevant subsumers; their stability, clarity, and discriminability) continue to operate during the retention period in which psychologically active assimilative processes are functional despite the lack of conscious awareness of same. This is the second or retention-forgetting phase of the assimilative processes (in the broad sense of the term), that are involved in, and that underlie, meaningful learning and retention. It matches in continuity of process the correspondingly overt cognitive acts of meaningful learning and retention.

Additionally, however, the dissociability strength of newly acquired meanings is generally decreased by assimilative processes over the course of time and is finally reduced to zero dissociability from those anchoring ideas themselves to which they had been linked. This is the case because it is much less burdensome to remember only an unelaborated general, or unqualified idea than one which is explicitly and specifically elaborated in these latter respects.

What is common to both phases—the meaningful learning and the retention-forgetting—that indicates the operation of assimilative processes is that stable and established ideas in cognitive structure selectively (by virtue of their relevance) interact with (assimilate) new ideas in the instructional material to produce the new meanings that constitute the goal of the learning process. The new meanings are then stabilized by linkage (storage) to these same stable anchoring ideas. They manifest maximum dissociability when first linked to the latter ideas, but gradually exhibit decreasing dissociability over the course of time thereafter for reasons of reducing cognitive strain generated by their particularity, qualifications, and elaborations. These processes are patently similar and assimilative in both cases because existing and established ideas in cognitive structure (established states of knowledge in the learner in particular disciplines) play a determinative process role in the acquisition and retention of new knowledge.

Cognitive variables, on the one hand, and motivational-personality-social variables, on the other, affect meaningful learning and retention through different mechanisms. Forgetting can also be influenced by certain factors (such as initial "learning shock," "repression," the elicitation of reproduction through recall versus recognition and hypnosis) that influence the threshold of availability without altering whatsoever the dissociability strength of the meanings in question.

COGNITIVE STRUCTURE FACTORS (VARIABLES) AND TRANSFER

Having considered the nature of meaning and meaningful learning, as well as the nature of reception learning and retention, we are now in a position to consider certain facilitating cognitive factors in classroom learning. Among these factors, the properties of the existing structure of knowledge at the time of learning (cognitive structure variables) are, perhaps, the most important consideration. Since this involves, by definition, the impact of all prior relevant learning experience on current learning processes, it is coextensive with the problem of transfer.

We have already hypothesized that all past learning experience influences, or has positive or negative effects, on new meaningful learning and retention by virtue of its impact on relevant properties of cognitive structure. If this is true, all meaningful learning necessarily also involves transfer. It is virtually impossible to conceive of any instance of such learning that is not affected in some way by existing cognitive structure. This current learning experience, in turn, results in new transfer by modifying cognitive structure. In meaningful learning, therefore, cognitive structure is always a relevant and crucial variable, even if it is not deliberately influenced or manipulated so as to ascertain its effect on *new* learning.

It follows, from the very nature of increments to the psychological structure of knowledge through the assimilation process, that existing cognitive structure itself—both the substantive content of an individual's structure of knowledge and its major organizational properties in a particular subject-matter field at any given time—is the principal factor influencing meaningful learning and retention in the same field. Logically meaningful material (subject-matter content in the context of school learning) is always, and can only be, learned in relation to a previously learned background of relevant concepts and principles in a particular learner, and also of pertinent information that makes possible the emergence of new meanings and enhances their organization and retention. It is evident, therefore, that the substantive and organizational properties of this background crucially affect both the precision and the clarity of these emerging new meanings and their immediate and long-term retrievability.

If cognitive structure is clear, stable, and suitably organized, precise and unambiguous meanings emerge and tend to retain their dissociability strength or availability. If, on the other hand, cognitive structure is unstable, ambiguous, disorganized, or chaotically organized, it tends to inhibit meaningful learning and retention. Thus, it is largely by strengthening relevant aspects of cognitive structure that new learning and retention can be facilitated.

It is, therefore, a commonplace that the details of a given discipline are learned as rapidly as they can be fitted into a contextual framework consisting of a stable and appropriate body of general concepts and principles. When we deliberately attempt to influence cognitive structure so as to maximize meaningful learning and retention as well as transfer, we come to the heart of the educational process.

In conclusion, therefore, in any given discipline, the cognitive structure of the learner can be influenced (1) substantively, by the inclusiveness, explanatory power, and integrative properties of the particular unifying concepts and principles presented to the learner; and (2) programmatically, by appropriate methods of presenting, arranging, and testing for the meaningful acquisition of subject matter, by using adequately programmed and pretested instructional material, and by suitably manipulating both the cognitive and motivational-personality-social variables.

COGNITIVE STRUCTURE VARIABLES

The most important cognitive structure variables considered in this book are (1) the availability in the learner's cognitive structure of specifically relevant anchoring ideas at an optimal level of inclusiveness, generality, and abstraction; (2) the extent to which such ideas are discriminable from both similar and different (but potentially confusable) concepts and principles in the learning material; and (3) the stability and clarity of the anchoring ideas.

Stability and clarity of the relevant anchoring ideas are largely determined by whether they were overlearned or consolidated by repetition and/or rehearsal both in the same and in different contexts. These cognitive structure factors are also important for their significant effect on the discriminability of similarities and differences between the new and the anchoring ideas. Stability and clarity are additionally influenced positively if the learner first masters the instructional material within a homogeneous context before turning to more heterogeneous settings and if sequentially and hierarchically organized learning materials are used. The above principles are obviously consistent with those of "mastery learning."

ADVANCE ORGANIZERS

Structure, Function, and Rationale for Use

An advance organizer is a pedagogic device that helps implement these principles by bridging the gap between what the learner already knows and what he needs to know if he is to learn new material most actively and expeditiously. The proximate situation that makes an advance organizer both desirable and potentially effective in bridging this gap is the fact that in most meaningful learning contexts, the existing relevant ideas in cognitive structure are much too general and lack sufficient particularity of relevance and content to serve as efficient anchoring ideas for the new ideas introduced by the instructional material in question. The advance organizer remedies this difficulty by playing a mediating role, i.e., by being more relatable to, and relevant for, the *particular* content of the specific learning task, on the one hand, and by additionally being relatable to the more *general* content of the potential anchoring ideas, on the other. It also facilitates learning by modifying the latter ideas in the direction of the particular content of the learning passage (as a result of the learner studying it in advance of studying the learning passage).

In order to function effectively for a variety of learners, each with a somewhat idiosyncratic cognitive structure, and to furnish or modify anchoring ideas at a superordinate level, *organizers are presented at a higher level of abstraction, generality, and inclusiveness than the new material to be learned.* Summaries and overviews, on the other hand, are ordinarily presented at the same level of abstraction, generality, and inclusiveness as the learning material itself. They simply emphasize the salient points of the material by omitting less important information. Thus, they largely achieve their effect by repetition and simplification.

The rationale for using organizers, therefore, is based primarily on:

1. The importance of having relevant and otherwise appropriate established ideas *already* available in cognitive structure to make *logically* meaningful new ideas *potentially* meaningful and *potentially* meaningful new ideas *actually* meaningful (i.e., yielding new meanings), as well as to give them stable anchorage.
2. The advantages of using the more general and inclusive ideas of a discipline in cognitive structure as the anchoring ideas or subsumers, suitably modified for the greater particularity of their relevance for the instructional material. Because of the greater aptness and specificity of their relevance, they also enjoy greater inherent stability, explanatory power, and integrative capacity.

3. The fact that the organizers themselves attempt both to identify already existing relevant content in cognitive structure (and to be explicitly related to it) and to indicate explicitly both the relevance of the existing content and of their own relevance for the new learning material.

Thus, an advance organizer is introduced to the learner prior to confronting him with the learning material itself. It primarily enhances the positive effects of the three cognitive structure variables considered above. Not only must it be more general, inclusive, and abstract than the ideas in the learning passage that it precedes, but it must also take into account potentially relevant existing ideas in the learner's cognitive structure (so that it itself is both learnable and can also explicitly mobilize all relevant content already available in that structure).

Equivocal findings on the effects of advance organizers largely reflect the failure both to adhere to these operationally stated criteria and to devise satisfactory methodological procedures for controlling other relevant variables. Where discriminability between anchoring ideas and new ideas in the instructional material is a serious problem, a *comparative* organizer that explicitly clarifies similarities and differences between the two sets of ideas can be used. Where this is not a special problem, an expository organizer usually suffices.

COGNITIVE DEVELOPMENT AND READINESS

The ability of the learner to process potentially meaningful ideas is obviously, in part, a function of his general developmental level of intellectual functioning or capacity. This developmental readiness or functional capacity naturally increases with age and experience (including school learning) and must be distinguished from the more specific subject-matter readiness considered above. The latter readiness refers to the availability in cognitive structure of specific subject-matter ideas or sophistication that are essential for the comprehension and manipulation of related new ideas in the same area or subarea.

Thus, in contradistinction to cognitive structure variables, cognitive readiness, in the developmental sense of the term, is not determined by the existing *state* of the learner's subject-matter knowledge in a given field, but rather by his *cognitive maturity* or the qualitative *level of intellectual functioning* required for undertaking the learning task at hand with a reasonable degree of effort and probability of success. This degree of developmental readiness obviously fails to occur in the absence of appropriate intellectual stimulation from the environment (e.g., from home or school).

STAGES OF COGNITIVE MATURITY AND READINESS FOR LEARNING

There is little disagreement about the fact that developmental readiness in cognition always crucially influences the efficacy of the learning process. Moreover, it often determines whether a given intellectual skill or type of school material is learnable at all at a particular stage of development. Most educators also implicitly accept the proposition that an age of readiness exists for every kind of learning. Postponement of learning experience beyond the age of readiness wastes valuable and often unsuspected learning opportunities, thereby unnecessarily reducing the amount and complexity of subject-matter content that can be mastered in a designated period of schooling. On the other hand, when a pupil is prematurely exposed to a learning task before he is adequately ready for it, he not only fails to learn the task in question (or learns it with undue difficulty), but also learns from this experience to fear, dislike, and avoid the task.

A given stage of cognitive maturity may be defined as qualitatively (discontinuously) different from adjacent stages. It typically occurs gradually at a certain critical point in continuous quantitative change. The sequence of stages is invariable; but the particular age at which a given stage appears within or between different cultures (and school systems), and in different subject-matter areas, varies depending on cultural, subcultural, and idiosyncratic experience (as well as on such factors as IQ and differential aptitude). Thus, in certain cultures or subcultures, and in retarded (or even in many intellectually normal) children, the most advanced stage may fail to emerge at all.

Concrete-Abstract Dimension

The most important dimension along which cognitive development proceeds in qualitatively discontinuous stages is the concrete-abstract dimension. The preschool child in our culture is generally unable to understand concepts unless he or she can spontaneously relate their abstracted criterial attributes to multiple specific but diverse examples of the concept *before* relating these same attributes to relevant ideas in his or her cognitive structure. Similarly, the preschool child is unable to understand relationships between propositional higher-order abstractions in the absence of particular examples of the concepts involved. The elementary-school child, on the other hand, is typically capable of understanding the meaning of a concept by directly relating its presented criterial attributes to cognitive structure, provided he or she is furnished with concrete empirical examples of these attributes. In most Western cultures and subcultures, however, beginning with the junior-high-school period, the learner can understand and manipulate abstract ideas (concepts and propositions) and the relationships between them directly, that is, without the benefit of any concrete-empirical props.

Although one may, thus, designate overall stages of cognitive maturity along the concrete-abstract dimension, it must be realized that in any particular learner the above maturational sequence in cognitive development largely occurs separately in each discipline. Hence, the older learner (high school or college) must undergo all three stages when first confronted with a new discipline. However, the factors that are responsible for maturational progress (the existence of a large body or "critical mass" of stable abstractions in cognitive structure and of sufficient transactional terms for relating them to each other, as well as considerable experience in comprehending and manipulating abstract ideas without the benefit of concrete props in other disciplines) are transferable to the new discipline. These factors, therefore, accelerate the transition from concrete to abstract comprehension and thought in the new subject-matter area. Thus, bearing the determinants of cognitive development in mind, it is possible, within limits, by providing appropriately constructed school experience shortly before the end of each stage, to accelerate the appearance of the next stage in the sequence.

Age-Level Changes in Cognitive Capacity

Hence, in appraising cognitive readiness, we would also consider all relevant age-level changes in ability to cope with different kinds and levels of subject matter that are reflective of growth in cognitive capacity or mode of cognitive functioning. Besides level of abstraction, there are several other examples of such changes in cognitive capacity that influence learning, retention, and thinking processes, and hence influence developmental readiness for learning different kinds and levels of subject matter. They include the following:

1. Increased widening and complexity of the cognitive field
2. Increased familiarity of the psychological world
3. Greater differentiation of cognitive structure
4. Greater precision and specificity of meanings
5. The possession of more abstract, higher-order concepts and transactional terms
6. Greater ability to comprehend and manipulate abstractions and relationships between abstractions without recent or current reference to concrete-empirical experience
7. Greater ability to deal with general propositions apart from particularized contexts
8. Decreased subjectivity in approach to experience
9. Increased attention span
10. Increased differentiation of intellectual ability

Some of these changes in cognitive sophistication (such as increased differentiation of cognitive content, structure, and intellectual ability, greater precision and specificity of meanings) have self-evident implications for general developmental readiness insofar as it bears on the breadth-depth issue in curriculum.

THE SUPERIORITY OF MEANINGFUL OVER ROTE LEARNING AND RETENTION

Many interrelated lines of evidence point to, and empirically suggest, the conclusion that meaningful learning and retention are more effective than their rote counterparts. The reasons for this self-evidently follow from our prior comparative analysis. First, the fact that the instructional material in meaningful learning is logically, and, hence, potentially meaningful, undoubtedly contributes something significant to this superiority; but it is primarily the superiority in meaningful learning *processes* (i.e., the learner's meaningful learning set and the nonarbitrary, nonverbatim relatability of the instructional materials to relevant anchoring ideas in cognitive structure) that basically accounts for the superior learning and retention outcomes.

Meaningful retention is superior to rote retention because of reasons stemming from their respective process considerations in each case. Newly emergent meanings resulting from the interaction between new ideas in the learning material and relevant (anchoring) ideas in cognitive structure are linked and stored with these highly stable anchoring ideas during the retention interval. This linkage obviously protects the new meanings from the arbitrary and verbatim interferences that proactively and retroactively beset rote associations.

Second, by virtue of the nonarbitrariness and nonverbatimness of the content of its learning material and of its learning and retention processes, a much greater quantity of instructional material can be learned and also retained over longer periods of time in meaningful as opposed to rote learning and retention situations. Also, as suggested earlier, linkage of the new meanings to the highly stable anchoring ideas protects them further from interference.

Third, meaning *per se,* on initial contact with the learning material and during the learning and retention periods, makes a positive subjective difference with respect to the effort to learn and remember. The learning experience in meaningful learning is subjectively pleasant and familiar and also arouses intellectual curiosity and the prospect of acquiring new knowledge instead of being reacted to as an unrewarding and unpleasant chore in rote learning that involves undue cognitive strain. Humans tend to work harder and are more highly motivated when the learning activities in which they engage make sense rather than nonsense and can be remembered and then articulated in their own words. This is basically the explanation offered by the Gestalt psychologists for the superiority of meaningful over rote learning and retention: when learning is accompanied by insight and the understanding of relationships, "stable traces" are formed that are remembered longer.

IMPORTANCE OF MEANINGFUL LEARNING AND RETENTION IN EDUCATION

Meaningful reception learning and retention are important in education because they are the human mechanisms *par excellence* for acquiring and storing the vast quantity of ideas and information represented by any field of knowledge. The acquisition and retention of large bodies of subject matter is really a very impressive phenomenon, considering first, that human beings, unlike computers, can apprehend, and immediately remember, only a few discrete items of information that are presented a single time, and second, that memory for rotely learned lists receiving multiple presentations is notoriously limited both over time and with respect to length of list, unless greatly overlearned and frequently reproduced. The tremendous efficiency of meaningful learning inheres in its two principal characteristics—nonarbitrariness and substantiveness (nonverbatimness).

THE ROLE, MEDIATION, AND EFFECTS OF PRACTICE (FREQUENCY) IN MEANINGFUL LEARNING AND RETENTION

To the proverbial man in the street, frequency of exposure to instructional material, i.e., practice) is not only a necessary or essential condition of most meaningful learning, and especially of meaningful retention, but is also the most important variable influencing these outcomes. From his standpoint, learning and retention can be demonstrated only rarely in the absence of frequency, as, for example, when the stimulus (learning) material is exceptionally vivid or unusual. For the most part, under ordinary circumstances, his stated opinion is right on target. Several exceptions, however, to this basic need for frequency in meaningful learning and retention should be noted: when the expected retention interval is very short; when the ideas in the learning material are relatively simple and easy to grasp; when precise retention of the instructional material is not required; and when transferability to other related topics or subject matter is not intended.

Conclusions

The mediational role of frequency is not entirely clear at this point in time. As indicated earlier, frequency is neither a necessary nor a sufficient condition for meaningful learning inasmuch as such learning can unequivocally occur without repetition under certain conditions specified above. Nevertheless, frequency is an essential and important variable in typical instances of meaningful learning especially when it is difficult, when overlearning or prolonged retention is desired, and when transferability is necessary. Further, frequency apparently has various distinctive effects on learning and retention delineated above, that do more than just provide an opportunity for the cumulated sub-threshold effects (such as continuity, reinforcement, drive reduction, cognitive confirmation, etc.) to influence the process and outcome of meaningful (and especially rote) learning and retention.

REFERENCES

Anderson, J. R., & Bower, G. H. *Human associative memory*. Washington, D.C.: V. H. Winston, 1973.

Anderson, R. C. *The notion of schemata and the educational enterprise*. In R. C. Anderson, R. J. Spiro, & W. E. Montague (Eds.), *Schooling and the acquisition of knowledge*. Hillsdale, N.J.: Lawrence Erlbaum & Associates, 1977.

Ashcraft, M. H. *Memory and cognition* (2nd ed.). New York: Harper Collins College Publishers, 1994.

Ausubel, D. P. *The psychology of meaningful verbal learning*. New York: Grune & Stratton, 1963.

Baddeley, A. D. *Working memory*. Oxford: Oxford University Press, 1986.

Bower, G. *Human memory: Basic processes*. New York: Academic Press, 1977.

Broadbent, D. E. *Perception and communication*. New York: Pergamon, 1958.

Brown, J. A. Some tests of the decay theory of immediate memory. *Journal of Experimental Psychology*, 1958, *10*, 12–21.

Brozova, V. Effect of organized learning on text understanding and processing. *Studia Psychologica*, 1995, *37*, 259–268.

Carroll, D. W. *Psychology of language*. Monterey, Calif.: Brooks-Cole, 1986.

Chance, P. *Learning and behavior* (3rd ed.). Pacific Grove, Calif.: Cole Publishing Co., 1994.

Collins, A. M., & Quillian, M. R. *How to make a language user*. In E. Tulving & W. Donaldson (Eds.), *Organization of memory*. New York: Academic Press, 1972, pp. 309–351.

Gagné, R. M. *The conditions of learning* (3rd ed.). New York: Holt, Rinehart & Winston, 1977.

Greeno, R. L. *Human memory: Paradigms and paradoxes*. Hillsdale, N.J.: Lawrence Erlbaum Associates, 1992.

Kail, R. V., & Hagen, J. W. *Perspectives on the development of memory and cognition*. New York: Lawrence Erlbaum, 1977.

Kintsch, W. Text comprehension, memory, and learning. *American Psychologist*, 1994, *49*, 294–303.

Klatzky, R. L. *Human memory: Structures and processes*. San Francisco, 1975.

Moreno, V., & di Vesta, F. J. Analogies (adages) as aids for comprehending structural relations in text. *Contemporary Educational Psychology*, 1994, *19*, 179–198.

Neisser, U. *Cognition and reality*. San Francisco: Freeman, 1976.

Neisser, U. *Cognitive psychology*. New York: Appleton-Century-Crofts, 1967.

Norman, D. A. *Memory and attention*. New York: Wiley, 1968.

Paris, S. G., & Lindauer, B. K. Constructive aspects of children's comprehension and memory. In R. V. Kail & J. W. Hagan, *Perspectives on the development of memory and cognition*. New York: Erlbaum Associates, 1977.

Peterson, L. R., & Peterson, M. J. Short-term retention of individual items. *Journal of Experimental Psychology*, 1959, *58*, 193–198.

Richardson, J. T. E., Engle, R. W., Hasher, L., & Logie, R. H. *Working memory and human cognition*. New York: Oxford University Press, 1996.

Rosch, E. On the internal structure of perceptual and semantic categories. In T. E. Moore (Ed.), *Cognitive development and the acquisition of language.* New York: Academic Press, 1973.

Slamecka, N. J. Ebbinghaus: Some associations. *Journal of Experimental Psychology: Learning, Memory, and Cognition, 11,* 414–435.

Sternberg, S. High-speed scanning in human memory. *Science, 153,* 652ff.

Tulving, E. Episodic and semantic memory. In E. Tulving & W. Donaldson (Eds.), *Organization of memory.* New York: Academic Press, 1972.

Turvey, M. Ecological foundations of cognition. In H. L. Piek, Jr., P. Van den Brock, & D. C. Knill (Eds.), *Cognition: Conceptual and methodological issues.* Washington, D.C.: American Psychological Association, 1992.

Waugh, N. C., & Norman, D. A. Primary memory. *Psychological Review,* 1965, *76,* 89–104.

CHAPTER 2

INTRODUCTION: SCOPE AND OBJECTIVES

SCOPE AND RESEARCH STRATEGY

The principal goal of this book is to present a comprehensive theory of how human beings learn and retain large bodies of organized subject matter in classroom and similar learning environments. Its scope is limited to "reception" learning and retention of potentially meaningful instructional material. "Reception" learning refers to the situation where the total content of the learning task (what is to be learned) is presented to the learner rather than independently discovered by him. That is, the learner is merely required to comprehend the material meaningfully and to incorporate (internalize) it and make it available or functionally reproducible for future use.

An ancillary goal of this work (and of its 1963 precursor as well) is to produce a commonsensical and relatively jargon-free theory of meaningful learning and retention that teachers, psychologists, and scholars in other related disciplines could non-tortuously perceive and comprehend as recognizably and intrinsically related to the actual psychological processes whereby modern human individuals are able to acquire and retain for extensive periods of time substantial bodies of knowledge. Such a theory would presumably have explanatory potential both for a toddler's primitive conceptualizations of his physical and interpersonal worlds as well as for the scholar's more stable and sophisticated organization of knowledge in the discipline of his specialization. Introductory and simplified versions of subject matter that are embodied in the cognitive structures of elementary, secondary, and undergraduate students, would, on the other hand, occupy an intermediate position in this continuum. Now almost forty years after the publication of the first of these two books, the theory is currently being applied in a practical way by Third World governments to the organization of the curriculum and to classroom instruction in their schools and universities and by the management of large American corporations to employee training programs.

Other Theoretical Approaches to Meaningful Reception Learning

In the absence of such a theory of reception learning and retention, inappropriate explanatory principles have been uncritically extrapolated from experimental findings on nonverbal or on short-term, fragmentary, and rote verbal learning.[1] As a result, not only have advances in the more efficacious programming of subject-matter materials for classroom learning been impeded, but teachers have also been misled into perceiving potentially meaningful verbal materials as rote in character. The upshot of this situation has been that many teachers have persisted in using rote teaching methods, in rejecting didactic verbal exposition as unsuitable for meaningful classroom instruction, and in perceiving expository teaching as fostering rote learning.

It is true, of course, that the school is also concerned with developing the student's ability to use acquired knowledge in solving practical problems, that is, in enhancing his ability to think systematically, independently, and critically in particular fields of inquiry. This latter function of the school, although partly inseparable in practice from its transmission-of-knowledge function, is less central in terms of the amount of time that can be reasonably allotted to it, the objectives of education in a democratic society, and what can be realistically expected from most students.[2] Furthermore, since the transmission of knowledge largely requires a form of reception learning, other types of learning (e.g., discovery learning, problem solving, concept formation, etc.), that are based on very different explanatory principles, cannot be definitively treated in this volume that is devoted to theoretical aspects of meaningful reception learning and retention.

Thus, it should be evident that meaningful verbal[3] learning constitutes the principal means of augmenting the learner's store of knowledge both within and outside the classroom. The rote learning of lists of nonsense syllables or of arbitrarily paired adjectives is representative of few defensible tasks in modern classrooms. It is difficult indeed, therefore, to find supportive evidence for Underwood's (1959) assertion that "much of our educational effort is devoted to making relatively meaningless verbal units meaningful." Some representational classroom learning, to be sure, such as that of the letter symbols (graphemes), foreign language vocabulary, and the symbols used to represent the chemical elements, although meeting the minimal criteria of meaningful learning, does, of course, approach the rote level. Such low-level, rote-like meaningful learning, however, tends to form a very small part of the curriculum, especially beyond the elementary school years once children have mastered the basic letter and number symbols.

Furthermore, unlike the rote learning of paired associates, the associations formed under these circumstances are not wholly arbitrary but involve the learning of representational equivalence. In other words, they involve learning that particular symbols are equivalent in meaning to already meaningful concepts in cognitive structure (i.e., an individual's prevailing organization, clarity, and stability of knowledge in a given subject-matter area).

From a process standpoint, the scope of the theory of learning elaborated in this book is limited to various principles of cognitive organization and interaction and also to various mechanisms of cognitive accretion and decrement. It deals (1) with systematic changes in the emergence, identifiability, and availability of new meanings as *presented* ideational materials interact initially and repeatedly with (and are incorporated into) existing cognitive structure; (2) with factors increasing and decreasing the assimilation of these materials, as well as with their subsequent long-term stability or availability in memory; and (3) with the most efficacious ways of manipulating existing cognitive structure so as to enhance the incorporability and longevity of new instructional materials.

In addition to excluding rote and discovery learning from consideration in this book as topics in their own right, such noncognitive kinds of learning as classical and instrumental conditioning and motor skills learning, and such less complex kinds of learning involving minor substantive changes in the content of consciousness (e.g., perceptual and simple discrimination learning) are similarly excluded. These latter types of learning not only require different explanatory principles, but their relevance for classroom learning is, at best, only indirect and tangential. Hence, their consideration would so broaden the scope of the field that the total coverage would necessarily become superficial, fragmentary, unsystematic, and disjointed. The psychology of specific school subjects is also not considered since this book is concerned with general principles applicable to all kinds and all grade levels of meaningful subject-matter learning.

Additionally, although their importance for classroom learning is in no sense discounted, no detailed or systematic attention is paid (1) to emotional and attitudinal factors in learning; (2) to incentive, reinforcement, interpersonal, and individual differences in intellectual ability variables (including intelligence and scholastic aptitude); or (3) ego involvement and personality variables. These latter topics can be studied much more fruitfully and economically within the framework of another body of learning theory concerned with subjective rather than objective aspects of the learning process.

Cognitive and motivational-interpersonal factors undoubtedly influence the learning process concomitantly and they probably interact with each other in various ways. Classroom learning does not take place in a social vacuum but rather in relation to other individuals who themselves—in addition to manifesting various personal emotional ties—act largely as impersonal representatives of the culture.

During the course of personality development the individual also acquires a characteristic motivational orientation to learning. This not only affects his mode of acquiring new attitudes and value judgments, but also influences objectively the scope, the depth, and the efficiency of his more objective learning processes. Nevertheless, for purposes of logical analysis or empirical investigation, either set of factors can be systematically varied while the other is held constant.

Because relatively few well-controlled studies of meaningful reception learning and retention have been conducted, especially those of a long-term nature, it is obvious that the theory presented in this work must of necessity be highly tentative and exploratory in nature at this time and be regarded more in the nature of a series of hypotheses than reflective of a definitive body of research data. Yet, a beginning must be made somewhere. Relevant theory stimulates and gives direction to relevant research efforts, which, in turn, sharpen, modify, and expand the original theory.

The practical implications of such theory and research for actual teaching practices in the classroom are self-evident. Before we could ever hope effectively to manipulate the classroom learning environment for the optimal acquisition of potentially meaningful subject matter, we would first have to know a great deal more about the organizational and developmental principles whereby human beings acquire and retain stable bodies of knowledge. Such principles, however, will forever elude us unless we abandon the untenable assumptions that there is no real distinction either between the logic of a proposition and how the mind apprehends it or between the logical structure of subject-matter organization and the actual series of cognitive processes through which an academically unsophisticated and cognitively immature and developing individual incorporates information and propositions into his cognitive structure.

It is perfectly logical from the standpoint of a mature scholar, for example, to write a textbook in which topically homogeneous materials are segregated into discrete chapters and treated throughout at a uniform level of conceptualization. But, how congruent is this approach with highly suggestive findings that one of the major cognitive processes involved in the learning of any new subject involves progressive differentiation of an originally undifferentiated field?: Once we learn more about cognitive organization and development than the crude generalizations that educational and developmental psychology can currently offer, it will be possible to employ organizational and sequential principles in the presentation of subject matter that actually parallel both the existing structure and the developmental changes in the organization of the intellect. The issue of concreteness versus abstractness is relevant when both general and explanatory ideas, on the one hand, and relatively specific and factual material, on the other, are present in the same learning exercise and both influence the learner's cognitive structure and become incorporated within it.

A reasonable assumption here would be that if the general and explanatory ideas were assimilated first (before the factual), the former would also be available to subsume (assimilate) and, thus, facilitate the subsequent learning of the factual material. This would obviously not be the case if the reverse order of presentation were used. Educational psychologists, however, tend to divide unpredictably regarding preference for "downward" or "upward" order of presentation and subsequent organization in cognitive structure. Generally speaking, neobehavioristically-oriented psychologists have favored the upward order, and constructivists have favored the downward order.

The obvious danger of excessive or unnecessary concreteness in presenting cognitively mature students (adolescents or older) with a new idea of same is that it tends to restrict the generality of the newly introduced concept. Students tend to get the false idea that a *particularly* apt but specific and concrete exemplar is itself the new concept or a facsimile thereof. By their very nature, however, concrete exemplifications of new concepts, or concrete exemplars of the latter, are not constructed to express generality.

Since abstract (as opposed to concrete) thinking capacity represents developmentally man's highest or most mature level of cognition, making possible a comparably high level of thought or problem-solving that enables him to develop all possible interactions between *general* representations of relevant variables, it seems appropriate at each succeeding stage of education to use only the most mature level of abstraction in characterizing his level of discourse that is didactically possible. The major advantage of this approach is that if general principles at the highest degree of abstraction, generalization, and inclusiveness are presented first (as in the previous chapter of this book as a whole), then less abstract ideas can be assimilated more efficaciously. Students should obviously be encouraged to function developmentally at their highest intellectual level—not somewhere beneath this. Naturally, under unusual circumstances, e.g., exceptionally complex and/or difficult learning materials that defy conceptualization, concept generalization, thus, might conceivably be more effective if we use only concrete exemplars rather than favoring the abstract variety.

To avoid the cardinal sin of violating in my presentation the very pedagogic principles I apparently espouse, a genuine effort will be made to organize this book in accordance with the above-stated generalization about the acquisition of knowledge in a new, uncharted field. A preview of the basic principles and ideas of the theory was presented in Chapter 1 before separate components of the theory will be differentiated and elaborated in individual chapters.

RESEARCH STRATEGY IN CLASSROOM LEARNING

Why the Dearth of Hard Knowledge about Classroom Learning?

Three principal reasons account for the dearth of established knowledge about classroom learning. First, the vast majority of studies in the field of school learning have been conducted by teachers and other nonprofessional research workers in education. These studies have typically been characterized by serious inadequacies in conceptualization and rigorousness of research design. They have also been too narrowly oriented toward improving particular academic skills or methods of instruction rather than toward the discovery of more general principles affecting the improvement of classroom learning and instruction as a whole.

Second, the more rigorously conducted research in learning theory has been largely undertaken by psychologists unconnected with the educational enterprise. They have investigated problems quite remote from the type of learning that goes on in the classroom. Their focus has been on animal learning or on short-term, fragmentary, rote, and nonverbal human learning rather than on the learning and retention of organized bodies of logically and potentially meaningful material. Even those psychologists who were engaged in military and industrial training programs during and after World War II were, by and large, more concerned with developing efficacious methods of learning and teaching highly specific military-related skills, often of a motor or technical nature, rather than with the analysis and investigation of more general problems of cognitive learning and instruction. Hence, despite the large sums of money spent on such research, and its overall success relative to the limited and specific objectives envisaged, it has not had wide applicability to other learning situations and has had relatively little theoretical impact on the psychology of meaningful reception learning or the acquisition and retention of knowledge.

Experimental psychologists can hardly be criticized, however, if laboratory studies of short-term, fragmentary, and rote learning have had little applicability to the classroom. Like all pure research efforts in the basic sciences, these studies were designed only to yield general laws of behavior as ends in themselves, quite apart from any practical utility.[4] The blame, if any is to be assigned, must certainly lie with educational psychologists who, in general, have failed to conduct the necessary applied research and have been content with extrapolating the rote learning findings of their experimental colleagues to school learning.

Finally, until the middle Sixties, educational psychologists have been successively preoccupied with measurement and evaluation, personality development, mental hygiene, and social psychology. Despite the self-evident centrality of classroom learning and cognitive development for the psychological aspects of education, these latter areas were largely ignored, both theoretically and researchwise.

It is undeniably true that the distinction between "basic" and "applied" (classroom or subject matter) learning is becoming progressively more blurred; that applied psychological studies often deal with more fundamental and general scientific issues than their "basic" counterparts; and that many well-respected psychological journals are allegedly negatively disposed to publish articles by educational psychologists on "applied" subjects. Nevertheless this hierarchical distinction between "basic" and applied psychology still exists unchanged in the minds of many "basic" psychologists who generally tend to conceive of psychological studies in an educational context as involving an inferior ("applied") brand of learning psychology. This, of course, undoubtedly negatively influences their judgment as supposedly unbiased referees for articles on learning. This mental set undoubtedly reflects in part early deficiencies in research design that characterized many learning studies conducted by psychologically untrained teachers in the early naive days of psychoeducational research.

One questionable practice in this regard (still present occasionally) is the tendency for some "basic" psychologists to use a neobehavioristic theoretical orientation in interpreting the findings of their own and other studies, even though neobehaviorism as a viable and credible theoretical system in the learning field was almost completely defunct, even among "basic" psychologists.

Yet all of these latter considerations should not blind us to recognizing that there is still a quite valid and significant distinction between "pure" and "applied" sciences. The former group is only concerned with discovering knowledge as an end in itself, irrespective of any practical or social benefits that may be anticipated from "basic" studies. Applied scientists (e.g., educational psychologists), on the other hand, design their research so that their findings might provide answers for many practical and social goals and issues in education. Consistent with this biased outlook, of course, was the practice of some "basic" researchers in often failing to cite the relevant studies of educational psychologists in the reference lists of their articles and books.

"Basic Science" versus Applied Approach

The tendency among educational psychologists uncritically to extrapolate research findings from laboratory studies of simplified learning situations to the classroom learning environment accounts, in large measure, for our lack of knowledge about school learning processes. It reflects the fascination that many research workers feel for the "basic science" approach to research in the applied sciences as well as their concomitant failure to appreciate its inherent limitations.

Gage (1961), for example, argues that progress in educational psychology is made more rapidly by focusing indirectly on "basic science" problems in general psychology than by trying to come to grips directly with the applied problems that are more indigenous to the field. Spence (1959) perceives classroom learning as much too complex to permit the discovery of general laws of learning and advocates a straightforward application to the classroom situation of the laws of learning discovered in the laboratory. Melton's (1959) position is more eclectic. He would search for "basic science" laws of learning in both laboratory and classroom contexts and would leave to the educational technologist the task of conducting the research necessary for implementing these laws in actual classroom practice.

The research position adopted in this book is that the principles governing the nature and conditions of meaningful reception learning can be discovered only through an applied or engineering type of research that actually takes into account the distinctive attributes of this phenomenon as it occurs in the classroom (Ausubel, 1953). We cannot merely extrapolate general "basic science" laws derived from the laboratory study of qualitatively different and vastly more simple instances of learning. Laws of classroom learning[5] at an applied level are needed by the educational technologist before he can hope to conduct the research preparatory to effecting scientific changes in teaching practices.

QUALIFICATIONS IN USING "BASIC SCIENCE" APPROACH IN APPLIED RESEARCH

Contrary to Spence's (1959) contention, the greater complexity and number of determining variables involved in meaningful verbal learning does not preclude the possibility of discovering precise laws with wide general applications from one educational situation to another. It simply means that such research demands experimental ingenuity and sophisticated use of modern methods of research design.

The "basic science" research approach is predicated on the very defensible notion that progress in the applied sciences is ultimately related to knowledge in the underlying sciences on which they are based. It can be convincingly demonstrated, for example, (1) that progress in clinical medicine is intimately related to progress in biochemistry and bacteriology, (2) that progress in engineering is intimately related to progress in physics and chemistry, and (3) that progress in education is similarly dependent upon advances in psychology, statistics, sociology, and philosophy. Two important kinds of qualifications, however, have to be placed on the value of "basic-science" research for the applied sciences: qualifications of purpose or orientation and qualifications of level of applicability.

By definition, "basic-science" research is concerned with the discovery of general laws of physical, biological, psychological, and sociological phenomenology as an end in itself. Researchers in these fields have no objection, of course, if their findings are applied to practical problems that have social value; in fact, there is reason to believe that they are motivated to some extent by this consideration.

The design of "basic-science" research, however, bears no *intended* relation whatsoever to problems in the applied disciplines, the aim being solely to advance knowledge in a general nonutilitarian sense. Ultimately, of course, such knowledge is applicable in a very broad way to practical problems; but since the research design is not oriented to the solution of these problems, this applicability is apt to be quite indirect and unsystematic and relevant only over a time period that is too long to be meaningful in terms of the short-range needs of the applied disciplines.

The second qualification concerns the level at which findings in the basic sciences can be applied once their relevance has been established. It should be self-evident that such findings manifest a much higher level of generality than the problems to which they can be applied. At the applied level specific ends and conditions are added that demand additional research to make manifest the precise way in which the general law operates in the specific case. That is, the applicability of general principles to specific problems is *not given* in the statement of the general principle; it must be specifically worked out for each applied problem. Knowledge about nuclear fission, for example, does not tell us how to make an atomic bomb or a atomic-powered submarine.

In fields such as education, the problem of generality is further complicated by the fact that practical problems often exist at higher levels of complexity with respect to the order of phenomenology involved than the "basic-science" findings requiring application. That is, new variables are added which may qualitatively alter the general principles from the basic science to such an extent that, at the applied level, they have only substrate validity but no explanatory or predictive value. For example, antibiotic reactions that take place in test tubes do not necessarily take place in living systems, and methods of rote learning in mazes, studied in psychological laboratories with animals, do not necessarily correspond to methods of learning children use in grappling with potentially meaningful verbal materials in classrooms.

The "basic-science" approach in educational research, therefore, is subject to many serious disadvantages. Its relevance is too remote and indirect because it is not oriented toward solving educational problems, and its findings, if relevant, are applicable only if much additional research is performed to translate general principles into the more specific form they have to assume in the task-specialized and more complex contexts of pedagogy (Ausubel, 1953).

Many of the better known generalizations in educational psychology—the principle of readiness, the importance of development in learning, the concrete to abstract trend in conceptualizing the environment—fit the above analogies very well. They are interesting and potentially useful ideas to curriculum specialists, but they have little practical utility in designing a curriculum until they are particularized at an applied level of operations.

The need for particularization is well illustrated by the principle of readiness. At the present time we can only speculate what curriculum sequences might conceivably look like if they took into account precise and detailed (but currently unavailable) research findings on the emergence of readiness for different subject-matter areas, for different subareas and levels of difficulty within an area, and for different approaches to teaching the same material.

Because of the unpredictable specificity of readiness as shown, for example, by the fact that four- and five-year-olds can profit from training in pitch but not in rhythm (Jersild & Bienstock, 1935), valid answers to such questions cannot be derived from logical extrapolation but require meticulous theory-related empirical research in a school setting. The next step would involve the development of appropriate teaching methods and materials to take optimal advantage of existing degrees of readiness and to increase readiness wherever necessary and desirable. But since we generally do not have this type of research data available, except perhaps in the field of reading, we can only pay lip service to the principle of readiness in curriculum planning.

Advantages of Basic Science Approach

The basic science-extrapolation approach, of course, offers several very attractive methodological advantages in verbal learning experiments. First, by using nonsense syllables of equal meaningfulness, it is possible to work with additive units of equal difficulty. Second, by using such relatively meaningless learning tasks (i.e., nonsense syllables equated for degree of meaningfulness), it is possible to eliminate, for the most part, the indeterminable influence of meaningful antecedent experience, which naturally varies from one individual to another. But it is precisely this interaction of new learning tasks with existing idiosyncratic cognitive structures that is the distinctive feature of meaningful learning.

Thus, although the use of nonsense syllables or paired adjectives adds undoubted methodological rigor to the study of learning, the very nature of this material limits the applicability of the findings in such experiments to a type of short-term, rote learning that is rare in everyday situations and even rarer in the classroom. Nevertheless, even though there are no a priori grounds for supposing that learning and retention occur in the same way for potentially meaningful and for relatively meaningless learning, the findings from rote learning experiments have been commonly extrapolated to potentially meaningful learning situations. One cannot have one's cake and eat it too. If one chooses the particular kind of methodological rigor associated with the use of rote learning materials, one must also be content with applying the findings from such experiments to only rote learning situations.

Much of the psychology of learning that teachers in training study today is based on findings from rote learning experiments that have been borrowed wholesale, and uncritically, without any attempt to test their applicability to the kind of learning situations that actually exist in classrooms. It would be a shocking situation, indeed, if a comparable procedure were followed in medicine, i.e., if physicians employed therapeutic technics validated only *in vitro* or by animal experimentation.

Unfortunately, the influence of theories of rote learning is not restricted to theoretical conceptions of, or experimental approaches to, school learning. The willingness of educational psychologists to extrapolate the findings of rote studies naturally led them to neglect almost entirely the nature and conditions of meaningful verbal learning and retention. This naturally delayed the discovery of more effective methods of verbal exposition, as well as helped to perpetuate the use of traditional rote approaches to teaching. These methods continue to dominate much of contemporary educational practice, particularly in the secondary school and university. Logically and potentially meaningful instructional materials are frequently taught by teachers and learned by students as if they were rote in character, and hence they are retained, if at all, both inefficiently and with unnecessary difficulty.

In still other educational circles *all verbal* exposition is perceived as *necessarily* fostering rote learning and is accordingly proscribed. Only relatively recently have curriculum specialists and educational psychologists concerned themselves with the substantive and programmatic aspects of the problem of facilitating the meaningful acquisition and retention of viable bodies of knowledge.

Psychology versus Educational Psychology

Since both psychology and educational psychology deal with the problem of learning, how can we distinguish between the special and legitimate research interests of each discipline in this area? As an applied science, education is not concerned with the general laws of learning, per se, but only with those properties of learning that can be related to efficacious ways of deliberately effecting stable changes in individuals (e.g., the acquisition and retention of knowledge) that have both personal and social value. Education, therefore, refers to guided or manipulated learning deliberately directed toward specific practical ends. These ends may be defined in part as the long-term acquisition of stable bodies of knowledge (ideas, concepts, facts), values, habits, skills, ways of perceiving, adjusting, and aspiring, and of the cognitive capacities needed for acquiring them.

The interest of psychologists in learning, on the other hand, is much more general. Many other aspects of learning apart from the efficient acquisition of designated knowledge, competencies, and capacities for cognitive growth in a directed context concern them. More typically, they investigate the nature of current, rote, fragmentary, or short-term learning experiences rather than the kinds of long-term learning involved in assimilating extensive and organized bodies of knowledge, values, habits, and skills. This former choice of research problems in learning by6 psychologists was largely determined by the reductionistic and unsubstantiated view that the higher mental processes can first be explained when more simple kinds of learning are understood.

The following kinds of learning problems, therefore, are particularly indigenous to *psychoeducational* research:

1. Discovery of the nature of those aspects of the learning process affecting the long-range availability, stability, and meaningfulness of organized bodies of knowledge, skills, etc., in the learner.
2. Long-range modification (improvement) of learning capacities.
3. Discovery of those personality and cognitive aspects of the learner and of the interpersonal and social aspects of the learning environment that affect motivation for learning and characteristic ways of assimilating instructional material.
4. Discovery of appropriate and maximally efficient review and feedback practices and ways of organizing, sequencing, and presenting learning materials, and of deliberately motivating and directing learning toward specified goals (Ausubel, 1953).

Thus, educational psychology is unequivocally an applied discipline. However, it is *not* general psychology applied to school learning—no more so than medicine is general biology applied to the prevention, diagnosis, and treatment of disease. Each applied discipline has its own independent body of theory and methodology that is just as basic as that underlying the parent discipline. The principal difference between them is that bodies of applied theory are less general in scope and are more relevant for the particular practical problems of a given applied discipline.

RELEVANT CURRENT TRENDS AND ISSUES IN EDUCATIONAL THOUGHT

The main focus of attention in this book, i.e., on the processes of meaningful reception learning and retention, and on ways of enhancing them, is largely in accord with three current trends of thought and opinion in education—increased emphasis on the importance and quality of intellectual training in the schools, greater stress on acquiring knowledge as an end in itself, and increased willingness on the part of the school to take more responsibility for the direction of learning. Concern with these issues has greatly reduced national preoccupation with, and heated public controversy about, such pseudoissues as whether students today learn as much in school as did prior generations of students, whether the curriculum has become "softer," whether Johnny can read, whether training in pedagogy is a necessary part of teacher education, and whether intellectual training should be the *exclusive* function of the school.

Greater Concern with Intellectual Training

Increased concern with the intellectual content and quality of the curriculum has been manifested in many different ways. First, scientists, scholars, curriculum experts, and psychologists have been collaborating sporadically for some time in a variety of curriculum reform movements placing greater emphasis on the basic, unifying principles of the various subject-matter disciplines, on more efficient programming of subject matter, and both on achieving consonance with recent advances in scholarly knowledge as well as on adequate depth of coverage.

Second, the subject-matter preparation of teachers has been receiving greater attention in the form of teachers' institutes in mathematics and science, fifth-year teacher education programs, and higher subject-matter requirements for high school teacher certification.

Third, numerous experiments have been conducted in classroom organization and administration, all of which are directed toward the more efficient teaching of subject matter, namely, team teaching, ungraded schools, the use of specialist teachers in elementary school science and mathematics, the differential grouping of pupils by subject, the organization of special programs for gifted students, the use of teacher's aides, and the more flexible scheduling of classes in terms of the number of pupils and the amount of time allotted to each.

Fourth, the subject-matter content of the curriculum has been increased through such measures as a longer school year and school day, the requirement of both more units and of more mandatory and fewer elective subjects for high school graduation,[6] the introduction into the elementary schools of foreign language and of more advanced mathematics and science instruction, the offering of college-level courses for capable senior high school students, and greater emphasis on homework.

Finally, there has been much frenzied activity in the area of teaching aids, e.g., films, education television, computer-assisted instruction, Cuisenaire rods and Stern blocks, and the use of tapes, records, and laboratory methods in foreign language teaching.[7]

These recent developments do not necessarily imply that the American school had previously repudiated intellectual training as its primary and distinctive function. It is true, of course, that this has often appeared to be the case because of the strident pronouncements of certain extreme proponents of the child-centered point of view who adopted a *laissez-faire* attitude toward the goal of attaining intellectual competence. These latter educators frequently derogated knowledge of subject matter, advocated the use of children's existing interests as the main criterion in constructing the curriculum, and placed major emphasis on the attainment of optimal personality development and social adjustment in a maximally permissive school environment.

Although this latter position had many adherents among professors of education, it never really prevailed, either in belief or practice, in more than a bare handful of public schools. Present concern in the more affluent suburban schools with intellectual competence and with the quality of the curriculum, therefore, is more a matter of increased emphasis than a radical shift in the objectives of American education.

Actually the child-centered and subject-matter approaches constitute a pseudodichotomy that causes serious disagreement only among extremists at either end of the continuum. No realistic advocate of the subject-matter approach, for example, suggests that the school should disregard the personality development and social adjustment of pupils or that subject matter should be taught without due regard for such relevant factors as readiness, individual differences in intellectual ability, and social-class motivation (or lack of motivation) for learning.

Similarly, constructive proponents of the child-centered approach largely emphasize noncognitive determinants and outcomes of learning because of their actual importance in learning subject matter. The difference again is more one of emphasis than of basic goals. The fact that noncognitive determinants and outcomes of learning are not exhaustively considered in this book does not mean that their significance is minimized or that an extreme subject-matter approach is adopted. Furthermore, much explicit emphasis is placed on the importance of developmental readiness and on individual differences in cognitive capacity as significant factors influencing meaningful reception learning.

This greater emphasis upon the quality of intellectual training is, of course, not without its dangers since it can be easily perverted to serve socially undesirable ends. In the first place, higher standards, harder objectives, and longer assignments *are not* ends in themselves. They are valueless and even pernicious (1) unless the content of the subject matter involved is worthwhile, leads to meaningful knowledge, and is consonant with the fruits of contemporary scholarship; (2) unless the standards themselves are differentially adjusted so as to demand from each child what he can actually do and the best of which he is capable. Raised standards must never be used as a lever to eliminate from school those pupils in the lower range of intellectual ability. Rather, new ways must be found to motivate such pupils adequately and to teach them academic subject matter more effectively.

Second, excellence is not synonymous with high examination scores irrespective of how they are achieved, the underlying motivation, or the kind of knowledge they reflect. In our present climate of frenzied competition for college entrance, there is a real danger that examination scores are being used as ends in themselves rather than as symbols of genuine accomplishment and of actual mastery of worthwhile knowledge.

Just as important as what pupils know at the end of the sixth, eighth, and twelfth grades is the extent of their knowledge at the ages of twenty-five, forty, and sixty, as well as their ability and desire both to learn more and to apply their knowledge fruitfully in adult life. In the light of these latter criteria, for example, in comparing the quantity and quality of our national research output in the pure and applied sciences with that of European countries, the American educational system stands up relatively well even though our school children are required to learn much less academic material.

Higher academic standards, therefore, seem to have relatively little impact on real learning if they are merely formalistic rituals. Hence, in setting our academic goals, we must be more concerned with the *ultimate* intellectual objectives of schooling, namely, with the *long-run* acquisition of stable and usable bodies of knowledge (and of intellectual skills) and with the development of the ability to think systematically, independently, and critically in particular fields of inquiry. The quality of instruction obviously influences the outcome of these objectives—not only in the substantive content of the subject matter that is offered, but also in the organization, sequence, and manner of presenting instructional material, its degree of logical meaningfulness, and the relative balance between ideational and factual materials.

Responsibility for Organizing the Curriculum and Selecting Subject Matter

One extreme point of view associated with the child-centered approach to education is the notion that children are innately equipped, in some mysterious fashion, for knowing precisely what is best for them in terms of intellectual content and type of instruction. This idea is obviously an outgrowth of the predeterministic theories of Rousseau, Gesell, and others that conceive of development as a series of internally regulated sequential steps that unfold in accordance with a predetermined design.

According to these predeterministic theorists, the environment facilitates development best by providing a maximally permissive field that does not interfere with the predetermined process of spontaneous maturation. From these assumptions it is but a short step to the claim that the children themselves must be in the most strategic position to *know* and *select* those components of the environment that are most congruent with their current developmental needs, and hence most conducive to optimal growth.

Empirical "proof" of this proposition is adduced from the fact that nutrition is adequately maintained and existing deficiency conditions are spontaneously corrected when infants are permitted to self-select their own diets. Thus, the argument runs: If children can successfully choose their own diets, they must certainly know what is best for them in all areas of growth and should, therefore, be permitted to self-select everything—including the curriculum.

First, even if development were primarily a matter of internal ripening, there would still be no good reason for supposing that the child is implicitly conversant with the current direction and facilitating conditions of development, and hence axiomatically equipped to make the most appropriate choices. Just because the individual is sensitive in early childhood to internal cues of physiological need, we cannot conclude that he is similarly sensitive to cues reflective of psychological and other developmental needs. Even in the area of nutrition, self-selection is a reliable criterion of such need only during early infancy.

Second, unless one assigns a sacrosanct status to "endogenous motivation," there is little warrant for believing either that it alone is truly reflective of the child's *genuine* developmental requirements or that environmentally derived needs are "imposed," authoritarian in spirit, and inevitably fated to thwart the actualization of his developmental potentialities. Actually, most needs originate from without and are internalized in the course of the child's interaction and identification with significant persons in his family and cultural environments.

Third, one can never assume that the child's *spontaneously* expressed interests and activities are completely reflective of *all* of his important needs and capacities. Just because existing capacities can *potentially* provide their own motivation does not mean that they always or necessarily do so. It is not the possession of capacities that is motivating but, rather, the anticipation of future satisfactions once they have been successfully exercised. However, because of such factors as inertia, lack of opportunity or appreciation of their existence, or preoccupation with other activities, many capacities may never be exercised in the first place. Thus, children typically develop only *some* of their potential capacities; consequently, their expressed interests cannot be considered coextensive with the potential range of interests they are capable of developing with appropriate stimulation.

In conclusion, therefore, the current interests and spontaneous desires of immature pupils can hardly be considered reliable guideposts and adequate substitutes for specialized knowledge and seasoned judgment in designing a curriculum. Recognition of the role of pupil needs in school learning also does not mean that the scope of the syllabus should be restricted to the existing concerns and spontaneously expressed interests that happen to be present in a group of children growing up under particular conditions of intellectual and social class stimulation.

One of the primary functions of education, in fact, should be to stimulate the development of motivations and interests that are currently nonexistent. It is true that academic achievement is greatest when pupils manifest felt needs to acquire knowledge as an end in itself. Such needs, however, are not endogenous but acquired—and largely through exposure to provocative, meaningful, and developmentally appropriate instruction.

Last, while it is reasonable to consider the views of pupils and even, under certain circumstances, to solicit their participation in the planning of the curriculum, it makes little developmental or administrative sense to entrust them with *sole* responsibility for significant policy or operational decisions.

Two additional related propositions in this regard, stemming from the activity program movement, are (1) that factual information and intellectual skills should always be acquired in the real-life, functional contexts in which they are customarily encountered (rather than through the medium of artificially contrived drills and exercises) and (2) that a pupil's progress should be evaluated only in terms of his own potentialities.

Contrived Drills and Exercises

Many teachers, however, have learned from their own experience not only that drills and exercises need not necessarily be rote in character, but also that they are essential for long-term retention and transferability and for acquiring many skills and concepts that do not occur frequently and repetitively enough in more natural settings and, hence, that structured practice or review is necessary.

Incidental versus Deliberate Learning

Similarly, they found it necessary to ignore much of the totally unsupported dogma disseminated about incidental learning. They discovered that although it is possible for children to learn some things incidentally, deliberate effort is required for the efficient learning of most types of academic material.

In Defense of School Marks and Group Norms

Finally, they had to discount much of the exaggerated condemnation of school marks and group norms as unqualified evils. They found that, stripped of their abuses, marks are both indispensable tools for evaluating the acquisition of valid, worthwhile knowledge and a quite necessary and unavoidable incentive for academic achievement in our competitive culture. They also found that although it is certainly useful to know how well a pupil is performing in terms of his own capabilities, this knowledge is not mutually preclusive with evaluation of his ability relative to the norm of his class or age group.

The battle cry of the progressivists that the student must assume full responsibility for his own learning has been distorted into a doctrine of pedagogic irresponsibility. It has been interpreted to mean that it is the student's responsibility to self-discover everything he has to learn, that is, to locate and organize his own instructional materials from primary sources, to interpret them independently, to design his own experiments, and merely to use the teacher as a consultant and critic.

Education, however, is not, and has never been, a process of complete self-instruction. Its very essence inheres in the knowledgeable selection, organization, interpretation, and sequential arrangement of learning materials by pedagogically sophisticated persons. The school cannot in good conscience abdicate these responsibilities by turning them over to students in the name of democracy and progressivism.

The student takes appropriate responsibility for his own learning

1. When he accepts the task of learning actively, seeking to understand the instructional material that he is taught.
2. When he genuinely attempts to integrate it with what he already knows.
3. When he does not avoid the effort and struggle of difficult new learning or demand spoon-feeding from his teacher.
4. When he takes it upon himself to ask the necessary questions about what he does not understand.

Another way in which educators have evaded responsibility for programming the content of instruction has been by advertising the slogan that the function of the school is to "teach children *how* to think—not *what* to think." This slogan also states a false dichotomy since the two functions are by no means mutually exclusive. Actually, as has been asserted above, the transmission of subject matter can be considered the more primary function of the school.

Most of the thinking that goes on in school is, and should be, supplementary to the process of reception learning, that is, concerned with having students assimilate subject-matter content in a more active, integrative, and critical fashion. Development of thinking or problem-solving ability can also, of course, be considered an objective of schooling in its own right, although it is a lesser objective than the learning of subject matter and is only partly teachable; but under no circumstances is it a proper substitute for reception learning per se or a feasible *primary* means of imparting subject-matter knowledge.

Fortunately, as evidenced by the phenomenal growth of curriculum reform movements several decades or more ago and of various forms of programmed instruction, leading educators are currently returning to the more traditional educational view that the content of the curriculum is the teacher's and not the student's responsibility.

KNOWLEDGE AS AN END IN ITSELF

Another encouraging trend on the current educational scene is a growing emphasis on the value of knowledge as an end in itself. The "life-adjustment" movement has performed a valuable service by pointing out that the school cannot afford totally to disregard the expressed interests, current problems, and future vocational, family, and civic concerns of high-school students, particularly those who have no intention of attending college. If young people perceive the school as uninterested in these problems, they react either by losing interest in academic studies or by feeling guilty for being preoccupied with supposedly trivial matters. If current concerns are not relieved, they inevitably serve as distractions from other constituted responsibilities.

Some extremists, however, carried this approach too far by adopting an anti-intellectual approach toward secondary-school education. Any branch of knowledge that had no immediate applicability to practical problems of everyday living was summarily dismissed as a waste of time. And in some instances the curriculum was diluted by the addition of various frills and leisure-time activities. It was held that only intellectually superior or college-bound students should be exposed to academic subjects and that these subjects are either valueless or too difficult for other students.

To be related to present needs and purposes, however, learning tasks need not necessarily deal solely with problems of adolescent adjustment. Academic knowledge can have relatedness to current motivations if its acquisition becomes, at least in part, a goal in its own right. It is unrealistic to expect that all school subjects can have, even remotely, utilitarian value or practical implications. The value of a great deal of school learning can be defended only on the grounds that it improves an individual's understanding of important ideas in his culture. If adolescents could be motivated to perceive academic knowledge in this light, it would constitute an important part of their current psychological field.

Furthermore, even if youths not bound for college do require some prevocational and life-adjustment education, this does not mean that they could not benefit from some academic subject matter. Appropriately taught and suitably modified in content to account for their intellectual ability, academic training is not only valuable as an end in itself, but, in a more general way, is just as important a preparation for adult living as education that is more explicitly related to immediate developmental tasks.

NOTES

[1]The attempt to reduce complex cognitive phenomena into simpler forms of rote learning, conditioning, or associationism is a form of scientific reductionism that currently lacks respectability among philosophers of science.

[2]It may be noted that problem-solving activity may also result in knowledge acquisition. Except in early childhood, however, it is not a conspicuous source of acquiring new ideas. For the most part, in the formal education of the individual the educational agency merely transmits ready-made concepts, categorical schemata, and derivative propositions.

[3]"Verbal" learning is used here in the more general sense of the term and is also inclusive of subverbal intuitive understanding and of other types of symbolic learning that is not expressed in the formal language of the culture.

[4]Many behaviorally-oriented psychologists, however, e.g., Skinner, have attempted explicitly to influence educational practice by applying behavioristic theory to classroom learning (e.g., automated teaching).

[5]These laws are just as "basic" as "basic science" laws. The term "basic" in this context refers to the distinction between "pure" and applied sciences. It does not mean "fundamental." In the latter sense applied research is just as "basic" as research in the pure sciences.

[6]In certain suburban and better-quality city high schools, the number of mandatory courses has, in fact, been reduced to permit greater concentration in a given intended area of college specialization.

[7]Admittedly most of this concern with, and effort to enhance, the acquisition and retention of subject-matter knowledge has been expended on the more affluent suburban, middle-class schools. Many inner-city schools still follow the principle of social promotion and seem quite content to produce functionally illiterate high-school graduates and dropouts.

REFERENCES

Ausubel, D.P. The nature of educational research. *Educational Theory,* 1953, *3*: 314–332.

Gage, N.L. Metatechnique in educational research. Urbana, IL: Bureau of Educational Research, University of Illinois, 1961.

Jersild, A.T., & Bienstock, S.F. The influence of training on the vocal ability of three-year-old children. *Child Development,* 1931, *2*: 277–291.

Jersild, A.T., & Bienstock, S.F. Development of rhythm in young children. *Child Development Monographs,* 1935, No. 2.

Melton, A.W. The science of learning and the technology of educational methods. *Harvard Educational Review,* 1959, *29*: 96–106.

Spence, K.W. The relation of learning theory to the technology of education. *Harvard Educational Review,* 1959, *29*: 96–106.

Underwood, B.J. Verbal learning in the educative process. *Harvard Educational Review,* 1959, *29*: 107–117.

CHAPTER 3

PREVIEW OF BASIC CONCEPTS OF MEANINGFUL RECEPTION LEARNING AND RETENTION

This chapter contains an exposition and elaboration of the major principles of meaningful reception learning and retention, i.e. of Assimilation Theory and its application to the acquisition and retention of knowledge in classroom-like situations. These principles will be presented largely at a descriptive level, with relatively little accompanying detail or supportive evidence; at this point in theoretical and research development explanatory aspects of the theory are still necessarily rudimentary and hypothetical. Nevertheless they still provide some needed specific and proximate ideational scaffolding for the meaningful learning and retention phenomena they purport to explain in the context of acquiring and retaining knowledge. More detailed and documented consideration of the separate components of the theory will follow in later chapters. Although this mode of organization inevitably makes for some redundancy, it more than compensates for this disadvantage by enhancing comprehensibility and meaningfulness.

NEOBEHAVIORISTIC VERSUS COGNITIVE ORIENTATIONS

Any attempt to understand the historical development and current theoretical status of the psychology of learning, retention, and instruction must of necessity begin with an examination of the contrasting views of cognitive and neobehavioristic theorists about the basic nature of cognitive processes and phenomena. The differences between these two theoretical orientations are as fundamental as they could possibly be, and cannot be explained away merely by saying that each group of theorists is essentially interested in elucidating basically different kinds of psychological phenomena.

It is true, of course, that over the years neobehaviorists have devoted most of their attention to such problems as classical and operant conditioning, rote verbal learning, instrumental learning, and discrimination learning, whereas cognitive psychologists have been traditionally preoccupied with such problems as thinking, concept formation, problem solving, and the learning of connected discourse. Nevertheless, representatives of both schools have attempted to extend their views to encompass the entire field of the psychology of learning and retention. In fact, much of the controversy that exists today about the psychology of cognition does so precisely because neobehaviorists have extended their views "upwards" to include the more complex cognitive processes, whereas their theoretical antagonists have extended their views "downwards" to include simpler kinds of learning.

The Neobehavioristic Theoretical Orientation

Like the behavioristic position from which it was derived, the neobehavioristic view focuses presumably on "real" behavioral responses, both overt and implicit, and their environmental instigators and reinforcers as the proper objects of scientific investigation in psychology. Consciousness, on the other hand, is regarded as a "mentalistic" concept that is both highly resistive to scientific inquiry and not very pertinent to the real purposes of psychology as a science; it is largely regarded as an epiphenomenon that is important neither in its own right nor as a determinant of behavior. Furthermore, according to neobehaviorists, it cannot be reliably (objectively) observed; and it is allegedly so extremely idiosyncratic as to render virtually impossible the kinds of categorization necessary for making scientific generalizations. In neobehavioristic terms, for example, a concept is not regarded as a generic or categorical *idea* in consciousness but rather as a common *response* to a class or family of stimuli.

Advocates of the neobehavioristic position obviously had little difficulty explaining such phenomena as classical and instrumental conditioning or rote verbal learning, but they initially experienced considerable difficulty with cognitive phenomena and processes, particularly those involving symbols. At first the only principles they could offer in explaining how responses could be evoked by stimuli that were not originally associated with them by means of contiguity and reinforcement, were the concepts of stimuli and response generalization. But this kind of transfer mechanism obviously depends on physical (or perceptual) similarity within the sets of stimuli or responses in question; and, hence, it could not be applied to such problems as symbolic representation (that is, equivalence in meaning between signs and significates), the inclusion of physically dissimilar exemplars within the same conceptual category, and problem solving involving the transfer of a given principle from one physically dissimilar situation to another.

Neobehaviorists attempted to solve these latter problems of symbolic representation, conceptual equivalence, and transfer by proposing a hypothetical mediational process that could render physically dissimilar situations equivalent by virtue of constituting the hypothetical common organismic response evoked by each situation. This mediational process was considered a form of implicit behavior (internal, stimulus-producing response) related to Hull's "fractional anticipatory goal response" and "pure stimulus act." Different neobehavioristic conceptions of meaning have been offered by Osgood (1957), Berlyne (1965), and Gagné (1977).

The Cognitive Position: Meaning as Differentiated Ideational Experience

Exponents of the cognitive viewpoint, on the other hand, take precisely the opposite theoretical stance. Using perception as their model, they regard differentiated and clearly articulated conscious experience (for example, knowing, understanding, thinking, etc.) as providing the most significant data for a science of psychology. Instead of focusing mechanistically on stimulus-response connections and their hypothetical "organismic" mediators, they endeavor to discover psychological principles of organization and functioning governing these differentiated states of consciousness and the underlying cognitive processes (for example, meaningful learning, abstraction, generalization) from which they arise.

From the standpoint of cognitive theorists, the attempt to ignore conscious states, or to reduce cognition to mediational processes reflective of implicit behavior, not only unwarrantedly excludes from the field of psychology that which is most worth studying, but also absurdly oversimplifies highly complex psychological phenomena. These neobehavioristic mediational processes are viewed by cognitive theorists as tortuous, implausible, and unparsimonious constructs made necessary both by the latter's stubborn refusal to recognize the centrality of consciousness in cognitive processes and by their attempt to reduce cognition to a set of implicit stimulus-stimulus or stimulus-response correlations that are applicable only to much simpler kinds of behavior.

In contrast to the neobehavioristic approach, the cognitive position with respect to the psychology of learning and meaning has a decidedly ideational and, by behavioristic standards, "mentalistic" flavor. Meaning, cognitive theorists assert, is not an implicit *response* but rather a clearly articulated and precisely differentiated conscious experience that emerges when potentially meaningful signs, symbols, concepts, or propositions are related to and incorporated within relevant components of a given individual's cognitive structure on a nonarbitrary and nonverbatim basis.

NEW MEANINGS AS THE PRODUCTS OF MEANINGFUL LEARNING

The acquisition of new meanings is, thus, held to be coextensive with meaningful learning, a process that is considered qualitatively different from rote learning in terms of the nonarbitrary and nonverbatim relatability of the content of what is to be learned to existing ideas in cognitive structure. New meanings, in other words, are the product of an active, integrative interaction between new instructional materials and relevant ideas in the learner's existing structure of knowledge. The conditions of learning presuppose additionally the existence of a meaningful learning set in the learner and of potentially meaningful learning materials. The latter condition, in turn, requires both (1) learning tasks that are sufficiently non-random, sensible, and plausible to be relatable nonarbitrarily and substantively to *some* relevant component of an existing body of knowledge in at least *some* learners and (2) the presence of this latter component in the cognitive structure of the *particular* learner.

Since subject-matter knowledge consists of a large number of interrelated concepts, propositions and representational symbols (e.g., concept names), and since rotely learned material is both drastically limited in terms of time (longevity) and item spans, and also requires much effortful repetition, it stands to reason that meaningful verbal reception learning is practically the most important mode of acquiring and retaining such knowledge in school or similar learning environments.

Meaning: Mostly Connotative or Mostly Denotative?

It is evident from the foregoing considerations that one major point of contention between the cognitive and neobehavioristic approaches hinges on whether the essential psychological attributes of meaning are primarily connotative in nature, and can, therefore, be conceptualized adequately in terms of implicit motor or affective responses (Suci, Osgood, & Tannenbaum, 1957) or whether they are basically denotative in nature and must necessarily be reflective of differentiated cognitive content. A related issue has to do with the applicability of the conditioning paradigm to the process whereby meanings are acquired, that is, whether the acquisition process is purely automatic or involves some implicit awareness and various active cognitive operations.

One major implication of the cognitive position is that the human psychological system, considered as an information-processing-and-storing mechanism, is so constructed and so functions that typically new ideas and information can be meaningfully learned and retained most efficaciously when appropriately relevant and typically more inclusive concepts or propositions are already available to play a subsuming role or to provide ideational anchorage to subordinate ideas (Ausubel, 1961, 1962). Subsumption thus, largely accounts for the acquisition of new meanings (or for the accretion of knowledge); for the extended retention span of meaningfully learned materials; for the very psychological organization of knowledge as a hierarchical structure in which the most inclusive concepts occupy a position at the apex of the structure and then subsume progressively downwards more highly differentiated subconcepts and factual data; and for the eventual occurrence of forgetting.

Forgetting, in process terms, is conceptualized as the second or "obliterative" phase of subsumption in which the distinctive import and substance of a meaningfully learned and subsumed idea is at first dissociable from the anchoring (subsuming) idea, then gradually loses this dissociability, and is finally assimilated completely by the more general meaning of its more stable and inclusive subsumer (Ausubel, 1962). Thus, forgetting is interpreted as a progressive loss in the dissociability of new ideas from the ideational matrix in which they are embedded and in relation to which their meaning emerges. The theory of meaningful learning and retention formulated above is referred to as "assimilation theory" (Ausubel 1963).

Newly Acquired Knowledge as a Basis for Transfer

A second major implication of the cognitive position is that the learner's acquisition of clear stable, and organized bodies of knowledge is not only the major long-term objective of education, but also that the learned properties of these bodies of knowledge, once acquired, constitute in their own right, and in their turn, the most significant *independent variables* influencing the meaningful learning and retention of *new* subject matter material. Hence, facilitation of sequential meaningful learning can be exercised most effectively by identifying and manipulating significant cognitive structure variables (e.g., availability, stability, clarity, and discriminability). This goal can be accomplished in two different complementary ways: (1) *substantively,* by showing concern for the "structure" of a discipline (that is, using for organizational and integrative purposes those unifying concepts and propositions that have the widest inclusiveness, explanatory power, generalizability and relatability for the subject-matter content of that discipline); and (2) *programmatically,* by employing suitable principles of organizing and ordering the sequence of subject matter, constructing its internal logic and organization and arranging practice trials (review).

Knowledge as Substantive Content or as Problem-Solving Capability

Both Gagné (1962) and Bruner (1959, 1960) depart significantly from the cognitive position presented above in their conception of the role of cognitive structure in transfer. This difference stems in part from their more behavioristic conception of the nature of knowledge as consisting of the *capability* of performing different classes of problem-solving tasks.[1] Thus, in fostering transfer, Gagné (1962, 1977) focuses on whether the learner possesses the component or subordinate problem-solving capabilities required for manifesting a given higher-order problem-solving capability. Concentrating more on the deductive aspects of transfer, Bruner (1959, 1960) emphasizes "generic learning" because it can facilitate derivative problem solving, that is, the solution of problems that are particular exemplars of a more general proposition.

From the standpoint of a cognitive approach, on the other hand, knowledge is viewed more as a substantive (ideational) state rather than as a problem-solving capability; and the transfer functions of cognitive structure are regarded as applying more significantly to reception learning than to problem solving in the typical classroom learning situation. Moreover, the learning of generic concepts and propositions is advocated more as a means of providing stable anchorage for correlative instructional materials (for example, extensions, elaborations, modifications, and qualifications of established ideas in cognitive structure) than to make possible the regeneration of forgotten derivative instances. The theoretical rationale for this preference is that the main problem of transfer in acquiring a body of knowledge involves the stabilization (through substantive and programmatic learning procedures) of those correlative ideas constituting the flesh and blood of a discipline that would otherwise undergo obliterative subsumption; much less crucial for transfer is enhancement of the ability to solve on demand those problems that can be successfully handled if the learner retains a bare skeleton of generic principles (derivative subsumption).

Neurophysiological Determinants and Correlates of Cognitive Phenomena

Apart from Hebb, neobehaviorists are generally less interested than were their predecessors in specifying the neurophysiological determinants or correlates of cognitive phenomena. They are usually content with stating that a basically behavioral organismic process underlies meaning, and they tend to be rather indefinite about defining this process in neurophysiological terms. Hebb (1949), on the other hand, aimed for thoroughgoing neurological explicitness in his theoretical system. He speaks, for example, about a process of "recruitment" in describing what happens in a hypothetical "cell assembly" during concept acquisition, and about the reorganization of cell assemblies into "phase sequences" in accounting for the development of Bartlett's (1932) "schemata."

Cognitive theorists, on the other hand, tend to doubt that the identification of cognitive events with hypothetical, speculative, and metaphorically related neurological entities can add much to our understanding of cognition. Even the postulation of nonphysiological organismic processes for cognitive phenomena strikes them as unnecessary and unparsimonious. They prefer to define cognitive events in terms of differentiated processes and states of consciousness—existing as organized systems of images, concepts, and propositions, etc., in cognitive structure—and of the cognitive processes on which they depend.

> Neurophysiological processes accompany, are correlated with, and make certain cognitive events possible but occur at a "substrate" level that has little or no *explanatory* value whatsoever for these higher-order phenomena. [Furthermore, although neurophysiological] correlates undoubtedly exist for the raw material (percepts and images) of cognitive operations, . . . the combination of, and interaction between images (percepts) and ideas involved in problem solving, concept acquisition, and thinking probably have no corresponding neural concomitants. They are essentially extraneural [non-material], psychological phenomena dependent on only sufficient substrate integrity of the brain to make [consciousness], perception, memory, [thinking], and the interrelation of their products possible. (Ausubel, 1961, 1962)

This, of course, is tantamount to almost complete repudiation of the reductionistic view that psychological phenomena must ultimately be explicable in neurophysiological terms.

Modern neuroscience's interest in the neurological basis of different psychological functions and deficiencies is not primarily in discovering differential neural nuclei, tracts, and connections (and the pathological lesions therein) that could explain the corresponding differences in psychological functioning and defects, as well as their underlying processes or mechanisms. This is the case because differential neural anatomy and physiology, in my opinion, play only a "substrate," non-explanatory role in psychological functioning. They need only manifest functional tissue (neural) integrity.

Differential psychological functioning, therefore, can be best explained, as well conceived of as determined and regulated primarily by psychological (rather than neural) processes, provided that their corresponding neural substrates are intact, and the person in question must obviously also be alive in order to play his substrate role in the differential psychological functioning.

THE NATURE OF RECEPTION LEARNING

Few pedagogic devices in our time have been repudiated more unequivocally by educational theorists than the method of expository verbal instruction. It is fashionable in many quarters to characterize verbal reception learning as parrot-like recitation and rote memorization of arbitrary and isolated facts that are completely unintelligible to the learner, and to dismiss it disdainfully as an archaic remnant of discredited educational tradition. In fact, quite apart from whatever intrinsic value they may possess, many educational innovations and movements of the twentieth century—activity programs, project and discussion methods, various ways of maximizing nonverbal and manipulative experience in the classroom, emphasis on "self-discovery," and on learning for and by *problem solving*—owe much of their origins and popularity to widespread dissatisfaction with the methods of verbal instruction. It has been commonly accepted for example (at least in the realm of educational theory) (1) that meaningful generalizations cannot be presented or "given" to the learner but can only be acquired as a product of problem-solving activity (Brownell & Hendrickson, 1950) and (2) that all attempts to master verbal concepts and propositions are forms of empty verbalism unless the learner has recent prior experience with the concrete realities to which these verbal constructs refer (Brownell & Hendrickson, 1950).

Critique of Expository Teaching and Reception Learning

Excellent reasons, of course exist for the general disrepute into which expository teaching and verbal reception learning have fallen. The most obvious of these is that, notwithstanding repeated policy declarations of educational organizations to the contrary, potentially meaningful subject matter is still very often presented to pupils in preponderantly rote fashion. Another less obvious but equally important reason why meaningfulness is perceived as an exclusive product of problem solving and discovery methods of learning stems from two serious shortcomings of modern learning theory. First, psychologists have tended to subsume many *qualitatively* different kinds of learning processes under a single explanatory model. As a result widespread confusion exists, even today, regarding basic distinctions between reception and discovery learning and between rote and meaningful learning. It has not always been sufficiently clear, for example, that such categorically different types of learning as problem solving and the understanding of presented verbal material have different objectives, and that conditions and instructional techniques facilitating one of these types of learning processes are not necessarily relevant or maximally efficient for the other.

Second, in the absence of an appropriate theory of meaningful verbal learning, many educational psychologists have tended to interpret long-term subject-matter (meaningful) learning in terms of the same concepts (e.g., retroactive inhibition, stimulus generalization, response competition) used to explain instrumental conditioning, paired-associate learning, rote serial learning, maze learning, and simple discrimination learning.

RECEPTION VERSUS DISCOVERY LEARNING

Until the late Fifties and early Sixties, and the first notable disavowal (Mandler, 1962) of the behavioristic attempt to reduce complex mental processes to the rote verbal learning model, many psychologists and educational psychologists implicitly accepted the proposition that comprehension, the acquisition and retention of knowledge, forgetting, concept formation, and problem solving could eventually be explained by the same principles that are operative in the learning and retention of nonsense syllables and paired adjectives. It is small wonder then that educators perceived subject-matter learning as an extension of rote learning and turned to such panaceas as "learning by discovery," "Every child is a creative thinker," and "process" approaches to the teaching of science, etc.

An attempt will, therefore, be made in this chapter to distinguish between reception and discovery learning, to sharpen the existing distinction between rote and meaningful learning, and to consider the distinctive role of each of these types of learning in the total educational enterprise. It should be clear by now that verbal reception learning can be genuinely meaningful without prior discovery experience or problem-solving activity and that the weaknesses attributed to the method of expository verbal instruction do not inhere in the method itself but, rather, are largely derived from various misapplications and misuses of it.

From the standpoint of enhancing intellectual development, no theoretical concern is more relevant or pressing in the present state of our knowledge than the need for distinguishing clearly among the principal kinds of school learning (e.g., rote and meaningful verbal learning, concept acquisition, and verbal and nonverbal problem solving) that take place in the classroom. One significant way of differentiating among the latter types of classroom learning is to make two critical process distinctions that cut across all of them—distinctions between reception and discovery learning and between rote and meaningful learning.

The first distinction is especially important because most of the understandings that learners acquire both in and out of school are presented (and the product of reception learning) rather than discovered. Also, since most learning material is presented verbally, it is equally important to appreciate that *verbal* reception learning is not necessarily rote in character and can be meaningful without prior nonverbal and problem-solving experience.

In reception learning (rote or meaningful) the entire content of what is to be learned is presented to the learner in final form. The learning task does not involve any independent discovery on his or her part. The learner is only required to internalize the material (e.g., a list of nonsense syllables or paired associates, a poem or geometrical theorem) that is presented to him so that it is available and reproducible at some future date.

The essential feature of discovery learning (e.g., concept formation, rote or meaningful problem solving), on the other hand, is that the principal content of what is to be learned is not given but must be independently discovered by the learner before he can internalize it. The distinctive and prior learning task, in other words, is to discover something—which of two maze alleys leads to the goal, the precise nature of a relationship between two variables, the common attributes of a number of diverse instances, etc.

The first phase of discovery learning, therefore, involves a process quite different from that of reception learning. The learner must rearrange a given array of information, integrate it with existing cognitive structure, and reorganize or transform the integrated combination in such a way as to create a desired end-product or discover a missing means–end relationship. After this phase is completed, the discovered content is internalized, just as in reception learning.

It should be clear up to this point, therefore, that reception and discovery learning are two quite different types of processes and that most classroom instruction is organized along the lines of reception learning. In the next section it will be shown that verbal reception learning is not necessarily rote in character, that much ideational material (e.g., concepts, generalizations) can be meaningfully internalized and made available without prior discovery experience, and that at no stage does the learner have to discover principles independently in order to be able to understand and use them meaningfully.

Reception and discovery learning are not only basically different in essential nature and process, but also differ with respect to their principal roles in intellectual development and cognitive functioning. Essentially, large bodies of subject matter are acquired in school through reception learning, whereas the everyday problems of living are solved through discovery learning.

Some overlap of function, however, does exist: The knowledge acquired through reception learning is also used in everyday problem solving, and discovery learning is commonly used in the classroom to apply, extend, integrate, and evaluate subject-matter knowledge and to test its comprehension. In laboratory situations discovery learning also leads to the contrived rediscovery of known propositions and, when employed by scientists, to significant new knowledge. Typically, however, the propositions discovered through problem-solving methods are rarely sufficiently original, significant, or worth incorporating into the learner's subject-matter knowledge. In any case, discovery technics hardly constitute an efficient primary means of transmitting the content of an academic discipline.

Discovery learning, therefore, is a psychologically more involved process than reception learning because it presupposes a problem-solving stage that precedes the interiorization of information and the emergence of meaning. However, reception learning, on the whole, appears later developmentally and, in most instances, implies a greater degree of cognitive maturity. The preschool child learns most new concepts and propositions inductively through autonomous discovery. Self-discovery, however, is not essential for concept formation in the elementary-school child if concrete-empirical props are available. Reception learning, on the other hand, although also occurring earlier developmentally, is not really prominent[2] until the child is both capable of internal mental operations and can comprehend verbally presented concepts and propositions with the benefit of current concrete-empirical experience. The typical contrast here, therefore, is between inductive concept *formation* with the aid of concrete-empirical props, on the one hand, and direct concept *assimilation* through verbal exposition (definition), on the other.

Presenting the case for the discovery or problem-solving approach to learning, Bruner argues that discovery is necessary for "real possession" of knowledge, has certain unique motivational advantages, organizes knowledge effectively for later use, and promotes long-term retention. Most of these specific claims, however, are untenable (Ausubel, 1961), but it is undeniable nevertheless that the discovery method does offer some unique motivational advantages, is a useful adjunctive instructional technique under certain educational conditions, and is necessary both for the development of problem-solving abilities and for learning how new knowledge is discovered. However, it is not an indispensable condition for the occurrence of meaningful learning and is much too time-consuming to be used efficiently as a primary method of transmitting subject-matter content in typical classroom situations.

Despite strident assertions on the part of discovery enthusiasts, most classroom teachers still appreciate that verbal exposition, supplemented where necessary by concrete-empirical props, is actually the most efficient way of teaching subject matter to elementary- and secondary-school pupils and leads to sounder and less trivial knowledge than when students serve as their own pedagogues.

Teachers generally reject such extreme assertions (e.g., Bruner, 1960) as (1) that children *really* understand what they learn only when they discover it autonomously (by themselves); (2) that learning the general "heuristics of discovery" is more important for purposes of transferability (and because of the so-called rapid obsolescence of knowledge) than learning the content of the various disciplines (e.g., the "process" approach to science teaching); (3) that learning by discovery should be the principal pedagogic device for transmitting the vast amount of knowledge that students must acquire; and (4) that science students learn science best by acting *as if* they were scientists and by doing the same things that the latter do. They reject the latter proposition because of major differences between scientists and students in their respective goals and levels of subject-matter sophistication.

Furthermore, research evidence that the availability of relevant background concepts and principles in the student's cognitive structure (supplemented somewhat by other cognitive capabilities and personality traits) accounts for most of the variance in problem-solving outcomes (Saugstad, 1955), (apart from discipline-specific, largely genically determined, and relatively unteachable cognitive and personality traits). It tends to deflate the claims of the "process" approach to teaching. Thus, "process" education or "teaching for problem solving" (or "creativity"), if it became the major instructional approach to education, could only result in a thoroughgoing educational disaster comparable to that occurring throughout the United States from the Thirties to the middle Fifties. At that time the expository teaching of concepts and principles in mathematics and the physical sciences fell into disrepute, and over-reliance was accordingly placed on a rote "type"-problem-solving approach and on cookbook performance of laboratory exercises for transmitting the substantive or ideational content of these disciplines. As a result an entire generation of high-school and college graduates were able to "solve" all of the required problems dealing, for example, with Ohm's Law, logarithms, exponents, functions, and differential and integral calculus, molar and molecular solutions, etc., without having the foggiest notions of the meaning of any of the concepts or principles in question.

All of this, of course, does not in the least detract from the legitimate use of contrived (arranged) discovery learning in teaching children scientific method in the various disciplines and in providing them with some notion of how new knowledge in a given field comes into being.

Can Reception Learning Be Meaningful?

It is frequently maintained, as already pointed out, that abstract concepts and generalizations are forms of empty, meaningless verbalisms unless the learner discovers them autonomously out of his own concrete, empirical, problem-solving experience. Careful analysis of this proposition reveals, in my opinion, that it rests on three serious logical fallacies: (1) A straw-man" representation of the method of verbal learning, (2) the prevailing tendency to confuse the reception–discovery dimension of the learning process with the rote–meaningful dimension, and (3) unwarranted generalization of the distinctive developmental conditions of learning and thinking in childhood to adolescence and adult life.

The use of the straw-man technic was, of course, the simplest and most effective way of discrediting the method of verbal exposition. Instead of describing this pedagogic method in terms off its essential characteristics, it became fashionable to picture it in terms of its worst abuses. Examples of such abuses were naturally not very difficult to find, since an appreciable number of teachers still rely on rote verbal learning in teaching potentially meaningful subject matter.

Some of the more flagrantly inept practices employed in such teaching include the following: (1) premature use of verbal technics with cognitively immature pupils, (2) arbitrary presentation of unrelated facts without any organizing or explanatory principles, (3) failure to integrate new learning tasks with previously presented materials, (4) the use of evaluation procedures that merely measure ability to recognize discrete facts or to reproduce ideas in the same words or in the identical context as originally encountered (Ausubel, 1961a).

Although it is entirely proper to caution teachers against the frequent misuses of verbal learning, it is not appropriate to represent them as inherent in the method itself. An approach to instruction that on logical and psychological grounds appears appropriate and efficient should not be discarded as unworkable simply because, like all pedagogic technics in the hands of incompetent or unintelligent teachers, it is subject to abuse. It would seem more reasonable to guard against the more common misapplications and to relate the method to relevant theoretical principles and research findings that actually deal with the long-term learning and retention of large bodies of potentially meaningful, verbally presented materials.

The distinction between rote and meaningful learning is frequently confused with the reception–discovery distinction discussed above. This confusion is partly responsible for the widespread but unwarranted twin beliefs that reception learning is invariably rote and that discovery learning is inherently and necessarily meaningful. Both assumptions, of course, are related to the long-standing erroneous doctrine that the only knowledge one *really* possesses and understands is knowledge that one discovers *by oneself.* Actually, each distinction constitutes an entirely independent dimension of learning.

A much more defensible proposition, therefore, is that *both* expository *and* problem-solving techniques can be either rote *or* meaningful depending on the conditions under which learning occurs. In both instances meaningful learning takes place if the learning task can be related in nonarbitrary, nonverbatim fashion to what the learner already knows and if the learner adopts a corresponding learning set to do so.

It is true, of course, that by these criteria much potentially meaningful knowledge taught by verbal exposition results in rotely learned verbalisms. This rote outcome, however, is not inherent in the expository method per se, but rather in such abuses of this method on the part of teachers, textbooks, and learners as fail to satisfy the criteria of meaningful learning. There is also much greater reluctance, on the other hand, to acknowledge that the aforementioned preconditions for meaningful learning also apply to problem solving and laboratory methods. It should seem rather self-evident, however, that performing laboratory experiments in cookbook fashion, without understanding the underlying substantive and methodological principles involved, confers precious little genuine understanding and that many students studying mathematics and science find it relatively simple to "discover" correct answers to "type" problems without really understanding what they are doing. They accomplish the latter feat merely by rotely memorizing these "type problems" and the appropriate procedures for manipulating the symbols of each type. Nevertheless, it is still not generally appreciated that laboratory work and problem solving are not genuinely meaningful experiences unless they are built on a foundation of clearly understood concepts and principles in the discipline in question and unless the constituent operations are themselves meaningful.

The art and science of presenting ideas and information meaningfully and effectively—so that clear, stable, and unambiguous meanings emerge and are retained over an appreciably long period of time as an organized body of knowledge—is really the principal function of pedagogy. This is a demanding and creative task rather than a routine or mechanical one. The job of selecting, organizing, presenting, and translating subject-matter content in a developmentally appropriate manner requires more than a rote listing of facts. If it is done properly, it is the work of a master teacher and is hardly a task to be disdained.

RECEPTION LEARNING AND COGNITIVE DEVELOPMENT

Finally, it is important to appreciate the relationship between reception learning and various developmental considerations that affect its meaningfulness. Learners who have not yet developed beyond the concrete stage of cognitive development are unable meaningfully to incorporate within their cognitive structures a relationship between two or more abstractions unless they have the benefit of current or recently prior concrete-empirical experience (Inhelder & Piaget, 1958). Thus, during the concrete stage, roughly covering the elementary school period, children are restricted by their dependence on concrete-empirical experience to a semiabstract, intuitive understanding of abstract propositions.

Even during the elementary school years the act of discovery is not indispensable for intuitive understanding and need not constitute a routine aspect of pedagogic technic. As every elementary school teacher knows, meaningful verbal reception learning—without any current or recently prior problem solving or discovery experience whatsoever—is perhaps the commonest form of classroom learning, provided that the necessary concrete props are available. A growing body of evidence suggests that improved instructional practices derived from meaningful verbal learning practices (Assimilation Theory) can enhance the ability of both children (even at the preschool level) and adults to engage in abstract verbal reception learning.

During the abstract stage of cognitive development, however, beginning in the late junior high school period, students acquire most new concepts and learn most new propositions by *directly* grasping higher order relationships between abstractions (Inhelder & Piaget, 1958). To do so meaningfully, they need no longer depend on current or recently prior concrete-empirical experience; hence, they are able to bypass completely the intuitive type of understanding reflective of such dependence. Through proper expository teaching they can proceed directly to a level of abstract understanding that is qualitatively superior to the intuitive level in terms of generality, clarity, precision, and explicitness. At this stage of development, therefore, it seems pointless and wasteful to enhance *intuitive* understanding by using discovery technics.

This is the point at which some of the more zealous proponents of Progressive Education took a disastrously false turn. John Dewey had correctly recognized that understanding of abstract concepts and principles in childhood must be built on a foundation of direct, empirical experience; for this reason he advocated the use of project and activity methods in the elementary school. But he also appreciated that once a firmly grounded foundation of abstract understandings was established, it was possible to organize secondary and higher education along more abstract and verbal lines.

Unfortunately, however, although Dewey himself never elaborated or implemented this latter insight, some of his disciples blindly generalized childhood limiting conditions, with respect to meaningful verbal reception learning, broadly enough to encompass learning over the entire life span. This unwarranted extrapolation, frequently but erroneously attributed to Dewey himself, provided a pseudonaturalistic rationale for, and, thus, helped perpetuate, the seeming indestructible myth that, under any and all circumstances, abstractions cannot possibly be meaningful unless preceded by direct, empirical experience.

THE ROTE-MEANINGFUL AND RECEPTION-DISCOVERY CONTINUA

Both the rote-meaningful and reception discovery dimensions of learning exist on a continuum rather than being dichotomous in nature. As will be indicated shortly, representational learning is much closer to the rote end of the continuum than is concept or propositional learning.

Also, it is quite possible to exhibit a rote and meaningful set simultaneously or successively (e.g., learning the multiplication table; an actor who first learns his lines meaningfully before memorizing them). Similarly, discovery learning may be entirely autonomous, as in the case of a research scientist, or wholly contrived or arranged as in the case of a typical science student performing a laboratory experiment.

Actually, *both* reception and discovery learning *each* exhibits many features of the reception mode. The only real difference between the two is that in reception learning the principal content of what is to be learned is presented to the learner, whereas in discovery learning the problem-setting proposition and the relevant background knowledge it activates must be reorganized to meet the demands of a means-end relationship. This latter generation and testing of problem-solving hypotheses is really the only true discovery aspect of so-called discovery learning.

IS RECEPTION LEARNING PASSIVE?

The emergence of meanings, as new concepts and ideas are incorporated into cognitive structure, is far from being a passive phenomenon. In view of the complex and variable nature of learners' intellectual backgrounds, much activity is obviously involved—but not the kind of activity characterizing discovery. Activity and discovery are not synonymous in the realm of cognitive functioning. Merely because potential meanings have been presented, we cannot assume that they have necessarily been acquired and that all subsequent loss is reflective of forgetting. Obviously, before meanings can be retained, they must first be acquired; and the process of acquisition is exceedingly active.

Meaningful reception learning involves more than the simple cataloguing of ready-made concepts within existing cognitive structure.

> First, at the very least, an implicit judgment of relevance is usually required in deciding under which existing concept or proposition to subsume new ideas in the instructional material.

Second, some degree of reconciliation with existing knowledge is also necessary, particularly if there are obvious discrepancies or conflicts.

Third, new propositions are customarily translated into a personal frame of reference consonant with the learner's idiosyncratic experiential background, vocabulary, and structure of ideas.

Last, some degree of reorganization under different, more inclusive concepts is sometimes required if a more simple basis for reconciliation cannot be found.

All of this cognitive activity, however, stops short of actual discovery or problem solving. Since the substance of the learning task is presented rather than discovered, the activity involved is limited to that required for understanding and generating new meanings and integrating them into existing cognitive structure. This is naturally of a qualitatively different order than that involved in independently discovering solutions to new problems, or in the task of integrating and reorganizing new information and existing knowledge to satisfy the requirements of new problem situations.

The extent of cognitive activity involved in meaningful reception learning obviously depends on the learner's general readiness and level of cognitive sophistication, as well as on the availability within his cognitive structure of relevant anchoring ideas. Hence, the degree of activity necessary would be substantially reduced if the presented material were appropriately programmed to fit his experiential background and level of readiness.

The extent to which meaningful reception learning is active is also a function of the particular learner's need for integrative meaning and of his or her self-critical faculty. Learners may either attempt to integrate a new proposition with all of their existing relevant knowledge or remain content with establishing its relatedness to just a single idea. Similarly, they may endeavor to translate the new proposition into terminology consistent with their own vocabulary and ideational background or remain satisfied with incorporating it as presented. Finally, learners may strive for the acquisition of precise, unambiguous meanings or be completely satisfied with vague, diffuse notions.

The main danger in meaningful reception learning is not so much that learners will frankly adopt a rote approach, but that they will delude themselves into believing that they have really grasped precise intended meanings when they have only grasped a vague and confused set of generalities and no real meanings whatsoever (Novak, 1998). In so doing, it is not so much that learners do not want to understand; rather, it is that they lack the necessary self-critical ability and/or are unwilling to put forth the necessary active effort involved in struggling with the material, looking at it from different angles, reconciling it with their existing and contradictory knowledge, and translating it into their own frame of reference. Thus, they find it easy enough to manipulate words so as to create an *appearance* of knowledge and thereby to delude themselves and sometimes others that they really understand.

A central task of pedagogy, therefore, is to develop ways of facilitating an active variety of reception learning supplemented by an independent and critical approach to the understanding of subject matter. This involves, in part, the encouragement of motivations for and of self-critical attitudes toward acquiring precise and integrated meanings, as well as the use of other technics directed toward the same end.

Precise and integrated understandings are, presumably, more likely to develop:

1. If the central, unifying ideas of a discipline are learned before more peripheral concepts and information are introduced.
2. If the limiting conditions of general developmental readiness are observed.
3. If precise and accurate definition is stressed and emphasis is placed on explicitly delineating similarities and differences between related concepts.
4. If learners are required to reformulate new propositions in their own words.

All of these latter devices come under the heading of pedagogic technics that promote an *active* type of meaningful reception learning. Teachers can help foster the related objective of critical thinking with regard to subject-matter content by encouraging students to recognize and challenge the assumptions underlying new propositions, to distinguish between facts and hypotheses, and between warranted and unwarranted inferences. Much good use can also be made of Socratic questioning in exposing pseudounderstanding, in transmitting precise meanings, in reconciling contradictions, and in encouraging a critical attitude toward knowledge.

MEANINGFUL VERSUS ROTE LEARNING

By "meaningful learning" we refer primarily to a distinctive kind of learning process as well as only secondarily to a meaningful learning outcome—attainment of a new meaning—that necessarily reflects the operation and completion of such a process. Meaningful learning as a process presupposes, in turn, *both* that learners employ a meaningful learning set and that the material they learn is potentially meaningful to them, that is, relatable to relevant anchoring ideas in their cognitive structures.

Thus, regardless of how much potential meaning may inhere in a given proposition, if the learner's intention is to memorize it arbitrarily and verbatimly, i.e., as a series of arbitrarily related and unalterable words, both the learning process and the learning outcome must necessarily be rote and meaningless. Conversely, no matter how meaningful the learner's set may be, neither the process nor outcome of learning can possibly be meaningful if the learning task itself consists of purely arbitrary associations as in a paired-associate or rote serial learning task or if relevant anchoring ideas are not present in his cognitive structure.

Meaningful Learning Set

In meaningful learning the learner has an obligatory set to relate nonverbatim (as opposed to verbatim) aspects of new concepts, propositions, information, or situations to relevant components of existing cognitive structure in various nonarbitrary ways that make possible the incorporation of derivative, elaborative, correlative, modifying, supportive, qualifying, superordinate, or representational relationships into his cognitive structure. Depending on the nature of the learning task (i.e., reception or discovery), the set may be either to discover or merely to apprehend (comprehend) and incorporate such relationships into his cognitive structure. In rote learning, on the other hand, the learner's set is either to discover an arbitrary solution to a problem, or to internalize verbal material arbitrarily and verbatim, as a discrete and isolated end in itself. Such learning, however, obviously does not occur in a cognitive vacuum. The material *is* related to relevant aspects of cognitive structure but not in a substantive (nonverbatim), nonarbitrary fashion permitting its incorporation in one of the existing cognitive structure relationships specified above. Where discovery learning is involved, the distinction between rote and meaningful learning corresponds to that between "trial and error" and insightful problem solving.

Potentially Meaningful Material

A meaningful intentional set or approach to learning, as already indicated, only eventuates in a meaningful learning process and outcome provided that the learning material itself is *potentially* meaningful. Insistence on the qualifying adjective "potential" in this instance is more than mere academic hairsplitting. If the learning material (task) were simply considered *already* meaningful, the learning process (apprehending and generating its meaning and making it functionally available) would be completely superfluous; the object of learning would obviously be *already* accomplished, by definition, before any learning was ever attempted irrespective of the type of learning set employed or the existence of prior relevant knowledge in cognitive structure. It is true, of course, that certain *component* elements of a current learning task as, for example, the individual words of a new geometrical theorem, may already be meaningful to the learner; but it is the meaning of the proposition as a whole that is the object of learning in this situation—not the individual meanings of its component elements.

Thus, although the term "meaningful learning" necessarily implies the processing of potentially meaningful learning tasks, it does *not* imply that the learning of meaningful as opposed to rote material is the distinctive feature of meaningful learning. Already meaningful learning material may, of course, be perceived as such and reacted to meaningfully; but the material cannot possibly constitute a *meaningful learning task* inasmuch as the very term "meaningful" denotes that the object of learning was previously consummated.

Two important criteria determine whether new learning can be considered potentially meaningful. The first criterion—nonarbitrary, nonverbatim relatability to *particular* relevant ideas in the learner's cognitive structure,[3] in the various potential relational ways specified above—is a property of the material itself and depends on whether it is plausible or sensible (nonarbitrary) and logically relatable to *any* appropriate cognitive structure. New material is *not* potentially meaningful if either the total learning task (e.g., a particular list of nonsense syllables, a list of paired adjectives, a scrambled sentence) or the basic unit of the learning task (arbitrarily paired adjectives) is only relatable to a hypothetical cognitive structure on a purely arbitrary basis. This criterion of potential meaningfulness applies to the current learning task as a whole—not to any of its component elements that may *already* be meaningful, such as the component letters of a nonsense syllable, each member of an adjective pair, or the component words of a scrambled sentence. In each instance, the meaningful components, although physically part of the learning material, do not constitute part of the psychological learning task in a functional sense.

The second important criterion determining whether learning material is potentially meaningful—its relatability to the *particular* cognitive structure of a *particular* learner—is more properly a characteristic of the learner than of the material per se. Phenomenologically, meaningfulness is an individual matter. Hence, for meaningful learning to occur in fact, it is not sufficient that the new material simply be relatable to relevant ideas in the hypothetical or *abstract* sense of the term (or to the cognitive structures of *some* learners). The cognitive structure of the *particular* learner must naturally include the requisite intellectual capacities, ideational content, or experiential background if it is to be considered relevant and relatable to the learning task. It is on this basis that the potential meaningfulness of learning material varies with such factors as age, intelligence, occupation, cultural membership, etc. In other words, it is subsumability within, or incorporability by, a *particular* learner's cognitive structure that converts "logical" into potential meaning and that (given nonarbitrary relatable learning material and a meaningful learning set) differentiates meaningful from rote learning.

As long as the learning set, learning material, and cognitive structure conditions of meaningful learning are satisfied, the learning outcome should be meaningful and the advantages of meaningful learning (i.e., economy of learning effort, more stable retention, and greater transferability) should accrue irrespective of whether the content to be internalized is presented or discovered and verbal or nonverbal.

PROCESS DIFFERENCES BETWEEN MEANINGFUL AND ROTE RECEPTION LEARNING

In view of the foregoing, plausible reasons exist for believing that rotely and meaningfully learned materials are processed and organized quite differently in cognitive structure and hence conform to quite different principles of learning and forgetting.

First, meaningfully learned materials are related to existing concepts in cognitive structure in ways making possible the apprehension and understanding of various kinds of significant ideational relationships (e.g., derivative, qualifying, correlative, superordinate, etc.) and the parallel emergence of corresponding new meanings. Most new ideational materials that pupils encounter in a school setting are nonarbitrarily and nonverbatimly relatable to a previously learned background of meaningful ideas and information. In fact, the curriculum is deliberately organized in this fashion to provide for the untraumatic introduction of new facts and ideas. Rotely learned materials, on the other hand, are discrete and relatively isolated informational entities that are relatable to cognitive structure only in an arbitrary, verbatim fashion, not permitting the establishment of the above-mentioned relationships. Second, because they are not anchored to existing ideational systems, rotely learned materials (unless greatly overlearned or endowed with unusual vividness) are much more vulnerable to proactive and retroactive interference and, hence, to forgetting; i.e., they have a much shorter retention span.[4]

These two differences between rote and meaningful learning categories have important implications for the underlying kinds of learning and retention processes involved in each category. Rotely learned materials are essentially isolated from existing conceptual and propositional entities within cognitive structure; consequently they are primarily influenced by the interfering effects of *similar* rote materials learned *immediately* before or after the learning task. Thus, it is not unreasonable to explain the learning and forgetting of discrete rote units in such stimulus–response terms as intratask and intertask similarity, response competition, and stimulus or response generalization.

With regard to meaningful learning and retention, however, it seems more plausible to suppose that learning materials are primarily influenced by the attributes of relevant and cumulatively established ideational foci in cognitive structure with which they interact. Compared to this type of extended interaction, concurrent interfering effects have relatively little influence and explanatory value.

THE ASSIMILATION PROCESS IN MEANINGFUL LEARNING AND RETENTION

We are now ready to consider the mechanisms of accretion and long-term retention of large bodies of ideational material. Why do high-school and university students, for example, tend to forget so readily previous day-to-day learnings as they are exposed to new lessons? Extrapolating from studies of short-term learning in animals and human subjects, the traditional answer of both experimental and educational psychology in the past has usually been that the forgetting in this example was caused by proactive and/or retroactive interference exerted by similar, but not identical, verbal material, immediately prior or subsequent to the learning of the instructional material in question.

It would be plausible to expect, however, that *meaningfully* learned ideas that are "anchored" to relevant ideas in cognitive structure, and are, thus, part of stable ideational systems, would be much less vulnerable to proactive and retroactive interference[4] than are discrete, rotely learned tasks, and would also be protected from such interference by the stability of the anchoring ideas in which they are embedded.

The model of cognitive organization proposed for the meaningful learning and retention of potentially meaningful materials assumes the existence of a cognitive structure that is hierarchically organized in terms of highly inclusive conceptual and propositional traces.[5] Under such are subsumed traces of less inclusive concepts and propositions, as well as traces of specific informational data. The major organizational principle, in other words, is that of progressive differentiation of trace systems of a given sphere of knowledge from regions of greater to lesser inclusiveness, each linked to the next higher step in the hierarchy through a process of subsumption.

It is incorrect, however, to conceive of this mode of organization as deductive in nature. The inductive–deductive issue is only relevant in considering the order of acquiring or presenting generalizations and supportive data and the hierarchical procedure adopted in problem solving. Irrespective of how they are acquired in the first place (inductively or deductively), new learning materials are incorporated into the total ideational organization in accordance with the same principle of progressive differentiation.

Meaningful reception learning typically occurs as potentially meaningful instructional material enters the learner's cognitive field and interacts with and is appropriately subsumed under a relevant and more inclusive conceptual system. The very fact that such material is subsumable in nonarbitrary, nonverbatim fashion (e.g., relatable to stable relevant elements in his or her cognitive structure) accounts for its potential meaningfulness and makes possible the establishment of meaningful relationships with anchoring ideas and the emergence of actual meaning. If it were not subsumable, it would constitute rote material and result in discrete and relatively isolated traces arbitrarily associated with ideational components in cognitive structure. Hence, it is postulated that both the learning and retention of potentially meaningful material are primarily influenced by the attributes of the particular relevant ideas in cognitive structure with which they interact and by the nature of this interactional process. Existing cognitive structure, in other words, is the major factor affecting meaningful learning and retention.

The initial effects of subsumption, therefore, may be described as facilitation of both learning and retention. Only orienting, relational, and cataloguing operations are involved at first. These preliminary operations are obviously essential for meaningful learning and retention since the hierarchical incorporation of new learning material into an existing relevant ideational system is the basis for the emergence of all meaning and must also necessarily conform to the prevailing principle of cognitive organization.

Furthermore, subsumption of the traces of the learning task under an established ideational system in cognitive structure provides anchorage for the new material, and, thus, constitutes the most orderly, efficient, and stable way of retaining them for future availability and/or use. For a variable period of time, these recently catalogued concepts and propositions can be dissociated from their subsuming (anchoring) ideas and are reproducible as individually identifiable entities. As a result of the assimilation process characterizing all of cognition, however, this gradual loss of dissociability with forgetting is probably a specific example of a more general reductionistic trend in overall cognitive processing. In concept formation, for instance, when the criterial attributes of the concept are finally induced from appropriate exposure to multiple examples of criterial and non-criterial attributes, the specific criterial instances tend to be gradually forgotten or to become non-dissociable from the final emergent form of the concept. Forgetting can be decelerated, nevertheless, by such factors as primacy, vividness and overlearning, and by positive cognitive structure factors of availability, stability, clarity, and discriminability.

The Nature of Forgetting

Thus, although the stability of meaningful material is initially enhanced by anchorage to relevant and stable conceptual foci in the learner's cognitive structure, such material is gradually subjected to the erosive influence of the ubiquitous reductionistic trend in cognitive organization. Because it is psychologically more economical and less burdensome to retain a single highly inclusive idea than to remember several more specific related ideas, the particular import (meaning) of the latter multiple ideas tends to be incorporated by the generalized meaning of the single idea. As a result, when this second, or *obliterative,* stage of subsumption begins, the specific items in their original specific form become progressively less dissociable as entities in their own right until they are no longer available and are said to be forgotten.

Forgetting, thus, is a continuation or later temporal phase of the same interactional process underlying the availability of the instructional material established during and for a variable period of time after learning; and the same subsumability that is necessary for meaningful reception learning somewhat paradoxically provides the assimilated basis for later forgetting.

This process of memorial reduction to the least common denominator capable of representing cumulative prior interaction of the subsuming (anchoring) ideas with relevant instructional material is very similar to the reduction process characterizing concept formation. A single abstract (generic) concept, for example, is much more manipulable for cognitive purposes (e.g., problem solving) than the dozen or more diverse instances from which its commonality is abstracted; similarly, the memorial residue of interiorized ideational interaction with exogenous ideational material is also more functional for future learning and problem-solving occasions when stripped of its tangential modifiers, particularized connotations, and less clear and discriminable implications.

Hence, barring repetition or some other special reason (e.g., primacy, vividness, uniqueness, enhanced discriminability, overlearning, or the availability of a specially relevant and stable subsumer) for the perpetuation of dissociability, specific items of meaningful ideational content that are supportive of or correlative to an established conceptional or propositional entity, tend gradually to undergo obliterative subsumption (assimilation). In contrast to the behavioristic theory of memory (that accounts satisfactorily perhaps for rote forgetting only), it is held that the forgetting of recently processed potentially meaningful material is attributable to obliterative subsumption by the generalities of the more inclusive and established (anchoring) ideas rather than to response competition or to stimulus or response generalization.

Unfortunately, the advantages of obliterative subsumption are gained at the expense of losing variable aspects of the detailed mass of differentiated concepts, propositions, and specific information that constitute the flesh if not the skeleton of any discipline. One of the chief problems in acquiring a firm grasp of any academic discipline, therefore, lies in combating this inevitable obliterative process that is characteristic of all meaningful learning. The traditional pedagogic approach used in the attempt to realize this objective—usually effective up to a point—has been repetition or the overlearning of instructional materials. An additional novel approach that is somewhat more consonant with Assimilation Theory, and is advocated later in this volume, relies on efficacious manipulation of existing cognitive structure variables in ways that maximize the learning and retention of new, potentially meaningful verbal material. It is also possible to increase the effects of this latter manipulation by using advance organizers that are prepared differentially to enhance the stability, clarity, or discriminability of relevant anchoring ideas in cognitive structure.

COGNITIVE STRUCTURE VARIABLES

Existing cognitive structure—an individual's organization, stability, and clarity of knowledge in a particular subject-matter field at any given point in time—is regarded as the major factor influencing the learning and retention of potentially meaningful new instructional material in this same field of knowledge. The properties of relevant cognitive structure determine both the clarity and longevity of the meanings that emerge as new material enters the cognitive field, as well as the nature of the interactional process that takes place.

If relevant aspects of cognitive structure are available, clear, and suitably organized, stable and unambiguous meanings emerge and tend to retain their particularity, idiosyncratic natures, and dissociability. If, on the other hand, cognitive structure is unstable, ambiguous, disorganized, or chaotically organized, it tends to inhibit learning and retention. Even under the best of circumstances, however, through the process of obliterative subsumption (assimilation), cognitive structure contributes to and helps account for the ordinary forgetting of knowledge. Hence, it is only by strengthening relevant aspects of cognitive structure in ways that retard the rate of this obliterative process that new learning and retention can be facilitated. When we deliberately attempt to influence cognitive structure so as to maximize meaningful learning and retention, we come to the heart of the educative process.

Cognitive Structure and Transfer

In meaningful reception learning cognitive structure is always a relevant and crucial variable, even if it is not deliberately influenced or manipulated either to facilitate or to ascertain its effect on new learning. It is always at least a "silent partner" when other variables (e.g., practice, instructional materials, teaching methods, motivation) are implicated—as, for example, in those short-term learning situations where just a single unit of material is learned and *transfer* to new learning units is not measured. In those circumstances, however, its influence is indeterminable; we can only ascertain the effect of those variables that are intentionally manipulated or are otherwise measurable in the context of transfer in the research design.

In the more general and long-term sense, cognitive structure variables refer to significant organizational and relational properties of the learner's *total* knowledge in a given subject-matter field and their effect on his or her future overall performance in the same area of knowledge. In the more specific and short-term sense, on the other hand, cognitive structure variables refer to the organizational properties of just the *immediately* (or proximately) relevant subconcepts within a particular subject-matter field and their effects on the learning and retention of relatively *small* new *units* of relevant subject matter. In either sense, however, long- or short-term, the learner's acquisition of a clear, stable, and organized body of knowledge constitutes *more* than just the major long-term *dependent* variable (or criterion) to be measured in evaluating the impact of all factors and conditions impinging on learning and retention. Cognitive structure is *additionally,* in its own right, the most significant *independent* variable influencing (facilitating, inhibiting, limiting) the learner's capacity for acquiring and retaining more *new* and transferable knowledge in the same subject matter field.

The importance of cognitive structure factors (as independent variables) has been generally underestimated in the past because preoccupation with noncognitive, rote, conditional, and motor types of learning has tended to focus attention on such current situational and intrapersonal factors as practice, drive, incentive, and reinforcement variables. It is true that the effects of prior relevant experience on current learning tasks is conventionally considered under the heading of positive and negative transfer (or proactive facilitation and inhibition); but such transfer is generally interpreted in terms of the *direct* interaction between the stimulus and response attributes of the two overlapping but essentially discrete learning tasks (i.e., the recently experienced and the current).

Quite unlike laboratory types of learning situations, school learning generally requires the learner's incorporation of new ideas and information into an existing and established cognitive framework with particular organizational properties. The transfer paradigm still applies here, and transfer still refers to the impact of prior learning experience upon current learning. Prior experience in this case, however, is conceptualized as a cumulatively acquired, hierarchically organized, and established body of knowledge that is inherently relatable to the new learning task rather than conceptualized as a recently experienced constellation of stimulus–response connections influencing the learning of another discrete set of similar connections.

Furthermore, the relevant aspects of past experience in this type of transfer paradigm are such organizational properties of the learner's subject-matter knowledge as availability, proximateness of relevance, clarity, stability, generalizability, inclusiveness, cohesiveness, and discriminability (i.e., cognitive structure variables)—rather than degree of similarity between the stimuli and responses of the two learning tasks. Recent prior experience is not regarded as influencing current learning by interacting *directly* with the stimulus–response components of the new learning task; rather it is considered an influence on current learning only insofar as it modifies significant attributes of relevant cognitive structure. Cognitive structure variables, in other words, are the principal factors involved in meaningful transfer; and transfer itself is largely a reflection of the influence of these variables.

Because training and criterion tasks in laboratory studies of transfer have usually been separate and discrete, we have tended to think in terms of how prior task A influences performance on criterion task B. If performance has been facilitated, in comparison with that of a control group which had not been exposed to task A, we say that positive transfer has occurred. Actually, however, in typical classroom learning situations, A and B are not discrete but continuous. Task A is a preparatory stage of task B and a precursive aspect of the same learning process; B is not learned discretely but in relation to A. Hence, in school learning we deal not so much with transfer in the literal sense of the term; rather we deal with the influence of prior knowledge on new learning in a continuous, sequential context.

Another confusing residue from laboratory studies is the fact that transfer of training has been traditionally tested by problem solving rather than by new reception learning and retention. Actually, the principal effect of existing cognitive structure on new cognitive performance is on the learning and retention of new *presented* material containing potential meanings to be processed—not on the solution of problems requiring the application and reorganization of cognitive structure to new problem-solving ends. A transfer situation thus exists whenever existing cognitive structure affects new cognitive functioning, irrespective of whether it is in regard to reception learning or problem-solving criteria.

Principal Cognitive Structure Variables Influencing Meaningful Reception Learning and Retention

One conspicuously important variable affecting the incorporability of new, potentially meaningful material is the *availability* in cognitive structure of relevant subsuming ideas at an appropriate level of inclusiveness (but at a somewhat higher level of generality or non-specificity) to provide optimal anchorage. The appropriate level of inclusiveness in this context may be defined as that level which is as proximate as possible to the degree of abstract conceptualization and generalization of the learning task itself—considered in relation to the existing degree of differentiation of the subject matter as a whole in the learner's experiential background and cognitive structure. Thus, the more unfamiliar the learning task (i.e., the more undifferentiated the learner's subject matter background and the fewer the relevant ideas in his cognitive structure), the more inclusive or highly generalized his subsuming ideas must be in order to be proximate. If appropriate, relevant and proximate subsumers are not present in cognitive structure, the learner tends to utilize the most relevant and proximate ones that are available.

Since it is not always the case at any given stage in the learner's differentiation of a particular sphere of knowledge that we can depend on the spontaneous availability of adequately relevant and proximate subsuming concepts, an efficient way of facilitating learning and retention under these circumstances is to introduce appropriate subsumers ("advance organizers") and make them part of existing cognitive structure prior to the actual presentation of the learning task. The products of the interaction between the introduced subsumers and existing cognitive structures, thus, become particularly targeted anchoring foci for the reception learning of the new material. In effect, they provide ideational scaffolding (anchorage) at the appropriate level of conceptualization.

A second important cognitive structure factor presumably affecting the learning and retention of a potentially meaningful learning task is the extent to which the relevant subsuming ideas in cognitive structure are *discriminable* from it. A reasonable assumption here, borne out by preliminary investigation (Ausubel & Blake, 1958; Ausubel & Fitzgerald, 1961), would be that if the distinguishing features of the new learning material (e.g., the doctrinal tenets of Buddhism) were not originally salient and clearly discriminable from their presumably stable subsuming foci (in this case the tenets of Christianity) in the learner's cognitive structure, they could be adequately represented by the latter for memorial purposes and would not persist as dissociable entities identifiable in their own right. In other words, only discriminable categorical variants of more inclusive anchoring ideas in cognitive structure would have long-term retention potential as instructional material. The discriminability of these new instructional ideas could be enhanced either by repetition or more explicitly in advance by comparative advance organizers indicating straightforwardedly the principal similarities and differences between Buddhism and Christianity (as its presumed subsumers in cognitive structure).

Last, the longevity of new meaningful material in memory has been shown to be a function of the stability and clarity of its subsumers (Ausubel & Blake, 1958; Ausubel & Fitzgerald, 1962). Ambiguous and unstable subsumers not only provide weak anchorage for related new materials, but also cannot be easily discriminated from them. Factors probably influencing the clarity and stability of subsuming ideas include repetition, the use of exemplars, and multicontextual exposure.

Advance Organizers

The original pedagogical strategy particularly advocated in this book for deliberately manipulating cognitive structure so as to enhance proactive facilitation or to minimize proactive inhibition involves the use of those introductory materials described above (i.e., advance organizers) that are administered prior to the presentation of the actual learning passage. These advance organizers consist of introductory material at a higher level of abstraction, generality, and inclusiveness than the learning task itself. The function of the organizer is to provide ideational scaffolding (anchorage) for the stable incorporation and retention of the more detailed and differentiated material that follows in the learning passage as well as to increase discriminability between the latter passage and relevant anchoring ideas in cognitive structure. The organizer must not only be explicitly related to the more specific learning passage that follows, but (to be learnable and stable) must also be relatable to and take relevant ideas in cognitive structure into account.

The usual condition creating difficulties in the meaningful learning and retention of new and unfamiliar (but potentially meaningful) ideas is that the possible subsumers in the learner's cognitive structure are lacking in the necessary and desirable degree of relevance and specificity (in addition to lacking discriminability from relevant established ideas in cognitive structure) to serve as effective anchoring ideas. The advance organizer is, therefore, introduced to bridge this gap, i.e., to be more specifically relevant and less general in relation to the new learning task than are existing relevant anchoring ideas in cognitive structure, but at the same time relatable to these latter ideas. Introducing the organizer in advance of the learning passage itself accomplishes both of these latter goals through the products of the interaction (1) between the organizer and relevant ideas in cognitive structure and (2) between the organizer and the unfamiliar new ideas in the learning passage.

In contrast to the "comparative" type of organizer used to increase discriminability between new ideas in the learning material and existing relevant subsumers in cognitive structure (as explained above), expository organizers are used to enhance the relevance (availability), stability, and clarity of anchoring ideas when discriminability is not the chief learning problem.

NOTES

[1]More recently Gagné (1968) has recognized the substantive nature of verbalizable knowledge but tends to discount it in favor of a hierarchy of problem-solving capabilities.

[2]Reception learning in the absence of concrete-empirical props first becomes possible at the junior high school level and beyond.

[3]This type of relatability to cognitive structure in the *general* sense of that term (i.e., to systems of ideas that lie within the realm of human learning capability) is referred to throughout as *logical* meaning. It is a property of relatability stemming from the content of the new instructional idea itself. In potential meaning, however, we are concerned with the type of idiosyncratic relatability to relevant ideas *actually* present in the cognitive structure of a *particular* learner. The interaction between the new instructional idea and the existing relevant idea in cognitive structure constitutes the meaningful learning process and yields the new meaning thereof.

[4]Greater retroactive or proactive interference *is* conceivable in *meaningful* learning in those relatively rare instances where either the interpolated or previously learned material engenders cognitive confusion in the learning and retention of the instructional task.

[5]The Gestalt term "trace" is used here simply as a hypothetical neuropsychological construct to account for the continuing representation of past experience in the nervous system and in present cognitive structure. No assumptions are made regarding the neurophysiological basis of the trace or regarding psychophysiological correlations; it is best expressed analogically in this context by the psychological concept of *idea.*

REFERENCES

Ausubel, D. P. Learning by discovery: Rationale and mystique. *Bulletin of the National Association of Secondary School Principles*, 1961, *45*, 18–58.

Ausubel, D. P. A subsumption theory of meaningful verbal learning and retention. *Journal of General Psychology*, 1962, *66*, 213–224.

Bartlett, F. C. *Remembering: A study in experimental and social psychology.* London: Cambridge University Press, 1932.

Berlyne, D. E. *Structure and direction in thinking.* New York: Wiley, 1965.

Brownell, W. A. Observations of instruction in lower grade arithmetic in English and Scottish schools. *Arithmetic Teacher*, 1960, *7*, 165–177.

Brownell, W. A., & Hendrickson, G. How children learn information, concepts, and generalizations. In *Learning and instruction*, 49th Yearbook, National Soc. Stud. Educ., Part I. Chicago: University of Chicago Press, 1950.

Bruner, J. S. Learning and thinking. *Harvard Educational Review*, 1959, *29*, 84–92.

Bruner, J. S. *The process of education.* Cambridge: Harvard University Press, 1960.

Dienes, Z. P. Insight into arithmetical process. *School Review*, 1964, *72*, 183–200.

Gagné, R. M. Learning hierarchies. *Educational Psychologist*, 1968, *6*, 1–3, 6, 9.

Gagné, R. M. The acquisition of knowledge. *Psychological Review*, 1962, *69*, 355–365.

Gagné, R. M. *The conditions of learning* (3rd Ed.). New York: Holt, Rinehart, & Winston, 1977.

Gates, A. I. The necessary mental age for beginning reading. *Elementary School Journal*, 1937, *37*, 497–508.

Gesell, A. The ontogenesis of infant behavior. In L. Carmichael (Ed.), *Manual of child psychology* (2nd Ed.). New York: Wiley, 1954.

Hebb, D. O. *The organization of behavior.* New York: Wiley, 1949.

Kinsella, P. J. A close look at preschool reading instruction. *Illinois Journal of Education*, 1965, *58*, 7–10.

Kintsch, W. Text comprehension in memory and learning. *American Psychologist*, 1994, 294–303.

Kintsch, W. *The representation of meaning in memory.* Hillsdale, N.J.: Erlbaum, 1974.

Mandler, G. From association to structure. *Psychological Review*, 1962, *69*, 415–426.

Milner, E. A study of the relationship between readiness in grade one school children and patterns of parent-child interaction. *Child Development*, 1951, *22*, 95–112.

Morphett, H. V., & Washburne, C. When should children begin to read? *Elementary School Journal*, 1931, *31*, 496–503.

Novak, J. D. *A theory of education.* Ithaca, N.Y.: Cornell University Press, 1977.

Novak, J. D. *Learning, creating, and using knowledge.* Mahwah, N.J.: Lawrence Erlbaum, 1998.

Olson, W. C., & Hughes, B. O. Subsequent growth of children with and without nursery school experience. In *39th Yearbook, Nat'l. Soc. Stud. Educ.* Chicago: University of Chicago Press, 1940.

Osgood, C. E., Suci, G. J., & Tannenbaum, P. H. *The measurement of meaning*. Urbana: University of Illinois Press, 1957.

Pines, M. How three-year-olds teach themselves to read and love it. *Harper's*, May 1963, *226*, 58–64.

Rambusch, N. H. *Learning how to learn: An American approach to Montessori*. New York: Halicon, 1962.

Saugstad. Problem solving as dependent upon availability of function. *British Journal of Psychology*, 1955, *46*, 191–198.

Sax, G., & Ottina, J. P. The arithmetic reasoning of pupils differing in school experience. *California Journal of Educational Research*, 1958, *9*, 15–19.

Tulving, E. Episodic and semantic memory. In E. Tulving & W. Donaldson (Eds.), *Organization of memory*. New York: Academic Press, 1972.

Tyler, F. T. Issues related to readiness. In *Theories of learning and instruction. 63rd Yearbook*, Natl. Soc. Stud. Educ., Part II. Chicago: University of Chicago Press, 1964.

Wood, B. D., & Freeman, F. N. *An experimental study of the educational influences of the typewriter in the elementary school classroom*. New York: Macmillan, 1932.

CHAPTER 4

THE NATURE OF MEANING AND MEANINGFUL LEARNING

Classroom or subject-matter learning is primarily concerned with the acquisition, retention, and use of large bodies of meaningful information such as facts, propositions, principles, and vocabulary in the various disciplines. It is important, therefore, that we make very explicit at the outset what we mean by meaning and meaningful learning. The concept of knowledge itself may refer either to the sum total of all organized subject matter and content possessed by an individual in a given field of inquiry or merely to the relative position and specific relationships of particular component elements in the hierarchical structure of the discipline as a whole.

In this chapter we shall consider the nature of meaning and the relationship of meaning to meaningful verbal learning. In addition, we shall also be concerned with such fundamental issues as the conditions of meaningful learning; the different kinds of meaning; how words, concepts, and propositions acquire meaning; the distinction between logical and psychological meaning; the academic and cultural significance of meaningful learning in acquiring knowledge; the relationship between perception and cognition; and the role of language in meaningful learning; hierarchical ways of relating new ideas to cognitive structure; and our three simple exemplars of meaningful learning.

THE NATURE OF MEANING

"Meaningful learning," by definition, involves the acquisition of new meanings. New meanings, conversely, are the end-products of meaningful learning. That is, the emergence of new meanings in the learner reflects the prior operation and completion of a meaningful learning process. After exploring in some detail what is involved in this process, we shall examine more explicitly both the nature of meaning itself and its relationship to meaningful learning.

THE CONDITIONS OF MEANINGFUL LEARNING

The essence of the meaningful learning process, as we have already seen, is that new symbolically expressed ideas (the learning task) are related in a nonarbitrary, and nonverbatim fashion, to what the learner already knows (his cognitive structure in a particular subject-matter field), and that the product of this active and integrative interaction is the emergence of a new meaning reflecting the substantive and denotative nature of this interactive product. That is, the instructional material is related either to some *specifically relevant existing* aspect or content of the learner's cognitive structure, i.e., to an image, an already meaningful symbol, a concept, or a proposition, or to some more non-specific but generally relevant background of ideas in his or her structure of knowledge.

Meaningful learning requires *both* that learners manifest a meaningful learning set (that is, a disposition to relate the new material to be learned, nonarbitrarily and nonverbatimly to their structure of knowledge) and that the material they learn be potentially meaningful to them, namely, relatable to their particular structures of knowledge on a nonarbitrary and nonverbatim basis (Ausubel, 1961a) (see A in Table 1). Thus, irrespective of how much potential meaning may inhere in a particular proposition, if the learner's intention is to memorize it arbitrarily and verbatimly (as a series of arbitrarily related words), both the learning process and the learning outcome must of necessity be rote or meaningless. Conversely, irrespective of how meaningful the learner's set may be, neither the process nor the outcome of learning can possibly be meaningful if the learning task itself is not potentially meaningful—if it is not nonarbitrarily and nonverbatimly relatable both to *any* hypothetical cognitive structure in the same subject-matter field as well as to the particular learner's idiosyncratic cognitive structure.

Meaningful Learning Set

One reason why pupils often develop a rote learning set in learning potentially meaningful subject matter is because they learn from prior unfortunate experience that substantively correct answers that do not conform in verbatim fashion to what the teacher or textbook states receive no credit whatsoever from certain teachers. Another reason is that because they have a generally high level of anxiety or because they have repeatedly failed in a given subject (reflective, in turn, of relatively low aptitude or inadequate teaching), they lack sufficient confidence in their ability to learn it meaningfully; hence, they believe that they have no alternative to panic apart from rote learning. (This situation is very familiar to mathematics teachers because of the widespread prevalence of "number shock" or "number anxiety" in school children as well as university students.)

In addition, pupils may develop a rote learning set if they are pressured into exhibiting glibness, or into concealing, rather than admitting, and gradually remedying existing deficiencies in genuine understanding. Under the circumstances just noted, it seems both less difficult and more important to generate a spurious impression of facile comprehension by rotely memorizing a few key terms or sentences, than to make a genuine effort at trying to understand what they mean. Teachers frequently overlook the fact that pupils become very skillful at using abstract terms with apparent appropriateness, when obliged to do so, although their understanding of the underlying concepts or propositions is virtually zero.

TABLE 1. Relationships Between Meaningful Learning, Potential Meaningfulness, Logical Meaningfulness, and Psychological Meaning

A	MEANINGFUL LEARNING or THE ACQUISITION OF MEANINGS	requires	(1) Potentially Meaningful Material	and	(2) Meaningful Learning Set
B	POTENTIAL MEANINGFULNESS	depends on	(1) *Logical Meaningfulness* (the nonarbitrary and substantive relatability of the learning material to correspondingly relevant ideas that lie within the realm of human learning capability)	and	(2) The availability of such relevant ideas in the *particular* learner's cognitive structure
C	PSYCHOLOGICAL MEANING (IDIOSYNCRATIC, PHENOMENOLOGICAL MEANING)	is the product of	Meaningful Learning	or of	Potential Meaningfulness and Meaningful Learning Set

Potential Meaningfulness

Whether the learning task is potentially meaningful, that is, both logically meaningful and nonarbitrarily and nonverbatimly relatable to the particular learner's cognitive structure, however, is a much more complicated matter than meaningful learning set. At the very least, it obviously depends on the two main factors involved in establishing a meaningful relationship between new and established knowledge, that is, on both the nature of the learning task itself and on the nature of the *particular* learner's structure of knowledge.

First, considering the nature of the instructional material, it must obviously be sufficiently nonarbitrary itself (i.e., nonrandom, plausible, sensible) so that it could be related on a nonarbitrary and nonverbatim basis to correspondingly relevant ideas that lie within the realm of what human beings are capable of learning (to correspondingly relevant ideas that at least *some* human beings are capable of learning if given the opportunity to do so). This aspect of the learning task itself that determines whether or not the material is potentially meaningful can be called *logical*[1] *meaningfulness;* it seldom, if ever, is lacking in the types of learning tasks found in schools and colleges since academic subject matter content, almost by definition, is logically meaningful.

Such is not the case, however, with respect to many tasks in the psychological laboratory and in regard to many everyday and laboratory learning tasks (for example, telephone numbers, paired adjectives, scrambled sentences, lists of nonsense syllables) that can be related to anyone's cognitive structure *only* on an arbitrary and verbatim basis. Much experimental research in psychological laboratories, for example, has used nonsense syllables for the very purpose of providing relatively *meaningless* but additive learning tasks of uniform difficulty that cannot be nonarbitrarily and nonverbatimly related to what the subjects already know and hence cannot yield new meanings. For this very reason most of the "laws" or theories based on such experimentation bear little or no relation to the processes involved in classroom learning.

The second factor determining whether learning material is potentially meaningful depends on the *particular* learner's cognitive structure rather than on the nature of the learning material itself. The acquisition of meaning is a phenomenon in nature that occurs in *particular* human beings—not in mankind generally. Thus, for meaningful learning to occur in fact, it is *not* sufficient that the new material simply be relatable in nonarbitrary and nonverbatim fashion to correspondingly relevant ideas in the more general or abstract sense of the term (to correspondingly relevant ideas that *some* human beings *could* learn under appropriate circumstances); it is also necessary for meaningful learning that relevant ideational content be available in the cognitive structure of the *particular* learner to serve this subsuming and anchoring function.

It is abundantly clear, therefore, that with respect to meaningful learning outcomes in the classroom, *the availability, and other significant properties, of relevant content in different learners' cognitive structures* are the most crucial variables determining potential meaningfulness. Hence, it is quite understandable that the potential meaningfulness of learning materials varies not only with prior educational background, but also with such factors as age, IQ, occupation, social class, and cultural membership.

The rationale for referring *only* to the *potential* meaningfulness of instructional materials (rather than to their *actual* meaningfulness) is an important condition of meaningful learning and retention and was provided in the previous chapter: If we had merely considered this aspect of the learning material as simply *meaningful,* without adding the qualifier, *potential,* the goal of the meaningful learning process would then obviously have been accomplished in advance, thereby rendering the learning process *per se* superfluous. This is the case because meaning itself is an emergent product of the interaction between the ideas to be learned in the instructional material and relevant subsuming (anchoring) ideas in the learner's cognitive structure.

Nonarbitrary and Nonverbatim Relationships

What, precisely, do we mean by saying that for learning material to be *logically* meaningful it must be nonarbitrarily and nonverbatimly relatable to correspondingly relevant ideas that lie within the realm of human learning capacity?

The first criterion—nonarbitrary relatability—simply suggests that if the material *itself* is sufficiently nonarbitrary (or nonrandom), an adequate and almost self-evident basis is present for relating it nonarbitrarily to the kinds of correspondingly relevant ideas in cognitive structure that human beings generally, or at least some beings, are capable of learning. Logically, meaningful learning material could, thus, be arbitrarily relatable to *specifically* relevant ideas as examples, derivatives, special cases, extensions, elaborations, modifications, qualifications, and more inclusive generalizations; or it could be relatable to a *wider background* of relevant ideas in the sense of being generally congruent with them.

The second criterion—*nonverbatim reliability*—suggests that if the learning task again is sufficiently nonarbitrary, an ideationally equivalent (synonymous) symbol or group of symbols could be related to the learner's cognitive structure without changing the meaning in any significant way. In other words, neither meaningful learning nor newly emergent meanings depend on the *exclusive* use of *particular* words and no others; the same concept or proposition could be expressed in synonymous language and would convey precisely the same meaning to the learner. Thus, for example, "canine," "Hund," and "chien" would induce the same meanings as "dog" in a person who has a reasonable command of English, German, and French; and "All of the internal angles of a triangle equal a straight angle" would have essentially the same meaning to most geometry students as "All of the interior angles of a triangle equal 180 degrees."

Rote learning tasks, of course, are not undertaken or mastered in a cognitive vacuum. They *can* be related to cognitive structure but *only* in that arbitrary, verbatim fashion that, as pointed out above, does not and cannot result in the acquisition of any new meanings. For example, inasmuch as the particular stimulus and response members of a given pair of adjectives in a paired-associate learning task are linked together in a purely arbitrary fashion, there is no possible basis for nonarbitrarily relating the learning task to anyone's structure of knowledge (unless the learner *invents* a mediating link that is meaningful); in addition, the learner must also remember verbatim the response to each stimulus word—he cannot, in other words, make use of synonyms.

This arbitrary and verbatim relatability of rote learning tasks to cognitive structure obviously has certain significant consequences for learning. First, since human cognitive "processing equipment," unlike a computer, cannot handle information very efficiently that is related to it arbitrarily and on a verbatim basis, only relatively short learning tasks can be mastered in this fashion, and these can be retained for only short periods of time unless greatly overlearned. Second, arbitrary and verbatim relatability to the learner's cognitive structure makes rote learning tasks highly vulnerable to interference from previously, concurrently, and subsequently encountered similar materials. As we shall see later, it is this basic difference in the kind of relatability to cognitive structure (arbitrary and verbatim versus nonarbitrary and nonverbatim) that accounts for the fundamental difference between rote and meaningful learning processes.

It is also quite possible, of course, that *already meaningful component* elements of a rote learning task (e.g., the adjectives in a paired adjective task) are relatable to cognitive structure in ways that do not involve any current learning of the arbitrary linkages between each of the adjective pairs, but, nevertheless, facilitate the rote learning of the task *as a whole.* It is by virtue of such relatability, for example, that the component letters of nonsense syllables are also *perceived* meaningfully and that the syllables as a whole elicit associations with similar meaningful words (and are thus perceived as partly meaningful themselves). For similar reasons—by enhancing the familiarity of the material, by eliminating the need for current learning of the component elements, and by making possible the combination of those elements into larger units (thereby reducing the total number of discrete associations to be linked)—the use of already meaningful component elements in learning materials facilitates rote learning.

THE RELATIONSHIP OF MEANING TO MEANINGFUL LEARNING

Our conclusion that new meanings are interactional products of a meaningful learning process, in which new ideas are related to, and interact with, relevant ideas in existing cognitive structure, sometimes gives rise to a charge of circularity or poses a "chicken and egg" type of problem. If new meanings can only emerge by new ideas interacting with existing meanings in cognitive structure, how then were the original meanings learned before any cognitive structure existed?

Any answer to this question must obviously be couched in terms of cognitive development. Before children form concepts they learn that particular objects and events that are perceptually similar are called by the same name and that other perceptually dissimilar objects and events have different names. From these two complementary generalizations, most children develop the insight at the close of the first year of life that everything has a name and that the name signifies psychologically whatever its referent does. Thus, even before they acquire genuine generic concepts, children learn that language has representational properties and, by relating particular object-name relationships as exemplars of this general insight, they begin to engage in representational learning.

The next step involves the acquisition of sufficient syntactical concepts and rules to combine words into rudimentary sentences expressing simple propositional ideas. Simultaneously children acquire concepts by hypothesis-generation and -testing; and gradually the standard cultural concept names they previously used over- or under-inclusively to designate particular objects and events now become the names of *generic* objects and events. With continued cognitive development they learn higher-order concepts in which perceptually *different* objects and events sharing certain inherently similarly criterial properties become members of a more inclusive class designated by its appropriate name. In this way a hierarchically organized cognitive structure develops which serves as a matrix for the acquisition of more new meanings. The steps in this process are considered in detail later in this chapter when the different kinds of meanings and their development are discussed.

Logical and Psychological Meaning

In our earlier discussion of this topic, the *potential* meaning inherent for *particular* learners in certain symbolic expressions and in the statement of certain propositions was differentiated from, on the one hand, *actual* (phenomenological or psychological) meaning, which is a product of a meaningful learning process, on the other. Actual meaning, according to this view, emerges when this potential meaning becomes transformed into new, differentiated, and idiosyncratic cognitive content within a *particular* individual, exhibiting a meaningful learning set, as a result of being nonarbitrarily and nonverbatimly related to, and interacting with, relevant ideas in his cognitive structure.

Our task in this section is simply to make explicit the analogous distinction between logical and psychological meaning (see Table 4.1). *Psychological meaning* is identical with actual or phenomenological meaning as defined above, whereas *logical meaning* corresponds to the meaning that learning material manifests if it meets the *general* or nonidiosyncratic requirements for potential meaningfulness. In short, logical meaning depends *only* on the "nature of the material" *per se,* independent of its relationships to the learner's cognitive structure (even if it makes sense). It is one of the two prerequisites that together determine whether learning material is potentially meaningful to a particular learner (the other prerequisite being the availability of the appropriate relevant content in this *particular* learner's cognitive structure to which it can be related).

Logical meaning, therefore, refers to the meaning that is inherent in certain kinds of symbolic (e.g., verbal) material by virtue of its very nature. Such material exhibits logical meaning if it can be related on a nonarbitrary and nonverbatim basis to correspondingly relevant ideas that lie within the realm of general human learning capability. For example, if propositional material itself consists of generally nonarbitrary relationships, then it can, almost by definition, also be related nonarbitrarily and nonverbatimly to the cognitive structure of at least some persons in a given culture and thus be logically meaningful.

Obviously excluded, therefore, from the domain of logical meaning is the almost infinite number of possible relationships between concepts that can be formulated on the basis of purely *random* or arbitrary pairings. This, of course, does not necessarily mean that all propositions with logical meaning are empirically *valid* or even logically defensible. The questions of empirical and logical validity are issues that simply are not germane in determining logical meaning. Propositions based on unvalidated premises or on faulty logic (e.g., the phlogiston theory of combustion) may conceivably abound in logical meaning.

Psychological (actual) *meaning,* on the other hand, is a wholly *idiosyncratic* cognitive phenomenon. Corresponding to the distinction between the logical and the psychological structure of knowledge, there is an equally important distinction between logical and psychological meaning. However, it is the possibility of relating, in nonarbitrary and nonverbatim fashion, logically meaningful propositions to a *particular* learner's cognitive structure (containing appropriately relevant anchoring ideas) that makes them potentially meaningful to him and thereby makes possible the transformation of logical into psychological meaning during the course of meaningful learning. Thus, the emergence of psychological meaning not only depends on presenting the learner with material that is logically meaningful, but also depends on the learner's actual possession of the necessary ideational background to subsume and anchor it.

It follows, therefore, that the more idiosyncratic a meaning is, the more thoroughly it reflects both the unique qualities of the particular learner's structure of knowledge, and hence the more idiosyncratically he has reformulated it and incorporated it into his unique ideational frame of reference and language usage. Thus, when any given individual learns logically meaningful propositions, it is quite apparent that they automatically tend to lose their nonidiosyncratic properties.

Psychological meaning is invariably an idiosyncratic phenomenon. Its idiosyncratic nature, however, does not rule out the possibility of social or shared meanings. The various individual meanings that different members of a given culture assign to the same concepts and propositions are ordinarily sufficiently similar to permit interpersonal communication and understanding. As we have had occasion to note earlier, this homogeneity of sharing meanings within a particular culture, and even between related cultures, reflects both the same logical meanings implicit in logically meaningful concepts and propositions as well as many common aspects of ideational background in different learners' cognitive structures.

MEANINGFUL LEARNING VERSUS THE LEARNING OF MEANINGFUL MATERIAL

As repeatedly emphasized throughout this volume, *meaningful learning* must not be regarded simply as the *learning of meaningful material.* It refers first of all to a distinctive learning process and to distinctive conditions of learning, and not primarily to the nature or characteristics of the material being learned. In meaningful learning also, the instructional material is only *potentially* meaningful. If it were *already* meaningful, the goal of meaningful learning—that is, the acquisition of new meanings—would be already accomplished, by definition, before any learning was ever attempted or ever took place.

Obviously, in most potentially meaningful learning tasks, the *component parts* (words of the material are *already* meaningful; but in these instances the *learning task as a whole* (the proposition) is only *potentially* meaningful. In learning a new geometrical theorem, for example, each of the component words is already meaningful, but the learning task *as a whole* (learning the meaning of the theorem) is yet to be mastered. Thus, *potentially* meaningful material (i.e., the propositional learning task), just like its already meaningful component parts, may be *perceived* or otherwise reacted to meaningfully, but it cannot be meaningfully *learned*.

This brings us to the important distinction between the *meaningful* learning of *potentially* meaningful material and the *rote* learning of tasks that contain *already meaningful components*. There are innumerable examples of the latter kind of rote or nonmeaningful learning. In learning a list of arbitrarily paired adjectives, for example, each adjective is already meaningful, but the relationship between the members of each pair and the learning task as a whole, are *not* potentially meaningful because these wholly arbitrary associations between adjectives are not relatable to any ideational aspect of the learner's existing knowledge in a nonarbitrary, nonverbatim sense. In learning a geometrical theorem, on the other hand, each component word is not only *already* meaningful but the learning task *as a whole* is also potentially meaningful. However, unless the learner exhibits a meaningful learning set in this latter instance, no meaning will emerge: He will merely learn and memorize rotely a series of arbitrarily connected words.

It is important, therefore, to differentiate between the *meaningful learning* of *potentially* meaningful material, on the one hand, and, on the other, the *rote* learning of *already* meaningful component elements of a learning task that, taken together, do not constitute a potentially meaningful learning task.

In the course of meaningful learning, a student must always relate the component elements of new concepts or propositions, as well as the concepts and propositions as wholes, to his own idiosyncratic cognitive structure. The outcome that results almost always involves at least some minor variation between how the learner internalizes the new information and how the teacher perceives and presents it. Thus, in later recall of statements or propositions the student's answer may vary somewhat from that expected by the teacher, even when the student's answer is substantively correct. Unfortunately, such responses are often scored wrong, and, as noted above, students may learn as a result to use rote (verbatim) learning approaches rather than to learn meaningfully.

MEANING VERSUS MEANINGFULNESS

What do investigators of rote verbal learning mean when they talk about the *meaningfulness* of the units (nonsense syllables, paired adjectives) that they employ in their research learning tasks? In using this term they obviously do not refer to the *substantive* meaning of a given symbol (the differential cognitive content it evokes in the learner after being meaningfully learned); rather, they refer to the *relative degree* of meaning it exhibits in comparison to that manifested by other symbols.

The meaningfulness of a word, for example, depends mostly on whether it has a concretely identifiable referent (such as "chair") or merely serves a transactional function (such as "since") (Epstein, Rock, & Zuckerman, 1960), and also on such factors as the frequency and variety of the contexts in which it is encountered (Bjorgen, 1964; Noble, 1953; Underwood & Schulz, 1960). A highly meaningful word, therefore, tends to be subjectively more familiar (Noble, 1953) and to elicit more associations (Glaze, 1928; Noble, 1953) than a less meaningful word. These are indices of its degree of meaningfulness rather than explanations of how it becomes meaningful in the first place.

One must be careful, in other words, not to confuse the psychological process whereby a word acquires meaning with the factors accounting for the relative degree of meaning it manifests. We have already referred to the reasons why meaningfulness may sometimes facilitate rote learning.

PSYCHOLOGICAL VERSUS LOGICAL ORGANIZATION OF KNOWLEDGE

It is necessary to recognize at this point that the idiosyncratic ideas acquired by a learner in a given field of inquiry may be substantially different from these same ideas as they are perceived by scholars in that discipline.

> It should not be forgotten . . . that in addition to organized bodies of knowledge that represent the collective recorded wisdom of recognized scholars in particular fields of inquiry, there are corresponding psychological structures of knowledge, represented by the organization of internalized ideas in the minds of individual students—ideas of varying degrees of both cognitive maturity and subject-matter sophistication in these same disciplines. I am making a distinction, in other words, between the formal organization of the subject-matter content of a given discipline, as set forth in authoritative statements in generally accepted textbooks and monographs, on the one hand, and the organized, internalized representation of this knowledge in the memory structures of particular individuals, especially students, on the other (Ausubel, 1964a).

As students gain increasing sophistication in a given field of knowledge, however, their cognitive structures show an increasing resemblance to the hierarchies and relationships recognized by "experts" in the discipline (Shavelson, 1972). This is particularly true in the case of good versus poor students.

Most textbooks are organized topically (logically) at a uniform level of conceptualization despite the commonly observed fact that, psychologically, the order in which different segments of knowledge in a given discipline are acquired is generally congruent with the principle of progressive differentiation (that is, hierarchically speaking, from the top downwards) as demonstrated by various advance organizer studies (see Chapter 5) and studies by Shavelson (1972). As a result, in the absence of available explanatory concepts and principles, much factual information and symbolic manipulation are learned rotely. Gagné and Briggs' (1974) model, on the other hand, assumes that cognitive structure is organized from the bottom upwards and that learning tasks should be similarly sequenced. This latter view is more applicable to rote and sensorimotor learning tasks in humans and to instrumental learning in infrahumans. Although some superordinate learning does occur at a meaningful level, all superordinate ideas eventually rise higher in the hierarchy of cognitive structure and become more stable than the corresponding subordinate ideas in relation to which they were originally acquired.

THE SIGNIFICANCE OF MEANINGFUL LEARNING IN ACQUIRING KNOWLEDGE

Meaningful learning is so important in the process of education because it is the human mechanism par excellence for acquiring and storing the vast quantity of ideas and information represented by any field of knowledge. The acquisition and retention of large bodies of subject matter is an extremely impressive phenomenon considering that

1. Human beings, unlike computers, can apprehend and immediately remember only a few discrete items of information that are presented just a single time.
2. Memory for rotely learned lists receiving multiple presentations is notoriously limited both over time and with respect to length of list, unless greatly overlearned and frequently reproduced.

The tremendous efficiency of meaningful learning as an information-processing and -storing mechanism can be largely attributed to its two distinctive characteristics—the nonarbitrariness and the nonverbatimness of the learning task's relatability to cognitive structure. First, by *nonarbitrarily* relating potentially meaningful material to relevant established (anchoring) ideas in their cognitive structures, learners are able effectively to exploit their own existing knowledge as an ideational and organizational matrix for the incorporation, understanding, retention, and organization of large bodies of new ideas. it is the very nonarbitrariness of this process that enables them to use their previously acquired knowledge as veritable touchstones for internalizing and making understandable vast quantities of new word meanings, concepts, and propositions with relatively little effort and few repetitions. Because of this factor of nonarbitrariness, the potential meaning of new ideas *as wholes* can be related to established meanings in cognitive structure (concepts, facts, and principles) *as wholes* to yield new meanings. In other words, the only way it is possible to make use of previously learned ideas in the processing (internalization) of new ideas is to relate the latter *nonarbitrarily* to the former. The new ideas, which become meaningful, in turn, also expand the base of the learning matrix.

If, on the other hand, learning material is *arbitrarily* related to cognitive structure, no *direct* use whatsoever can be made of established knowledge in internalizing the learning task. At the very best, already meaningful *components* of the learning task can be related to existing *unitary* ideas in cognitive structure (thereby facilitating indirectly the *rote* learning of the task as a whole); but this in no way either makes the newly internalized arbitrary associations *themselves* relatable as a whole to established meaningful content in cognitive structure or makes them usable in acquiring new knowledge. And because the human mind is not efficiently designed to interiorize and store arbitrary associations, this approach permits only very limited amounts of material to be internalized and retained for short periods of time, and then only after much effortful repetition and/or reinforcement.

Also, the fact that a new idea becomes *meaningful* (becomes a clear, differentiated, and sharply articulated content of awareness) after it is meaningfully learned, presumably makes it intrinsically less vulnerable than internalized arbitrary associations are to interference from other arbitrary associations, and hence makes it more retainable. In addition, as will be indicated later in discussing the assimilation process, the maintenance of this same *nonarbitrary relatability* advantage through the *anchorage* of the new meaning to its corresponding (anchoring) established idea in cognitive structure during the storage period further extends the span of retention.

Second, the *nonverbatim* nature of, thus, relating new material to, and incorporating it within, cognitive structure also circumvents the drastic limitations imposed by the short-item and time-spans of rote memory on the processing and storing of information. Much more can obviously be apprehended and retained if the learner is required only to assimilate the substance of ideas rather than the exact words used in expressing them.

The distinctively human capacity for meaningful verbal learning is dependent, of course, upon such cognitive capabilities as symbolic representation, abstraction, categorization, and generalization. It is the possession of these latter abilities that ultimately makes possible the original discovery and subsequent learning of generic concepts and propositions and, hence, the later acquisition of the more detailed, relatable information and ideas comprising the bulk of knowledge.

Another means of compensating for the information-processing and -storing limitations of the human brain in comparison with a computer has been described by Miller (1956). It is called "chunking" and is derived from information theory. "Chunking" refers to the process of rearranging the stimulus input successively into a smaller and more efficiently organized "sequence of chunks." Miller suggests that linguistic recoding is the most powerful device that human beings possess for extending the amount of information they can process and remember and thus for acquiring large bodies of knowledge.

Miller and Selfridge (1950) argue against the importance of meaning in learning by applying this type of information-theory analysis to the problem of explaining why meaningless connected discourse is remembered better than strings of linguistically unconnected words as well as meaningful prose. In this instance chunking is accomplished by grouping a series of words that are sequentially dependent on each other into larger units (phrases) and then remembering the phrases rather than individual words. The recoding scheme under these circumstances is derived from the contextual constraints that characterize linguistically connected discourse and that are both built into the structure of a language and implicitly learned by all persons who use it. These contextual constraints are defined in terms of "dependent probabilities," that is, the statistical dependency of the choice of a particular word upon the words that precede it or the extent to which the choice of a given word is determined by the occurrence of the preceding words.

As degree of contextual constraint or order of approximation to English increases in a given sequence of words, learning is progressively facilitated. This is the case because the message "preserves the short-range associations of the English language that are so familiar to us" (Miller & Selfridge, 1950) and hence permits chunking or phrasing. "In fact, when short-range contextual dependencies are preserved in nonsense material, the nonsense is as readily recalled as is meaningful material." From this it is argued that contextual dependencies extending over five or six words permit positive transfer, and that it is these familiar dependencies rather than the meaning that facilitates learning (Miller & Selfridge, 1950).

It is evident from careful analysis of these findings, however, that compensatory mechanisms such as chunking merely increase the learner's *rote* capacity for apprehending and retaining information. For example, although Miller and Selfridge demonstrated unequivocally that nonsense material, manifesting the same contextual constraints as potentially meaningful prose, is recalled just as readily as meaningful prose, it is important to bear in mind that they demanded *verbatim* recall of the prose material. Such verbatim, or *rote,* learning of potentially meaningful connected discourse obviously precludes all of the information-processing and -storing advantages of meaningful verbal learning; it (the latter) is superior (in the same way that the rote learning of connected *nonsense* material is also superior) to the rote learning of linguistically *unconnected* words solely because the sequential flow of the connected material conforms to the familiar contextual constraints of the language that make phrasing possible.

True meaningful learning, on the other hand, presupposes *both* that the learning task is potentially meaningful and that the learner exhibit a meaningful learning set. Thus, irrespective of how much potential meaning may inhere in a given passage of connected discourse, the material is still rotely learned as long as the learner's set is to assimilate it verbatim. In short, because of their *rote learning set,* the subjects of this experiment never had a fair opportunity to demonstrate that *meaningful* learning of prose material really is superior to the *rote* learning of linguistically connected nonsense.

Consequently, one cannot apply Miller and Selfridge's conclusion that "it is these familiar dependencies rather than the meaning that facilitates learning" to any situation other than the artificial one involved in verbatim or rote learning. The acquisition of large bodies of knowledge is simply impossible in the absence of meaningful learning. The connectedness of discourse, by making chunking possible undoubtedly facilitates learning and retention to some degree but not nearly enough to make possible the acquisition and retention of a body of knowledge constituting a discipline. Unless learning can be meaningful, very little knowledge, organized or otherwise, can be assimilated.

TYPES OF MEANINGFUL LEARNING

The most fundamental type of meaningful learning, upon which all other kinds of meaningful learning depends, is *representational* learning, that is, learning the meanings of single symbols (typically but not necessarily words)[2] or learning what they represent.

Single words in any language, after all, are conventional or socially shared symbols, each representing a unitary object, situation, concept, or other symbol in the physical, social, and ideational worlds. To any *uninitiated* individual, however, what a given symbol means, or represents, is *at first* a completely unknown quantity to him; it is something that he has to learn. The process whereby he learns this is called representational learning. It is coextensive with the process whereby new words gradually come to represent to the learner the corresponding objects or ideas to which the words refer (their referents); that is, the new words come to signify to him the same things and properties that the referents do or to evoke the same differentiated cognitive content that the latter do.

For example, when children first learn the meaning of the word "dog," it is proposed to them by verbally more sophisticated persons in their environment that the sound of the word (which is potentially meaningful but as yet has no meaning for them) represents, or is equivalent to, a particular dog-object that they are perceiving at the moment and, hence, that it signifies the same thing (an image of this dog-object) that the object itself does. They, in turn, actively relate—in relatively nonarbitrary and nonverbatim fashion—this proposition of representational equivalence to relevant content in their cognitive structures.[3] Thus, when the initial phase of meaningful learning is completed, the word "dog" is reliably capable of evoking differentiated cognitive content (a composite image of the various dogs in his experience) that is approximately equivalent to that elicited by particular dog-objects. Once the more generic meaning of the word "dog" is acquired, this symbol also serves as a concept label (name) for the criterial attributes of the cultural concept "dog."

How representational learning actually occurs, and how children develop a capacity for such learning, will be explored later in this chapter. At this point we wish only to distinguish between three basic kinds of meaningful learning: *representational learning, concept learning,* and *propositional learning.*

Representational learning refers to the meanings of unitary symbols or words, and *propositional learning* refers to the meanings of ideas expressed by groups of words combined into propositions or sentences. In the first case (as in naming, defining, and labeling activities) learning the meanings of single words requires learning what they represent. It means learning that particular symbols represent or are equivalent in meaning to particular referents.

Another type of meaningful learning that is prominent in the acquisition of subject matter consists of *concept learning.* Concepts (unitary generic or categorical ideas) are also represented by single symbols in the same way that other unitary referents are. Except in very young learners, as a matter of fact, most individual words (apart from proper nouns), that are commonly combined in sentence form to constitute propositions, actually represent concepts rather than particular objects or situations; thus, propositional learning largely involves learning the meaning of a composite idea generated by combining into a sentence single words each of which typically represents a concept.

In *propositional learning* the meaningful learning task at hand is not to learn what words singly, or in combination, represent but, rather, to learn the meaning of new ideas expressed in propositional form. Thus, in true propositional learning the object of the learning activity is not to learn propositions of representational equivalence, but to learn the meaning of verbal propositions that express ideas other than those of representational equivalence. In other words, the meaning of the proposition is not simply the sum of the meanings of its component words.

In true verbal propositional learning one is, therefore, learning the meaning of a new composite idea in the sense (1) that the proposition itself is generated by combining or relating to each other multiple individual words (concepts), each representing a unitary referent; and (2) that the individual words are combined in such a way (usually in sentence form) that the resulting new idea is more than just the sum of the meanings of the component individual words. It is obvious, therefore, that before one can learn the meanings of verbal propositions one must first know the meanings of their component terms or what the terms represent. Thus, representational and concept learning are basic to, or a prerequisite for, true propositional learning when propositions are expressed in verbal form.

At this point, it is necessary to explain how concept learning is related to representational learning. Since concepts as well as objects and situations are represented by words or names, learning what *concept words* mean (learning which concept is represented by a given new concept word or learning that the new concept word is equivalent in meaning to whatever the concept itself means) is self-evidently a major type of *representational learning*. It typically follows concept learning itself, since it is very convenient to be able to represent the multiple criterial attributes of a newly learned concept by a single word that is equivalent to it in meaning. But learning what the concept *itself* means, which, in effect, consists of learning what its criterial (distinguishing or identifying) attributes are, requires a very different type of meaningful learning that, like propositional learning, is substantive in nature and intent rather than nominalistic or representational.

These two types of meaningful learning (concept and propositional) differ in that in the former instance the *criterial attributes* of a new concept are related to relevant ideas in cognitive structure to yield a new generic but *unitary* meaning, whereas in the latter instance a new *proposition* (or composite idea) is related to cognitive structure to yield a new *composite* meaning. They are *both* very different from representational learning, even though concept learning is typically followed by a form of representational learning in which the newly learned concept is equated in meaning with the concept word that represents it. If we think of a rote-meaningful learning continuum, representational learning would usually be closer to the rote end of the continuum, and concept or propositional learning would constitute the highest form of meaningful learning.

COGNITION VERSUS PERCEPTION IN MEANINGFUL VERBAL LEARNING

The distinction between perceptual and cognitive processes[4] in meaningful verbal learning is particularly difficult to define because both kinds of processes involve interaction between verbal stimulus input and cognitive structure. We both perceive verbal messages *and* cognitively learn their meaning as a result of interpreting them in the light of existing knowledge. The difference between the two processes is one of immediacy and complexity. Perception involves an *immediate* content of awareness *before* the intervention of such complex cognitive processes as are even involved in reception learning (comprehension of presented ideas). Cognition, on the other hand, involves such processes as relating the new material to relevant aspects of existing cognitive structure, ascertaining how the resulting new meaning can be reconciled with established knowledge, and recoding it in more familiar and idiosyncratic language.

Hence, if verbal meaning results when potentially meaningful verbal materials are related to, interact with, and are incorporated within existing cognitive structure (thereby generating new and differentiated cognitive content), and if this process of learning (acquiring) meanings is conceded to be *cognitive* in nature, when, where, and how in this sequence of events does *perception* play a role in meaningful verbal learning? Whether a given intellectual operation involves an immediate content of awareness (perception), on the one hand, or more complex and deferred intellectual processes (cognition), on the other, depends to a great extent on the complexity of the learning task relative to the learner's cognitive maturity and on whether the new material is first being learned or is *already* meaningful (Ausubel, 1968).

Learning that particular auditory symbols (spoken words) represent particular objects is a *cognitive* problem to a child first learning the meanings of new words with perceptual referents. Similarly, functional understanding of the distinctive syntactic properties of words in a sentence is, however, a cognitive problem to the same child; it presupposes both minimal mastery of the syntactic code and of the ability to apply such knowledge in syntactically decoding the sentence at hand.

Later on, however, when both the spoken words and the syntax are *already* thoroughly mastered, the child is able to grasp their denotative meanings and syntactic functions immediately on a purely *perceptual* basis. This sequence of events with regard to cognition and perception is then repeated as he or she learns to *read* words and sentences in school. In other words, once the symbols, spoken or written, are encountered many times and become meaningful, they become immediately and effortlessly (that is, perceptually) apprehensible (meaningful) on subsequent encounters.

The situation is somewhat more complicated in understanding propositions expressed in sentence form. The proposition itself is *always* a *new* learning task the meaning of which remains to be acquired, even if the meanings and syntactic functions of the component words are already known and can thus be apprehended (understood) perceptually. Thus, the understanding of a sentence is a two-stage process involving perception and cognition successively. The first stage involves the perception of the potentially meaningful material, and the second stage involves relating perceived potential meanings to relevant existing propositions in cognitive structure. In the first stage the learner perceives what the message is, or what he has to learn; in the second stage he understands what he perceives, that is, he acquires its meaning. Thus, perception precedes cognition in the meaningful learning of new propositions. The product of the perceptual process is not propositional meaning itself, but rather the immediate content of awareness that follows from preliminary interpretation of the *sensory* input (visual or aural) furnished by the potentially meaningful learning task. This perceptual content of awareness is intermediate, both temporally and in terms of complexity of process, between primitive sensation and the actual emergence of meanings. It consists of awareness both of the separate meanings of the component words and of the syntactic relations among them, but it stops short of apprehension of the meaning of the propositional message as a whole.

Hence, in order to understand a sentence, one must be able:

1. First, to perceive the potential propositional meaning it communicates (understand the denotative meanings and the syntactical functions of its *component* words).
2. Then, second, to incorporate this perceived potential meaning within existing cognitive structure.

The first step implies both adequate knowledge of vocabulary and a functional, if not a formal, knowledge of syntax. The second step implies relating the perceived proposition to relevant anchoring ideas in cognitive structure.

It should be noted, however, that repeated encounters with, or exposure to, the *same* potentially meaningful propositions change the above-specified relationship between cognition and perception. During the first encounter the potentially meaningful message is first perceived, and the perceived content is then incorporated into cognitive structure to yield a corresponding meaning. Once the message becomes essentially meaningful, perhaps as early as on the second presentation, the two processes, cognition and perception, become telescoped into one. That is, as a result of the initial emergence of meaning and the concomitant change in cognitive structure, the learner becomes *sensitized* to the potential meaning in the message on subsequent encounters with it. Its meaning having already been grasped, the message no longer presents a cognitive problem; it *immediately* (without the intervention of any cognitive processes) conveys *actual* (psychological) rather than merely potential meaning when next perceived.[5] Hence, although the *acquisition* of meanings is a cognitive process, it is proper and correct to refer to the cognitive content evoked by an already meaningful proposition as a product of perception rather than of learning.

To summarize, once children master the syntactical code and a basic vocabulary, the only cognitive aspects of understanding a sentence are associated with relating the ideas it contains to a relevant existing proposition (idea) in cognitive structure. The denotative meanings and syntactical functions of the component words are already meaningful and can, therefore, be apprehended perceptually. Even the understanding of the propositional meaning itself becomes a purely perceptual process after the message is repeated one or more times.

THE ACQUISITION OF MEANINGS

In this section we propose to explore more systematically some of the problems involved in the acquisition of word, concept, and propositional meanings. Thus far, the acquisition of these types of meanings has just been considered illustratively and in general terms in clarifying the nature of meaning and in contrasting the three main types of meaningful learning.

Vocabulary or Representational Learning

It has already been suggested that learning the meanings of single words, or learning what single words represent, involves the meaningful learning of particular propositions of representational equivalence—learning that particular words represent and thereby signify psychologically the same things that their referents do. It was also suggested that, as a result of such learning, words come to evoke approximately the same differentiated cognitive content that their referents do. At this point it is necessary to relate more explicitly this particular type of meaningful learning, namely, representational learning, to the more general paradigm of the meaningful learning process and to the previous discussion of the nature of meaning itself. In other words, how do human beings acquire vocabulary? How do they actually learn what single words mean, and how does such learning exemplify meaningful learning in general?

To begin with, there is the matter of genic endowment without which no amount of appropriate experience would suffice. Human beings, we have reason to believe, have a genically determined potentiality for representational learning.[6] As stated earlier, representational learning implies learning that a given pattern of stimulation (such as the distinctive pattern of sounds in the symbol "dog") represents and thereby signifies approximately the same thing (a dog-image) that an entirely unrelated pattern of stimulation (such as the referent dog-object) signifies.

The major step in actualizing this potentiality for representational learning is typically taken near the end of the first year of life. At this time the child acquires the *general insight* that it is possible to use a symbol (word or name) to represent any object or event and that the symbol signifies to him or her whatever its referent does. He or she acquires this insight by generalizing, subverbally and intuitively, from multiple exposures to the two complementary forms of the proposition of representational equivalence that more proficient users of the child's native language arrange for him or her—that different referents have *different* names and that different exemplars of the same referent have the *same* name.

Once this insight is firmly established in a given child's cognitive structure, it lays the necessary foundation for all subsequent representational learning. Thereafter, when a particular new proposition of representational equivalence is presented to him (e.g., that "dog" is representationally equivalent to different dog-objects and, hence, to their corresponding dog-images), the child is able nonarbitrarily and nonverbatimly to relate such a proposition as an exemplar to the already established and more general statement of the same proposition in his cognitive structure. The resulting product of the interaction between the two propositions is the differentiated cognitive content that "dog" signifies or is representationally equivalent to, a composite dog-image; and presentation of the word "dog" will subsequently elicit this image.

At this stage, a particular proposition of representational equivalence may often be learned and retained for a surprisingly long period of time, even though it is put to the child only once and in connection with only a single exemplar of the significate in question, provided, of course, that the object or event is familiar to him. This situation is in marked contrast to the situation that applies to the process of conditioning or associative rote learning which typically requires multiple exposures for even retention over relatively short intervals of time.

Types of Vocabulary Learning

In the early stages of vocabulary learning, words tend to represent particular and noncategorical objects and events; hence they tend to be equated in meaning with the relatively concrete and specific images such referents signify. Thus "naming," the earliest form of vocabulary learning in children, involves the establishment of representational equivalence between first-order symbols and concrete images.

As children advance in age and as words begin to represent concepts or generic ideas, such words become concept names and are equated in meaning with more abstract, generalized, and categorical cognitive content. The word "dog" to a toddler may just signify a cognitive image of his own pet and of the particular dogs in his neighborhood; to the older preschool child, however, it refers to the *criterial attributes* of a composite dog-image which he himself has discovered inductively from his own concrete-empirical experience with dogs. (This latter discovery process is called "concept formation.")

Correlated with the *denotative* meaning of "dog" that emerges when the criterial attributes of this concept are meaningfully learned are various idiosyncratic affective and attitudinal reactions that the term evokes in each child depending on his particular experience with the species. These reactions constitute the *connotative* mean-ing of "dog." It should be noted, however, that in older children the connotations of most words, for instance, "democracy," "totalitarianism," "alcohol," are not acquired through first-hand experience; they are rather typically assimilated uncritically from prevailing evaluative attitudes in their immediate familial or cultural environment.

After the preschool years most new words are meaningfully acquired by definition or by being encountered in appropriate and relatively explicit contexts. Representational equivalence is established in cognitive structure between synonyms and already meaningful words or between new concept words and their meanings conveyed by their respective definitions or contexts.

An adequate definition or context provides, in turn, the criterial attributes of the new concept expressed in already meaningful words or combination of such words. In learning the meaning of the new concept *word* "president" (a form of representational learning typically following concept learning itself), for example, a pupil equates the word in meaning to whatever "chief of state" or "chief executive of a republic or institution" means to him. He does so *after* he learns what these attributes presented in the definition[7] mean (concept learning). Only the representational learning that *follows* concept learning (namely, the process of equating the concept word in meaning with what the concept itself means), however, can be legitimately considered part of vocabulary learning. By any reasonable standard, vocabulary learning can be regarded only as synonymous with representational learning. According to the generally accepted meaning of the expression, acquiring a vocabulary consists of learning a body of word meanings which, by definition, refers to learning what the words mean and not to learning what their referents mean. Thus, to use the term "vocabulary learning" to encompass concept learning as well as learning what concept words mean, although very commonly done, only generates confusion.

Learning what concept words mean obviously demands more sophisticated *prior knowledge* about their corresponding referents than does other forms of representational learning, since learning the meaning of concept words differs in one important respect from learning the meaning of words that do not represent concepts (e.g., proper nouns). Where the referent of a given word happens to be an *actual* object or event, on the other hand, learning that the word signifies approximately the same thing as the referent itself does not really involve a prior *substantive* task of *learning* what the referent itself signifies; getting to know what an object or event signifies is merely a simple matter of perception. An object, thus, simply signifies the corresponding perceptual image it elicits when present, or the corresponding memory image that remains, and can be otherwise evoked, when the object is no longer present.

When the referent of a word is a concept (an abstraction or a generic idea that does not actually exist), however, learning that the concept word signifies the same thing as the referent *does* involve a prior substantive task of learning what the referent signifies. One can, in this instance, get to know what the concept itself signifies only by *learning* what its criterial attributes are and what they mean. This, by definition, is a substantive form of meaningful learning. Hence, learning the meaning of a concept word always presupposes that the learner *first meaningfully learns* what its referent (the concept) signifies, namely, its criterial attributes, even though the actual *representational* learning involved is essentially no different in process than that involved in learning the meaning of words that do not represent concepts (e.g., words like "the," "when," etc., proper nouns).

The practical and educational significance of distinguishing carefully between learning the meanings of concepts and learning the meanings of concept words can be illustrated by citing several everyday and educational examples. First, it happens quite frequently, particularly in concept formation, that pupils acquire particular concepts meaningfully without learning for some time what their names are. Thus, simply because they do not know what particular concept *words* mean, it cannot be assumed that they necessarily do not know the corresponding concept *meanings* (criterial attributes).

Second, it is very possible either to forget what a given concept word means but to remember its corresponding concept meaning or to remember a concept word but to forget its meaning. Third, in teaching native language synonyms as well as foreign language equivalents of native language words, it is important to appreciate that pupils only have to learn new concept words—not new concepts. Thus, it is only necessary for them to equate in meaning the old concept words and the corresponding new synonyms or foreign language equivalents; it is superfluous and wasteful of time for them to equate in meaning the new concept words and the referents of the old concept words.

Finally, if concepts are rotely learned as a result of failure to relate their criterial attributes substantively and nonverbatimly to cognitive structure, it necessarily follows that their corresponding concept words are also rotely learned. It is unlikely that a learner will nonarbitrarily and nonverbatimly relate a concept word to other relevant concept words in his cognitive structure unless it has been meaningfully learned. Knowing about the two separate kinds of rote learning involved here helps one understand why rotely learned concept words that have been equated with rotely learned concepts have such little utility and are forgotten so quickly.

Vocabulary Learning as Meaningful Learning

It is clear from the preceding discussion that vocabulary learning, or the acquisition of concept word meanings, is not regarded in this book as an expression of conditioning or rote verbal learning. It reflects, rather, a meaningful and active cognitive process involving the establishment in cognitive structure of representational equivalence between a new symbol and the idiosyncratic, specifically relevant cognitive content its referent signifies.

It is true, of course, that most verbal symbols do represent their referents on a somewhat arbitrary and verbatim basis. There is typically no nonarbitrary reason why a given word is chosen to represent the corresponding object or idea to which it refers,[8] and verbatim reproducibility is also essential if representational symbols are to function as surrogates of the referents, since only a very slight change (e.g., a single letter of a word) may drastically change or even reverse the meaning. On both counts, therefore, vocabulary (representational) learning is the kind of meaningful learning most closely related to rote learning.

Representational learning, nevertheless, still satisfies the minimum criteria of nonarbitrary, nonverbatim relatability of the learning task to cognitive structure that is necessary for meaningful learning. This is true because (1) any particular proposition of representational equivalence is nonarbitrarily relatable to a more general proposition of the same nature that is typically established in cognitive structure quite early in childhood and (2) even quite young children growing up in a bilingual environment seem implicitly to appreciate that second-language symbols manifest the same representational relationship that the first-language symbols do, both to the referents in question and to what the referents signify.

In any case, the acquisition of representational equivalence between new symbols and what their referents signify is a much less arbitrary learning task than either the serial learning of nonsense syllables or the learning of a list of paired associates. The type of meaningful cognitive process involved in representational learning is obviously basic to and, prerequisite for, the learning of all units of meaning in any symbolic system. Furthermore, it is only because the meanings of single words can be learned in this way that, by combining such meanings, it becomes possible to generate verbally both conceptual and propositional ideas that are inherently less arbitrary and can, therefore, be learned more meaningfully.

Concept Learning

We define concepts as objects, events, situations, or properties that possess common criterial attributes and are designated by the same sign or symbol. Essentially there are two methods of concept learning: (1) concept formation that takes place primarily in young (preschool) children and (2) concept assimilation, which is the predominant form of concept learning in school children and adults.

In concept *formation* the criterial attributes of the concept are acquired as a consequence of direct experience through successive stages of hypothesis generation, testing, and generalization. Thus, the young child comes to know the concept "dog" through successive encounters with dogs, cats, cows, etc., until he can generalize those criterial attributes that constitute the cultural concept of "dog." In this case the sign (word) "dog" is usually acquired before the concept itself. The reverse may occur, however,, for other concepts such as "argument" or "mammal."

As the child's vocabulary increases, new concepts tend to be acquired more frequently through the process of concept *assimilation* since the criterial attributes of new concepts can be ascertained by use in new combinations of existing referents (words as well as images) available in the child's cognitive structure. Although concrete-empirical props must be used to facilitate concept assimilation in elementary-school children, it is also possible with older pupils to use other existing relevant concepts in their cognitive structures to accelerate the process of defining the criterial attributes of new concepts.

Older children and adults learn very few new concepts through the process of concept formation. Typically, only gifted or creative adults in our culture discover new concepts inductively or even deductively, by analysis and synthesis.

Propositional Learning

Although somewhat more complex than learning the meaning of new words, the meaningful learning of presented new verbal propositions is similar to representational learning in that (given a meaningful learning set in the learner) their meanings emerge after a potentially meaningful learning task is related to, and interacts with, relevant ideas in cognitive structure on a nonarbitrary and nonverbatim basis. In this case, however, the learning task, or potentially meaningful proposition, consists of a *composite* idea and is expressed verbally in a sentence containing both denotative and connotative word meanings and the syntactic functions of and relations between words. The differentiated cognitive content resulting from the meaningful learning process (in which the new instructional ideas and the established ideas in cognitive structure interact), and constituting its meaning, is the product of the *particular* way in which the content of the new proposition is related to the content of the relevant established (anchoring) ideas in cognitive structure. The relationship in question may be either subordinate, superordinate, a combination of these two, or combinatorial.

DIFFERENT HIERARCHICAL WAYS OF RELATING NEW INFORMATION TO EXISTING (ANCHORING) IDEAS IN COGNITIVE STRUCTURE

Emergent meaning has been defined above as the principal product of an active and integrative interactional process between new ideas in the instructional material and relevant existing (anchoring) ideas in the learner's cognitive structure. The type and degree of meaning that emerges in meaningful learning and retention, its status in the hierarchy of related internalized ideas and ideational relationships in its particular subject matter field, its longevity, and its relative ease of acquisition largely depend on such factors as: (1) the particular hierarchical and substantive relationships between the new and the existing (anchoring) ideas in the interactional process; (2) the degree of particularized relevance of the anchoring ideas in the learner's cognitive structure for the new ideas in the instructional material to which they are related; (3) whether the new instructional material is related to relatively *specific* (particularized) anchoring ideas in the meaningful learning process or to more general and diffuse background knowledge in the learner's relevant memory store; and (4) such cognitive structure variables as the availability, stability, longevity, and clarity of the anchoring ideas and their discriminability from both new ideas in the learning material and relevant anchoring ideas in cognitive structure.

Subordinate Learning or Subsumption

In both concept and propositional learning, new, potentially meaningful information is most frequently anchored to more general and inclusive relevant ideas in the learner's existing cognitive structure. This process of relating new information to relevant preexisting superordinate segments of cognitive structure has been referred to above as *subsumptive* learning. Since cognitive structure itself tends to be hierarchically organized with respect to level of abstraction, generality, and inclusiveness of ideas, the emergence of *new* propositional meanings most typically reflects a *subordinate* relationship of the new material to more superordinate existing ideas in cognitive structure.

This outcome, in turn, results in the further hierarchical organization of cognitive structure when the subsumed ideas themselves become subsumers. The efficiency and longevity of subsumptive learning can probably be attributed to the fact that once subsuming (anchoring) ideas are themselves adequately established in cognitive structure, they:

1. Have maximally specific, particularized, and direct relevance for subsequent learning tasks.
2. Possess enough explanatory power to render otherwise arbitrary factual detail potentially meaningful.
3. Possess sufficient inherent stability to provide the firmest type of anchorage for newly learned and highly particularized meanings.[9]
4. Organize related new facts around a common theme, thereby integrating the component elements of new knowledge both with each other and with existing knowledge.

It is necessary at this point to differentiate between two basically different kinds of subsumption that may occur in the course of meaningful learning and retention. *Derivative* subsumption takes place when the new learning material is understood either as a specific exemplar of an established concept or proposition in cognitive structure or as supportive or illustrative of a previously learned concept or general proposition. In either case the new learning material is directly and self-evidently derivable from, or implicit in, an already established and more inclusive preexisting anchoring concept or proposition in cognitive structure. Under these circumstances the meaning of the derivative material emerges quickly and *relatively* effortlessly, but tends to be quickly forgotten both because it can be adequately represented by the subsumer itself and because a new exemplar can be easily regenerated when needed.

More typically, however, new subject matter is learned by a process of *correlative* subsumption. The new learning material here is an extension, elaboration, modification, or qualification of previously learned concepts or propositions. It also interacts with, and is incorporated by, more relevant and inclusive subsumers in cognitive structure; but its meaning is not implicit in, and cannot be adequately represented by, these latter subsumers. Thus, unlike the case in derivative subsumption, the forgetting of correlative ideas is not innocuous because they cannot be regenerated from the anchoring ideas themselves. When the learning material attempts explicitly to enhance discriminability between the new instructional ideas and the presumed relevant subsuming ideas in cognitive structure by means of a series of comparisons involving the explicit exposition of the similarities and differences between them, it may be considered a *comparative* subtype of correlative subsumption.

Superordinate and Combinatorial Learning

New learning bears a *superordinate* relationship to cognitive structure when an individual learns an inclusive new proposition under which several preexisting, established, but less inclusive ideas may be subsumed. Superordinate learning takes place in the course of inductive reasoning, when presented material is organized inductively, involves the synthesis of component ideas, and in the learning of higher-order abstractions. The acquisition of superordinate meanings occurs more commonly in *concept* than in propositional learning, such as when children learn that the familiar concepts of carrots, peas, beans, beets, and spinach may all be subsumed under the new superordinate concept of "vegetable" although they are perceptually very different.

The meaningful learning of new propositions that bear neither a subordinate nor a superordinate relationship to *particular* relevant ideas in cognitive structure (that cannot be subsumed under inclusive or established concepts or propositions, or cannot themselves subsume specific and less inclusive ideas) gives rise to *combinatorial* meanings. They are potentially meaningful because they consist of sensible new combinations of previously learned ideas that can be nonarbitrarily related to a *broad background* of *generally* relevant content in cognitive structure by virtue of their *general congruence* with such content as a whole. Unlike subordinate or superordinate propositions, they are not relatable to *particular* relevant ideas within cognitive structure. The availability here of only generally and nonspecifically relevant anchoring ideas in cognitive structure presumably makes combinatorial propositions less relatable or anchorable to previously acquired knowledge. Hence, at least initially, they are more difficult to learn and remember than subordinate or superordinate propositions. This latter inference follows directly from the previously described conditions of meaningful learning and from evidence indicating that the availability of appropriately relevant *specific* content in cognitive structure is a crucial variable in meaningful learning.

Many of the inclusive and broadly explanatory *new* generalizations that students learn in science, mathematics, social studies, and the humanities are nevertheless examples of combinatorial learnings—for example, relationships between mass and energy, heat and volume, genic structure and phenotypic variability, demand and price, etc. Although acquired with greater difficulty than subordinate or superordinate propositions, they exhibit, once adequately established, the same inherent stability as any inclusive or superordinate (subsuming) idea in cognitive structure (see above). Further elaboration of these ideas typically results in derivative or correlative subsumption (analysis, differentiation) and less commonly in superordinate learning (generalization, synthesis).

Since propositions can presumably be learned and retained most readily when they are subsumable under *specifically* relevant ideas in cognitive structure, and since the *hierarchical* organization of cognitive structure is itself largely reflective of the prevailing subsumptive process in meaningful learning and retention, it seems reasonable to suggest that the subsumptive mode of meaningful learning be utilized wherever possible for instructional purposes.

Some school learning that is frequently labeled "rote learning" (and which under many circumstances *is* purely rote) is actually intended to be a simple form of meaningful propositional learning, as, for example, certain aspects of the learning of addition and multiplication facts. It is true that some rote learning may be encouraged as a means of accelerating speed of response and calculation; but in most modern schools the multiplication table, for instance, is learned *after* a clear understanding of number ideas and relationships is acquired. Since this type of learning—relating pairs of numbers to their product--can be nonarbitrarily and nonverbatimly related to existing concepts of number relationships in cognitive structure, it is hardly analogous to the rote learning of paired associates or nonsense syllables. It is, rather, much more comparable to an actor's verbatim memorization of his lines after he acquires a meaningful grasp of the story or plot. Learning sets, therefore, need not be purely rote or purely meaningful. Learners may simultaneously or successively choose to learn both meaningfully and rotely.

Some readers may perceive some similarity between the concepts of subordinate (subsumptive) and superordinate learning in relation to assimilation theory, on the one hand, and Piaget's contrasting notions of assimilation and accommodation, on the other. Actually the resemblance is more terminological (nominalistic) than real. Piaget uses these terms solely to describe different kinds of *developmental* changes in schemata rather than to describe *contemporaneous* learning processes. Hence, he makes no reference whatsoever to the conditions of, or mechanisms underlying, these learning processes.

Discovery Learning

Propositional learning as described above is typical of the situation prevailing in reception learning when substantive propositions are *presented* to the learner and he is required only to learn and remember their meaning. It is important to realize, however, that propositional learning is also a major type of verbal problem solving or discovery learning. The main difference between propositional learning as found in reception learning situations, on the one hand, and in discovery learning situations, on the other, inheres in whether the principal content of what is to be learned is discovered by learners themselves or is presented to them. In reception learning this content is presented to learners in the form of a substantive or non-problem-setting proposition that they need only understand and remember. In discovery learning, on the other hand, they must first discover this latter content themselves by generating propositions that represent either solutions to the problems that are set or successive steps in their solution.

Actually, the reception and discovery varieties of propositional learning are not dichotomous. They involve both varieties of propositional learning successively at different stages in the problem-solving process. To begin with, problem-solving propositions are not typically generated *de novo*. Their generation involves, rather, a transformation (restructuring, reorganization, synthesis, integration) of relevant and available *substrate* propositions (propositions undergoing transformation). Substrate propositions, in turn, are of two main types: (1) *problem-setting* propositions, defining the nature and conditions of the current problem situation; and (2) *background* propositions, consisting of relevant aspects of previously acquired knowledge (information, principles) that bear on the problem.

The meaningful learning of problem-setting propositions, in school and similar learning environments, typically involves only reception learning.[10] That is, these problem-setting propositions are presented to the learner and he need only learn and remember what they mean by relating them nonarbitrarily and nonverbatimly to relevant subsuming ideas in his cognitive structure. Unlike *substantive* reception learning situations, however, that *end* with the learning and retention of the propositions in question, the meaningful internalization of *problem-setting* propositions first sets in motion a discovery learning process. A new *problem-solving* proposition, embodying a potentially meaningful means-end relationship, is then generated through various transformational operations on the internalized problem-setting and background propositions. The final step in this meaningful learning sequence, namely, learning and retaining the meaning of the newly-generated successful problem-solving proposition, is again a matter of meaningful reception learning. In fact, the only real discovery aspect of this entire sequence of meaningful discovery propositional learning, apart from generating the successful problem-solving proposition, consists of the actual process of transforming the substrate propositions into a potentially meaningful problem-solving proposition.

In meaningful discovery learning, as opposed to more typical (substantive) instances of meaningful reception learning, the learner, thus, nonarbitrarily and nonverbatimly relates problem-setting propositions to his cognitive structure—not for the purpose of understanding and remembering what they mean *as an end in itself,* but for the purpose of transforming them (in conjunction with and with the benefit of previously acquired relevant background knowledge) into successful new problem-solving propositions that are potentially meaningful to him.

THE ROLE OF LANGUAGE IN COGNITIVE FUNCTIONING

Although preverbal cognitive functioning does exist and does characterize the behavior and "thought" of infrahuman organisms and of young children, it plays a relatively minor role in school learning. For all practical purposes, the acquisition of ideas and of subject-matter knowledge depends on verbal and other forms of symbolic learning. In fact, it is largely because of language and symbolization that most complex forms of cognitive functioning become possible.

> Translation of experience into symbolic form, with its attendant means of achieving remote reference, transformation, and combination, opens up realms of intellectual possibility that are orders of magnitude beyond the most powerful image-forming system. . . . Once the child has succeeded in internalizing language as a cognitive instrument, it becomes possible for him

to represent and systematically transform the regularities of experience with greater power and flexibility than before (Bruner, 1964a).

Evidence from various other sources indicates that somewhere between the fourth and fifth years of life, language assumes a much more dominant role in cognitive functioning. Luria (1959) has shown that the "internalization" of speech at this age (that is, the ability of the child to manifest speech on a nonvocal and noncommunicative basis) coincides with the emergence of language as the principal directive factor in instigating, controlling, and organizing behavior. The same shift from stimulus to verbal-cognitive control of behavior is exhibited in discrimination learning (T. S. Kendler, 1963) and in the ability to transpose a learned relationship to an analogous pair of stimuli (Alberts & Ehrenfreund, 1951). For example, after the "verbal" child learns to choose the larger member of a pair of two blocks, he can transfer this learned relationship to similar pairs of *any* absolute size.

Experimental findings in discrimination learning (Kendler & Kendler, 1961), transposition learning (Spiker & Terrell, 1955), and concept formation (Weir & Stevenson, 1959) suggest that the superiority of verbal learning to preverbal cognitive functioning is attributable to the fact that symbolic learnings can be identified, transformed, and differentially responded to much more efficiently than can the concrete stimuli or situations represented by the symbols.[11] Finally, by this age (five years), the child has also mastered the syntax of language sufficiently well to understand and generate fairly complex propositional statements.

Parallel analysis of the development of language and thought (Inhelder & Piaget, 1958; Vygotsky, 1962) also suggests that growth in logical thinking is, in large measure, tied to growth in language capability. On purely theoretical ground, it would be difficult indeed to deny some degree of cause-effect relationship in such linguistic developments as symbolical representation, the mastery of syntax, the internalization of language, and the acquisition of more abstract and relational linguistic terms, on the one hand, and such developments in cognitive functioning as the internalization of logical operations, emergence of the ability to understand and manipulate relationships between abstractions without the benefit of current or recent concrete-empirical experience, and attainment of the capacity to think in terms of hypothetical relations between variables, on the other hand.

Much of the failure to appreciate the important facilitative impact of language in cognitive functioning is, of course, a reflection of the view popularized by the "progressive education" movement that verbal learning necessarily consists of rotely memorized glib verbalisms. In large part, however, it also *reflects confusion between the labeling and process functions of language.* Hendrix, for example, argues that "in the natural order of events, the abstraction comes first and *then* a name for it is invented" (Hendrix, 1950). According to her, the understanding and discovery of ideas is completely a "subverbal, internal process"; the *entire* substance of an idea inheres in subverbal insight. Language becomes involved in the process only because of the need to attach a symbol or label to the emerging subverbal insight so that it can be recorded, verified, classified, and communicated to others. Verbalization, she asserts further (1947), is not only unnecessary for the generation and transfer of ideas and understanding, but is also positively "harmful" when used for *these* purposes. "The resulting problem then becomes one of how to plan and execute teaching so that language can be used for its necessary *secondary* (labeling) functions without damage to the dynamic quality of the learning itself" (Hendrix, 1961).

How plausible are these propositions? Let us grant at the outset that a subverbal type of insight exists and that this type of insight is exhibited by rats, monkeys, and chimpanzees in experimental learning situations and by household pets, barnyard animals, wild beasts, children, and adults in a wide variety of everyday problem-solving situations. But is it because of *this* type of insight that human beings have created cultures and are able to discover and assimilate knowledge in such fields as physics, chemistry, biology, mathematics, and philosophy quite beyond anything yet approached by horses, chickens, or apes? Or is it because of the qualitatively superior transfer power of *verbal* or symbolic generalization?

What Hendrix is referring to, of course, is simply the representational ("labeling" or "naming") function of language in thought. The choice of a particular arbitrary symbol to represent a *new* abstraction obviously comes *after* the process of abstraction itself and is not intrinsically related to it. This, however, is not the *only* role of language in the abstraction process, nor is it the *first* time that it is used in this process. Verbalization does more than verbally gild the lily of subverbal insight; it does more than just attach a symbolic handle to an idea so that one can record, verify, classify, and communicate it more readily. It constitutes, rather, an *integral* part of the very process of acquiring new abstract ideas and influences both the nature and the product of the cognitive processes involved in generating new concepts and abstract propositions. One of the important influences of language on concept development has been carefully studied by Whorf, particularly in contrasting Native American Indian languages and European or English. Whorf (Carroll, 1964) asserts that "concepts of 'time' and 'matter' are not given in substantially the same form by experience to all men but depend upon the nature of the language or languages through the use of which they have been developed."

The actual act of assigning an arbitrary name to a newly generated abstraction is not, of course, an integral part of the abstraction process itself. At this point language *does* have merely a *labeling* function. Language, though, is also involved, in at least two others ways: in the *process* aspects of abstraction and thought. First, the fact that abstractions have names—that their meanings can be represented by words—plays a very important role in the *process* of generating new concepts from their constituent abstractions. When we look backwards, for example, to the abstraction process preceding the labeling of a given, newly generated concept, it is evident that this process itself could never have originated were it not for the representational power of words. In the abstracting, categorizing, differentiating, and generalizing aspects of combining and transforming existing known concepts into new abstractions, generic ideas are simply not sufficiently *manipulable* themselves to be handled in these designated ways unless they are first named;[12] it is only because complex concept meanings can be represented by single words that these combinatorial and transformational operations become possible. Thus, by exploiting the unique manipulability of representational symbols, it is possible to generate new concepts and propositions that transcend by far—in inclusiveness, generality, clarity, and precision—the level of abstraction that could be achieved if concepts were unnamed. The naming of ideas, therefore, is a significant *prerequisite* for their later *use* in conceptualization and other forms of thinking, except, of course, in the case of generating new concepts and propositions at a very low level of abstraction.

Second, language plays an important role in verbalizing or encoding into sentences, the new intuitive or subverbal products (concepts or propositions) that emerge from the transformational operations involved in thinking. Verbalizing subverbal ideas (*expressing* them verbally in propositional form as opposed to the later act of *naming* them) is a *refining* process that results in their becoming much clearer, more explicit, more precise, and more sharply delineated. It is, therefore, a serious mistake to believe that the *entire* substance of an idea as well as *all* of its transfer power inhere in its subverbal form, as Hendrix asserts (1961). The old philosophical notion that verbalization "merely mirrors thought" or "clothes it in outer garments" is charmingly poetic but has little psychological utility or explanatory value today. By means of its significant refining functions, verbalization adds a great deal both to the meaning and transferability of the products of thought; thus, it must be considered an integral part of the process of thinking.

In conclusion, therefore, it can be stated that language contributes in three important ways to concept formation and problem solving:

1. The representational properties of words facilitate the transformational processes involved in thought.
2. Verbalization of the emerging subverbal products of these operations, prior to naming them, refines and enhances their meanings and thereby increases their transfer power.
3. In a larger sense, the acquisition of language also enables developing human beings to acquire through *reception* learning, and to use in *discovery* learning, a vast repertoire of concepts and principles they could never discover by themselves in their own lifetimes.

The latter is the case because the human capacity for representational symbolism and verbalization makes possible both (1) the *original* generation (discovery) of ideas at a uniquely high level of abstraction, generality, and precision and (2) the cumulation and transmission of these ideas during the course of cultural history. The scope and complexity of the ideas acquired through reception learning make possible and foster, in turn, a general level of individual cognitive development that would be utterly inconceivable in the absence of language. (3) last, the kinds of concepts an individual learns in a particular culture, as well as his thought processes, are profoundly influenced by the vocabulary and structure of the language to which he is exposed in his particular culture (Whorf, 1956).

NOTES

[1]The use of the term *logical* to designate a kind of potential meaning inherent in the knowledge to be learned is obviously not the same usage that is employed in philosophy but rather is an idiosyncratic usage adopted for this particular context. To be "logically" meaningful, learning material need not be either logically valid or empirically true as long as it is sensible, plausible, and non-random, e.g., the phlogiston theory of combustion, the Lamarckian theory of evolution, pre-Galilean theories of the solar system, pre-Columbian theories of the shape of the earth, etc.

[2]E.g., algebraic and chemical symbols, geometrical figures, etc.

[3]As explained in an earlier section, this specific proposition of representational equivalence is additionally related to the more general proposition in the learner's cognitive structure that all objects and events have names and that these names signify whatever their referents do (Ausubel, 1968).

[4]The distinction between perception and cognition is particularly important because most "cognitive" psychologists, such as Norman (1965) and Neisser (1970), appear to subsume many perceptual processes under the term "cognition."

[5]Partly as a result of this telescoping effect (i.e., the immediate perceptual emergence of meaning), repetition has a particularly consolidating effect on learning and retention: The learner does not have to acquire meanings on subsequent trials and can concentrate solely on trying to remember them.

[6]Whether this capacity is also allegedly present in qualitatively similar fashion in chimpanzees, dolphins, and other higher mammals is still an open question. In any case it is apparent now that the cognitive capacities of these animals in this respect have been grossly exaggerated in the past.

[7]When the criterial attributes of a concept are presented to the learner by definition or context, rather than discovered by him, as in the case of concept formation, concept learning is referred to as "concept assimilation." In both instances, however, whether the criterial attributes are discovered or presented, it is self-evident that they must be meaningfully related to relevant ideas or images in cognitive structure before concept meanings emerge.

[8]In some instances, where new words are derived from already meaningful roots, either native or foreign, the representational relationship between word and referent is not arbitrary, provided that the individuals learning such words are aware of the derivations in question.

[9]Interested reader may consult Bellugi (1971), Chomsky (1957, 1972), Cocking (1972), McNeill (1970), Manyuk (1971), and Nelson (1973). It should also be realized that although five-year-old children are functionally competent in the major syntactical patterns of their native language, syntactical development continues well

into the elementary school years (Laban, 1966; O'Donnell, 1967; Palermo & Mofese, 1972; Slobin, 1976).

[10]The superior inherent stability of superordinate or inclusive ideas in cognitive structure is demonstrated by their greater resistance to forgetting over protracted time intervals, as shown by qualitative analysis of experimental and classroom subject-matter forgetting.

[11]In more informal learning situations as well as in research laboratories (where discovery is genuinely autonomous), the learner himself formulates problem-setting propositions that are followed by a preliminary type of discovery learning and by meaningful reception learning of the products of discovery.

[12]As we shall see later (Chapter 5) in discussing the relevant research, verbalization is an important factor in transferring learned principles to new problem-solving situations, even those of a motor or mechanical nature. These findings challenge the widely accepted tenet of "progressive education" that verbal learning is necessarily rote in character and that only nonrepresentational experience is transferable from one problem-solving situation to another.

REFERENCES

Alberts, C. A., & Ehrenfreund, D. *Transposition in children as a function of age.*

Ausubel, D. P. *Educational psychology: A cognitive view.* New York: Holt, Rinehart & Winston, 1968.

Bernard, W. Psychological principles of language learning and the bilingual reading method. *Modern Language Journal,* 1951, *35,* 87–96.

Bjorgen, I. A. *A re-evaluation of rote learning.* Oslo: Oslo University Press, 1964.

Bower, G. *Human memory: Basic processes.* New York: Academic Press, 1977.

Brozova, V. Effect of organized learning on text understanding and perceiving. *Studia Psychologica,* 1995, *37:* 259–268.

Carroll, J. B. The analysis of reading instruction: Perspectives from psychology and linguistics. In *Theories of learning and instruction.* 63rd Yearbook, Nat'l. Soc. Stud. Educ., Part I. Chicago: University of Chicago Press, 1964.

Chomsky, N. A. *Language and mind.* New York: Harcourt, 1972.

Chomsky, N. A. *Syntactic structures.* The Hague: Mouton, 1957.

Epstein, W., Rock, I., & Zuckerman, C. B. Meaning and familiarity in associative learning. *Psychological Monographs,* 1960, *74* (Whole No. 491).

Gagné, R. M., & Briggs, L. J. *Principles of instructional design.* New York: Holt, Rinehart & Winston, 1974.

Glaze, J. A. The association value of nonsense syllables. *Journal of Genetic Psychology,* 1928, *35,* 255–267.

Greeno, J. G. Situations, mental models and generative knowledge. In D. Klahs & K. Hotovsky (Eds.), *Complex information processing: The impact of Herbert A. Simon.* Mahwah, N.J.: Lawrence Erlbaum Associates, 1989.

Greeno, J. *Human memory: Paradigms and paradoxes.* Hillsdale, N.J.: Lawrence Erlbaum Associates, 1992.

Hendrix, G. A new clue to transfer of training. *Elementary School Journal,* 1947, *48,* 197–208.

Hendrix, G. Learning by discovery. *Mathematics Teacher,* 1961, *54,* 290–299.

Hirt, E. R., McDonald, H. E., & Erikson, G. A. How do I remember thee? The role of encoding, set, and delay in reconstructive memory processes. *J. Exp. Soc. Psychol.,* 1995, *31:* 379–409.

Inhelder, B., & Piaget, J. *The growth of logical thinking from childhood to adolescence.* New York: Basic Books, 1958.

Kendler, H. H., & Kendler, T. S. Effect of verbalization on reversal shifts in children. *Science,* 1961, *134,* 1619–1620.

Kendler, T. S. Development of mediating responses in children. *Monographs of the Society for Research in Child Development,* 1963, *28,* No. E. 33–48.

Lennenberg, E. H. On explaining language: The development of language in children can best be understood in the context of developmental biology. *Science,* 1969, *164,* 635–643.

McNeill, D. *The acquisition of language.* New York: Harper & Row, 1970.

Miller, G. A. The magical number seven plus or minus two: Some limits in our ability for processing information. *Psychological Review*, 1956, *63*, 81–97.

Miller, G. A., & Selfridge, J. A. Verbal context and the recall of meaningful material. *American Journal of Psychology*, 1950, *63*, 176–185.

Moreno, V., & Di Vesta, F. J. Analogies (adages) as aids for comprehending structural relations in text. *Contemporary Educational Psychology*, 1994, *19*, 179–198.

Neisser, U. *Psychology of cognition*. New York: Appleton-Century-Crofts, 1970.

Noble, E. E. The familiarity-frequency relationship. *Psychological Review*, 1953, *60*, 80–98.

Norman, D. *Memory and attention*. New York: Wiley, 1968.

Rosch, E. On the internal structure of perceptual and semantic categories. In T. E. Moore (Ed.), *Cognitive development and the acquisition of language*. New York: Academic Press, 1973.

Shavelson, R. G. Some aspects of the correspondence between content structures and cognitive structures in physics instruction. *Journal of Educational Psychology*, 1972, 225–234.

Spiker, C. C., & Terrell, G. Factors associated with transposition behavior of preschool children. *Journal of Genetic Psychology*, 1955, *86*, 143–158.

Underwood, B. J., & Schulz, R. W. *Meaningfulness and verbal learning*. Philadelphia: Lippincott, 1960.

Vygotsky, L. S. *Thought and language*. New York: Wiley, 1962.

Weir, M. W., & Stevenson, H. W. The effect of verbalization in children's learning as a function of chronological age. *Child Development*, 1959, *30*, 143–149.

Whorf, B. L. *Language thought and reality: Selected writings of Benjamin Lee Whorf*. Cambridge, Mass.: Massachusetts Institute of Technology Press, 1956.

CHAPTER 5

ASSIMILATION THEORY IN MEANINGFUL LEARNING AND RETENTION PROCESSES

Having already described the nature of meaning and the kinds of conditions and processes involved in the meaningful learning of words, concepts, and propositions, we shall want to explore in greater detail the psychological mechanisms whereby large quantities of subject-matter knowledge are retained in cognitive structure over extended periods of time. How is such knowledge assimilated and organized in cognitive structure, and why is it subsequently forgotten? Is there more than one valid explanation for the discrepancy between learned and remembered content, that is, are there different kinds of forgetting? Lastly, how does meaningful learning as a process differ from rote learning, and why does it yield superior learning and retention outcomes?

THE ASSIMILATION PROCESS IN THE ACQUISITION, RETENTION, AND ORGANIZATION OF KNOWLEDGE

To account more completely for the acquisition, retention, and organization of meanings in cognitive structure, it is necessary to develop further the principle of *assimilation*. This can be done most efficaciously and understandably below using simple representational symbols.

When a new idea *a* is meaningfully learned by being related to and interacting with relevant established idea *A* in cognitive structure, both ideas are modified, and *a* is *assimilated* into established *A*. This would typically be an instance of derivative or correlative subsumption, and, as indicated in Chapter 4, both the anchoring idea *A* and the new idea *a* are modified somewhat in forming the interactional product *A'a'*. For example, if *A* is a child's existing concept of Christian sin in his cognitive structure, *a* may be a presentation of Buddhist concepts of sin, thus modifying slightly the child's concept of Christian sin (*A'*), in addition to yielding a new idiosyncratic meaning for Buddhist sin (*a'*).

In more precise terms, the *actual* or total interactional product of the new idea in the learning material and the established idea in cognitive structure is hypothesized as being greater and more complex (i.e., *A'a'*) than as originally described in Chapter 4. This is where the retention phase of the assimilation process enters the picture; and, hence, we must examine more closely the new concept of *a;* the later dissociability of *a*′ (the new meaning) from *A*′ (the modified anchoring idea); and the eventual loss of dissociability of *a*′ from *A*′.

As previously noted, not only the potentially meaningful idea *a* but also the established idea *A* in cognitive structure (to which it is anchored) is changed as well by the interactional process. This is indicated by use of a prime sign in each case. More importantly, both interactional products *a*′ and *A*′ remain in relationship to each other as co-members of a linked composite unit or ideational complex, *A*′*a*′. In the more complete sense of the term, therefore, the actual interactional product of the meaningful learning process is not just the new meaning *a*′ but also includes the modification of the anchoring idea and is, thus, coextensive with the composite meaning *A*′*a*′.

In the further course of subsumptive learning, a new composite idea emerges which may undergo further change over time during the retention and forgetting intervals. Therefore, *assimilation* is not complete after meaningful learning occurs but continues over a time period that may involve further new learning and/or retention (e.g., as after review) or varying degrees of intact retention or storage, or eventual loss of the retrievability of the assimilated subordinate ideas.

Most of the learning material presented in schools and similar institutions is in the form of concepts and *propositions* (which consist of concepts that in combination have some new composite meaning). Thus, to learn the meaning of a potentially meaningful new proposition requires more than just the learning of the meanings of its component concepts. It presupposes the availability in cognitive structure of relevant anchoring concepts and propositions that are related both to the component parts of the new proposition to be learned, as well as to the composite meaning of the latter proposition as a whole.

At the core of assimilation theory, therefore, is the idea that new meanings are acquired by the *interaction* of new, potentially meaningful ideas (knowledge) with previous learned concepts and propositions. This interactional process results in a modification of both the potential meaning of the new information and of the meaning of the concepts or propositions to which it is anchored, and also creates a new ideational product which constitutes its new meaning to the learner. The process of sequential assimilation of new meanings from successive exposures to new, potentially meaningful materials results in *progressive differentiation* of concepts or propositions, in the consequent refinement of meanings, and in enhanced potentiality for providing anchorage for further meaningful learning.

When concepts or propositions are learned through successive new subsumptive, superordinate, or combinatorial learning processes, new and different meanings may develop; and conflicting meanings may possibly be resolved through a process of *integrative reconciliation*. In time, as the assimilation process continues to operate, the meanings of component concepts or propositions may no longer be dissociable (retrievable) from their anchoring ideas, and *obliterative* assimilation or meaningful forgetting is said to have occurred: The relatively complete assimilation of the specificity of the new meaning renders it no longer dissociable (retrievable) from the generality of the more inclusive anchoring idea in cognitive structure (due to obliterative subsumption) and is, therefore, considered to be forgotten.

The Explanatory Value of the Assimilative Process

Assimilation theory has considerable explanatory value for elucidating the nature of both meaningful learning and retention phenomena because it helps account for the acquisition, retention, and forgetting of meaningfully learned ideas and also for the way in which knowledge is organized in cognitive structure. Assimilation of a new idea could conceivably enhance retention in three different ways. First, by becoming "anchored," so to speak, to a modified form of an existing and highly stable and relevant idea in cognitive structure, the new meaning vicariously partakes of the stability and longevity of the latter idea.[1] Second, this type of anchorage, by *continuing* during the storage interval the *original* nonarbitrary and substantive relationship between the new and the established ideas, also protects the new meaning from the relatively mild interference exerted by previously learned (proactive), concurrently experienced, or subsequently encountered (retroactive) similar contradictory ideas. This interference is what is so much more damaging when learning material is arbitrarily related to cognitive structure, as is the case in rote learning.

Last, the fact that the newly emergent meaningful idea is stored in linked relationship to the *particular* idea(s) in cognitive structure to which it is most relevant—that is, to the idea(s) to which it was originally related in acquiring its meaning—presumably makes retrieval a less arbitrary and more systematic process as well as accounts for obliterative assimilation when retrieval is not possible. Assimilation explains the phenomenon of forgetting (or loss of retrieval capacity in relation to the newly learned meaning) by hypothesizing that the unique particularity and specificity of the latter meaning is displaced (obliterated) in varying degrees by the generality of its anchoring idea(s).

The assimilation hypothesis can also help explain how knowledge is organized in cognitive structure. If new ideas are *stored* in linked relationships to correspondingly relevant existing ideas in cognitive structure [and if it is also true both that one member of the linked pair is typically superordinate to or more inclusive than the other and that the superordinate member (at least, once it is established) is the more stable member of the pair], then it necessarily follows that the cumulative residue of what is learned, retained, and forgotten (the psychological structure of knowledge or cognitive structure as a whole) conforms to the organizational principle of progressive differentiation.

Thus, if the principle of assimilation is actually operative in the storage of meaningful ideas, it would then be quite understandable why an individual's organization of the content of a particular subject-matter discipline in his or her own mind exemplifies a hierarchically ordered pyramid. In this pyramid the most inclusive and broadly explanatory ideas occupy a position at the apex of the pyramid and subsume progressively less inclusive, or more highly differentiated, ideas, each linked to the next higher step in the hierarchy through relational bonds that are assimilative in nature.

As already suggested, the assimilation or anchoring process probably also has a generally facilitating effect on retention. To explain how newly assimilated meanings actually remain available during part or all of the retention period, it is necessary to assume that for a variable period of time they are *dissociable* from their anchoring ideas and, hence, are reproducible as individually identifiable entities. The newly learned and assimilated meaning *a'* is initially dissociable from its linked relationship to anchoring idea *A'*; the interactional product *A'a'*, in other words, can dissociate into *A'* and *a'*. Universal experience indicates that degree of dissociability or dissociability strength is at a maximum shortly after learning and, therefore, that newly acquired meanings, even in the absence of direct or indirect practice (review), are maximally dissociable at that time.

The newly learned meaning, modified by obliterative assimilation emanating from its anchoring idea, and linked to the latter idea during the retention and storage intervals, therefore shares vicariously in the high stability of the anchoring idea. Thus, in this respect, contrary to the loss of dissociability strength caused by the aforementioned obliterative assimilation, retention of the emergent new meanings is facilitated by the protection against highly similar and apparently contradictory ideas afforded by the linkage of this new meaning to its anchoring idea.

MEMORIAL REDUCTION: OBLITERATIVE ASSIMILATION OR FORGETTING

The theoretical attractiveness of the postulated assimilation process inheres not only in its ability to account for the superior (long-term) retention of meaningfully, as opposed to rotely learned ideas, but also in the fact that it implies a plausible retention and forgetting mechanism that is both continuous and compatible with the acquisition (learning) process, and also with the subsequent forgetting of these ideas (namely, with the gradual "reduction" of their meanings to the meanings of the corresponding anchoring ideas to which they are linked). Thus, although the retention of newly learned meanings is initially enhanced by anchorage to highly stable relevant established ideas in the learner's cognitive structure, such knowledge is still subject to the erosive influence of the general reductionist trend in cognitive organization. Because it is psychologically more economical and less burdensome merely to remember reduced variants of the more stable and general anchoring concepts and propositions than to remember the new, more highly differentiated ideas (new meanings) that are obliteratively assimilated by them, the meaning of unrehearsed or unoverlearned new ideas tends to be assimilated or reduced, over the course of time, to the more stable meanings of the established anchoring ideas.

Some time after learning occurs, therefore, when this second, *obliterative* stage of assimilation is beginning to take place, the newly-learned ideas start to become progressively less dissociable (retrievable) from their anchoring ideas as entities of their own right until they are no longer available and are said to be forgotten. When the dissociability strength of *a'* falls below a certain critical level (the threshold of availability), it is not retrievable at all. Eventually zero dissociability is reached, and *A'a'* is further reduced to *A'* or *A* itself, the original anchoring idea.

It should be additionally noted that in *meaningful* learning the potential meanings in the original new instructional material *a* may never be retrievable in precisely the same form in which they were originally presented. The very process of subsumption occurring in the assimilation of *a* may result in some drastic alteration of *a* to *a'*, and, hence, in a sense, obliterative subsumption may really ***begin*** at the time meaningful learning itself occurs. For this reason evaluation practices that require verbatim reproduction of presented information or ideas tend to discourage meaningful learning. Further, forgetting of meaningfully learned material also tends to leave a residue of modified sub-threshold anchoring ideas.

The additional concept of a variable threshold of availability is especially useful because it can explain transitory fluctuations in the availability of memories that are attributable to general cognitive, affective, or motivational variables (e.g., attention, anxiety, change of set or context, release of repression) without the occurrence of any significant change in dissociability strength (the intrinsic retrievability strength of the item in memory itself). By the same token, it explains why items of low dissociability strength, that are ordinarily not available under typical conditions of consciousness, are available under hypnosis, and why many memory items can often be recognized but not recalled.

Forgetting is thus a continuation or later temporal phase of the same assimilative process underlying the availability of newly learned ideas during an earlier phase of the retention interval. The same nonarbitrary relatability to, and interaction with, a relevant established idea in cognitive structure that is necessary for the meaningful learning of a new idea, and that leads to its enhanced retention through the process of anchoring the emergent meaning to the meaning of the established (anchoring) idea, somewhat paradoxically provides the mechanism for most later forgetting.

We observe in the principle or process of assimilation, therefore, an economy of explanation or theoretical parsimony; for the same basic principle of assimilation explains many different aspects of meaningful learning and retention and why there are individual variations in meaningful learning performance (depending in part on differential availability, stability, and discriminability of relevant subsumers) in particular learning situations; and why differential periods of retention should be expected (depending in part on similar factors influencing obliterative assimilation).

In the case of subordinate and combinatorial learning, the process of obliterative assimilation, as a reduction phenomenon, seems straightforward enough: The less stable (and more specific) meaning of a subordinate idea is gradually incorporated within or reduced to the more stable (and more general and inclusive) meaning of the superordinate and relevant idea in cognitive structure that assimilates it; and the less stable (and more specific) meaning of a combinatorial idea is similarly assimilated within or reduced to the more stable (and more generalized) meanings of the broader, less specifically relevant body of ideas in cognitive structure to which it is related. The forgetting of *superordinate* learnings, however, that, by definition, are more

TABLE 2. Forms of Meaningful Learning as Viewed in Assimilation Theory

1. Subordinate Learning:

A. *Derivative subsumption*

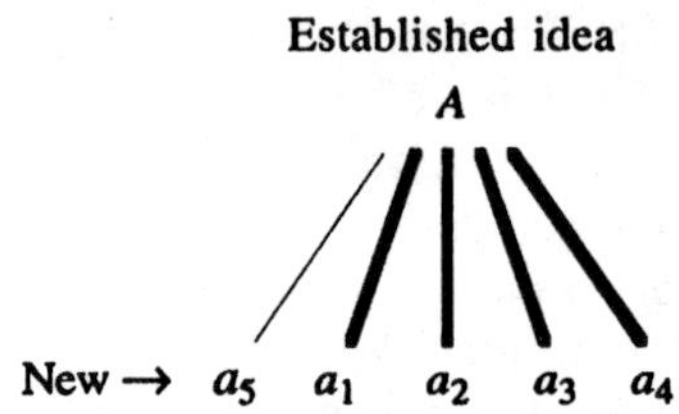

In derivative subsumption, new information a_5 is linked to superordinate idea A and represents another case or extension of A. The criterial attributes of the concept A are not changed, but new examples are recognized as relevant.

B. *Correlative subsumption*

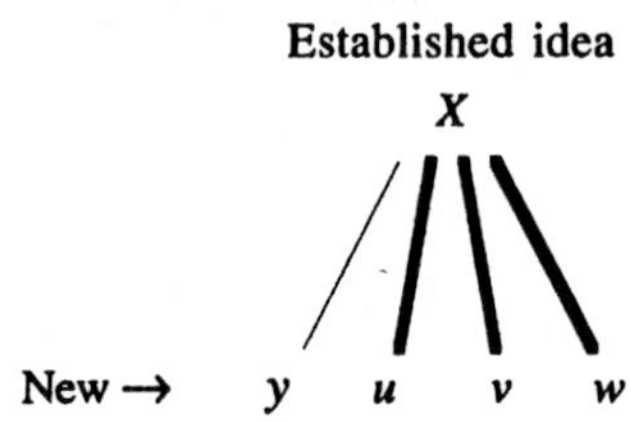

In correlative subsumption, new information y is linked to idea X, but is an extension, modification, or qualification of X. The criterial attributes of the subsuming concept may be extended or modified with the new correlative subsumption.

2. Superordinate Learning:

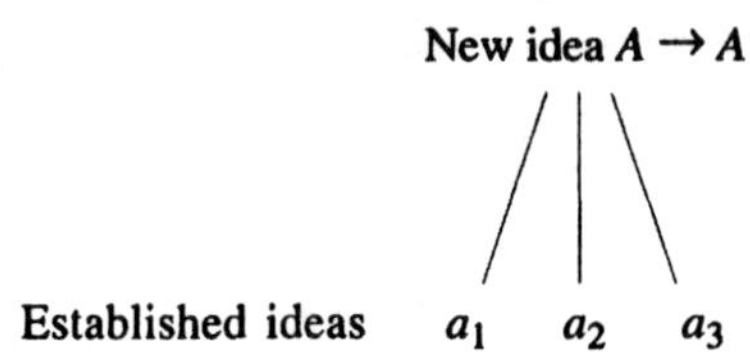

In superordinate learning, established ideas a_1, a_2, and a_3 are recognized as more specific examples of new idea A and become linked to A. Superordinate idea A is defined by a new set of criterial attributes that encompass the subordinate ideas.

3. Combinatorial Learning:

New idea $A \rightarrow B - C - D$

Established ideas

In combinatorial learning new idea A is seen as related to existing ideas B, C, and D but is neither more inclusive nor more specific than ideas B, C, and D. In this case, new idea A is seen to have some criterial attributes in common with preexisting ideas.

4. Assimilation Theory:

New information is linked to *relevant, preexisting* aspects of cognitive structure and both the newly acquired information and the preexisting structure are modified in the process. All of the above forms of learning are examples of assimilation. Most meaningful learning is essentially the assimilation of new information.

generalized and inclusive at the time of learning than the established subordinate ideas in cognitive structure that subsume them must be explained differently. Here the process of obliterative assimilation must obviously conform to a somewhat different paradigm, since the more stable anchoring ideas in this case are *less* general and inclusive than the new superordinate meanings they assimilate.

At least in the beginning, therefore, while the emergent new superordinate meanings are relatively unstable, they are reduced to their less inclusive (subordinate) anchoring ideas during the process of obliterative assimilation. Later, however, if and when the emergent new superordinate meanings are further consolidated and differentiated, they tend to become more stable than the subordinate ideas that originally assimilated them, inasmuch as the stability of an idea in memory, everything else being equal, tends to increase with its level of generality and inclusiveness (Kintsch, 1974; Meyer & McConkie, 1973). Thus, at this point, the direction of obliterative assimilation is reversed: The less inclusive, and now less stable, meanings of earlier learned subordinate ideas tend to be incorporated within or reduced to the more generalized meanings of the later learned and now more stable meanings of the superordinate ideas (see Table 2).

The dynamics underlying the meaningful learning, retention, and forgetting of newly learned ideas can be appreciated more fully by considering certain detailed aspects of the interactional and assimilation processes that have not been mentioned as yet. For example, consider the natural history of a potentially meaningful correlative concept or proposition a that a learner relates to (subsumes under) a specifically relevant and more inclusive and stable established proposition A in his cognitive structure. As a result of the subsumption process, an interactional product, $A'a'$, is formed in which both original components entering into the interactional process are modified as a consequence of the interaction.

It is obviously an oversimplification of convenience, however, to suppose that new learning idea a forms only a single interactional product with A. Actually to a lesser extent, it forms additional interactional products with other less relatable and relevant ideas in cognitive structure called B, C, D, E, and so forth, the degree of assimilation in each case being roughly proportional to the latter's place on a gradient of relevance. In this broader view of the interactional process also, the assimilating ideas could be modified considerably by particular new experience, thereby resulting, for example, in the correction of over- or underinclusive concepts or propositions. The defining attributes of the subsuming idea in cognitive structure may be broadened, for example, to include new features that were formerly excluded, or may be made less inclusive by excluding features that were originally included.

In the new interactional product, $A'a'$, it must be understood that a', once formed, does not lose its identity completely or since a dissociation equilibrium, $A'a' \leftrightarrow A' + a'$, is set up at the outset in which a', depending on prevailing threshold conditions, has a given degree of retrievability as an identifiable entity for a given period of time. As will be explained in greater detail later (Chapter 6), the original degree of dissociability strength of a', after meaningful learning occurs, varies with such factors as the relative relevance of the anchoring idea *A*, its stability, clarity, and the extent to which *A* is discriminable from the learning material (that is, from *a*).

Actually, assimilated items become unavailable (forgotten) long before the point of zero dissociability is reached since they are no longer retrievable when they fall below the prevailing *threshold of availability* (the critical level of dissociability strength a given item must exhibit in order to be retrievable). Much residual dissociability strength exists between this below-threshold level and the point of zero dissociability, but not enough to make the new meaning available (retrievable) under ordinary conditions of recognition or recall. The existence of below-threshold dissociability may be demonstrated, however, by the use of hypnosis (Nagge, 1935; Rosenthal, 1944), which greatly lowers the threshold of availability for all or most memory items, with the result that many items that were ordinarily below the level of availability become available under hypnosis. Relearning also demonstrates subthreshold dissociability strength (Burtt, 1941). The fact that forgotten materials can be *relearned* more effectively and in less time than that required for original learning is ample evidence of the existence of subthreshold dissociability strength; because of its presence, less new learning is required to reach any given threshold level than would otherwise be the case.

This concept of a dissociation equilibrium, in which an assimilated idea gradually becomes less dissociable from the established ideational system to which it is anchored and from which it derives its meaning, and, eventually is forgotten, has considerable heuristic value. It accounts *both* for the original availability of a newly learned meaning and for the subsequent *gradual* decline in its availability during the retention interval until forgetting ensues.

As will be indicated later, assimilation theory differs markedly in principle from the Gestalt theory of forgetting in this respect. Gestalt theory holds that the assimilative process induced by interaction between traces is a matter of all-or-none replacement of a given trace by another more potent trace, on the basis of the similarity existing between them.

The familiar Gestalt phenomena of "leveling" and of "sharpening," in which forgetting is manifested by reduction to a more familiar and stable idea or by accentuation of a specially salient characteristic, can be easily reinterpreted in terms of assimilation theory. In the process of *leveling* (Allport & Postman, 1947; Wulf, 1922), for example, *a*, which is a specific derivative or illustration of *A* or a slightly asymmetrical or incomplete variant of *A*, becomes *a'* after it is learned and is simply reduced to *A'* in the course of forgetting; whereas in the process of *sharpening* a more striking or conspicuous aspect of *a* becomes its criterial feature and is remembered in accentuated form because it is subsumed under, and eventually reduced to, a preexisting representation of this feature in cognitive structure. Continuous and inverse principles, and principles with qualifying conditions, similarly tend to be remembered more as discontinuous, direct, and unqualified in nature with the passage of time (Tomlinson, 1962).

Learning versus Retention

In meaningful reception learning the distinctive interactional phenomenon in both learning and retention sequences is a gradual increase in the availability or future reproducibility of the meanings derived from the ongoing learning process. Learning is the process of *acquiring new actual meanings* from the potential meanings presented in the learning material and of *making them more available.* It represents an *increment* in the availability of these new meanings—the situation that prevails when they first emerge or are first established, or when their dissociability strength is subsequently increased by repetition or by conditions enhancing their stability, clarity, or discriminability. Retention, on the other hand, refers to the process of *maintaining the availability* of a replica of the acquired new meanings. Thus, forgetting represents a *decrement* in availability, that is, the situation that prevails between the establishment of an emergent new meaning and its later reproduction or between two presentations of the learning material.

Retention, as we have already noted, is largely a later temporal phase and variably diminished aspect of the *same* phenomenon or functional capacity involved in learning itself. Later availability is always, for the most part, a function of initial availability. In the absence of intervening practice, therefore, delayed retention cannot possibly surpass immediate retention. For example, the common phenomenon of *reminiscence* (the superiority of delayed over immediate retention) is not, in all probability, reflective of a later increase in the dissociability strength of newly learned material. It reflects, rather, the subsequent lowering, at a later retesting of retention, of temporarily elevated thresholds of availability immediately after learning is completed.

Meaningful retention is not only a later attenuated manifestation of the same availability function established during learning, but is also a later temporal phase of the *same interactional process* underlying this availability. During the learning phase the meaning of the potentially meaningful instructional idea(s) forms an interactional product with its relevant anchoring idea and exhibits a given degree of dissociability from it. Continued spontaneous interaction between the successive meanings of the new instructional materials and their anchoring ideas during the retention interval results in a gradual decrease in the dissociability of the new meanings (that is, in forgetting) until the interactional product is reduced to the least common denominator capable of representing it, namely, to the anchoring (assimilating) idea itself. The *same* cognitive structure factors (the availability, relevance, stability, clarity, discriminability, and degree of differentiation of anchoring ideas) determining the original degree of dissociability strength of the new meaning immediately after learning (initial interaction) also determine the rate at which dissociability strength is subsequently lost during retention (later interaction).

In *rote* learning, on the other hand, the *same* interactional process is *not* involved in both learning and retention. Hence, rote learning represents an increment in availability (associative strength) after learning, involving one discrete interactional process and set of variables; and rote forgetting represents a loss in this availability due to interference from *another* discrete process (and group of variables) set in motion shortly before or after learning.

Three reasons, therefore, probably account for the superiority of retention resulting from meaningful learning in contrast to retention after rote learning. First, since meaningful learning is more efficacious, because of the advantages inherent in the nonarbitrary and nonverbatim relatability of the new ideas to relevant, established ideas in cognitive structure, a greater quantity of material is incorporated more easily and also made more available immediately after learning (more learning occurs originally).

Second, since the same relationship between new and established ideas is maintained by the assimilation process during the retention interval as during learning itself, and since the same variables influence both initial and later dissociability strength, this same continuing nonarbitrary, nonverbatim relatability advantage *further* enhances the efficiency of the process whereby acquired meanings are subsequently *retained.* Finally, a new presented idea subjected to assimilation by a well-established, relevant idea will vicariously tend to acquire some of the inherent stability of the original anchoring idea and, hence, will be retained longer.

Similarly, when dealing with different learning conditions affecting meaningful learning itself, we would expect these same three sources of retention superiority to be operative whenever a cognitive variable, for example, degree of discriminability, influences the learning-retention process. Johnson (1973) found that textual prose material with the highest level of meaningfulness was recalled three to eighteen times more quantitatively than material with the lowest level of meaningfulness. Aulls (1975) obtained similar findings with more meaningful, logically structured prose passages.

Depending on the method used to measure meaningful retention, one may obtain either quantitative or qualitative indices of the assimilation process that are elicitable during the retention interval. If one merely counts the number of concepts or propositions in a learning passage the meanings of which the learner can recognize or identify correctly, one ascertains what proportion of the newly learned material maintains sufficient dissociability strength to exceed the threshold of availability. If, on the other hand, one examines the *kind* of recognition or recall errors that are committed, and the organization of what is recalled, one also obtains a picture both of the *direction* of memorial changes induced by the assimilation process and of its qualitative aspects (e.g., cohesiveness, integrativeness). These latter changes include both the end products of obliterative assimilation (reduction to a more general or less qualified idea) as well as the various intermediate stages reflective of different degrees of dissociability strength. They must, of course, be differentiated from changes reflective of selective reconstruction of the memories that are available at the time of reproduction.

The distinction between learning and forgetting is obviously much greater in discovery than in reception learning. In discovery learning repeated encounters with the learning task give rise to successive stages in an autonomous or contrived arranged problem-solving process, whereas in reception learning repetition (apart from some possible changes in degree and precision of meaning) primarily increases the future availability of the material. Thus, the forgetting aspect of discovery learning hardly constitutes just a later continued phase of an original learning process that merely requires the learner to internalize and make presented material more available. Forgetting in this latter instance, therefore, has little in common with that part of discovery learning in which meaning must first be discovered by problem solving before it can be made available and retained.

Retention versus Forgetting

A distinction was made earlier between derivative and correlative subsumption. Derivative subsumption takes place when the learning material is understood to be a specific example of an established concept or proposition in cognitive structure or when the new material is supportive or illustrative of a previously learned general proposition. New learning proceeds easily in derivative subsumption, but forgetting may take place more rapidly unless this new material is greatly overlearned. The reason for this rapid *obliterative* subsumption is simply that the meaning of the new material can be very adequately represented by the more general and inclusive meaning of its established subsumer in cognitive structure, and that this latter process of memorial representation is more efficient and less burdensome than the actual retention of the derivative, supportive, or illustrative data themselves. If such data are needed at a later date, they can be synthesized or reconstructed by appropriately manipulating specific elements of past and present experience so that they exemplify the desired concept or proposition. For example, in recounting a long past incident, one ordinarily retains only the ideational substance or core of the experience and from this reconstructs or invents plausible details that are consistent with its general import and setting.

New subject matter, however, is more typically learned by a process of *correlative* subsumption. The new learning material in this case is incorporated by, interacts with, and is assimilated by relevant and more inclusive subsumers in cognitive structure, but its meaning is not implicit in and cannot be adequately represented by these latter subsumers. Nevertheless, in the interests of economy of cognitive organization and of reducing the burden on memory, the same trend toward obliterative subsumption occurs. This trend is particularly evident if the subsumers are unstable, unclear, or insufficiently relevant or if the learning material itself is lacking in discriminability or is not overlearned. In this latter instance, however, the consequences of forgetting (i.e., obliterative subsumption) are not as innocuous as in the case of derivative subsumption. When correlative propositions lose their idiosyncratic identifiability and can no longer be dissociated from their subsumers, a genuine loss of knowledge occurs. The subsumers under these conditions cannot adequately represent the meaning of new, previously presented correlative propositions; hence, the mere availability of the subsumers alone in memory does not make possible a reconstruction of the substance of the forgotten material. The same situation also exists when new superordinate and combinatorial meanings are forgotten. In the latter cases we are basically not dealing with a subsumptive learning process; consequently it might be more appropriate to speak of *obliterative assimilation* rather than of subsumptive learning in these contexts, although the basic forgetting process is similar to that following derivative or correlative subsumption, on the one hand, or superordinate or combinatorial learning, on the other.

The acquisition of a body of knowledge, therefore, after learning is completed is largely a matter of counteracting the trend toward obliterative assimilation in retaining correlative, superordinate, and combinatorial learnings. Thus, Bruner's exclusive emphasis on "generic learning" or on acquiring "generic coding systems," as a means of facilitating school learning, is unrealistic in our opinion, because it focuses on derivative aspects of subsumption that are atypical both of the assimilation process in general and of most instances of assimilating new subject matter.

It is true, as Bruner asserts, that most specific content aspects of subject matter can be forgotten with impunity as long as they are derivable, or can be reconstructed when needed, from those generic concepts or formulae that are remembered. The analogous forgetting of correlative, superordinate, or combinatorial content, however, results in a loss of knowledge that cannot be regenerated from residual generic concepts. The reductionist trend in memory (that is, obliterative assimilation) that is functional or, at the very worst, innocuous in the case of derivative material, constitutes the principal difficulty in retaining a body of knowledge consisting largely of correlative, superordinate, or combinatorial concepts and propositions.

Hence, the problem of meaningful learning and retention cannot ordinarily be solved by incorporating "a representation of the criterial characteristics of [a] situation [or] a contentless depiction of the ideal case" (Bruner, 1960) and then ignoring the loss of specific content that occurs. The main purpose of learning generic concepts and propositions is *not* so much to make possible the later reconstruction of forgotten derivative instances as to provide stable anchorage for learning the correlative, superordinate, or combinatorial material that follows; and it is any decrement in the rate of obliterative assimilation resulting from the interaction between the instructional material and the anchoring ideas that provides teachers with one of their major opportunities for enhancing the dissociability strength of pupils' assimilation of presented subject matter.

ASSIMILATION OF ABSTRACT VERSUS FACTUAL MATERIALS

The extent to which learning material is either abstract or factual in nature has an important bearing on its longevity or on the rate at which obliterative assimilation takes place. Comparison of the relative retention spans of substance and verbatim items invariably shows that the longevity of different components of the learning material, all other factors being equal, varies directly with degree of abstractness or superordination (Kintsch et al., 1975; Meyer & McConkie, 1973). The principal distinction between abstract and factual items is in terms of level of particularity or proximity to concrete-empirical experience. Typically, abstract material is also characterized by greater connectedness or less discreteness than is factual material.

All factual material, furthermore, is not of one piece. Some factual material can be learning meaningfully, whereas other factual material cannot possibly be related to cognitive structure in nonarbitrary, nonverbatim fashion and, hence, must be rotely learned if at all. But even if factual matter is potentially meaningful, it is more likely to be rotely learned than is abstract material—because it is undeniably more difficult to relate it to existing ideational materials in cognitive structure.

The previously made distinction between derivative and correlative subsumption is also important in accounting for differences in relative susceptibility to obliterative subsumption of different kinds of potentially meaningful factual material. Derivative facts undergo obliterative subsumption more rapidly because, unlike similar correlative matter, their meaning can be adequately represented by the existing relevant ideational material in cognitive structure that subsumes them. In any case a degree of factual reconstruction that is satisfactory enough for most purposes of communication is usually possible when reproduction is required or attempted.

The greater retention longevity of abstract than of factual material can, therefore, be partly accounted for in terms of the superiority of meaningful over rote learning and retention. Another credible explanation is that abstractions tend more often than factual material to be correlative rather than derivative in nature. Hence, because they are, from the very beginning, much less close than factual matter to the end-point of obliterative subsumption, they can be retained for longer periods of time.

THE THRESHOLD OF AVAILABILITY: REMINISCENCE

It has already been observed that in order for assimilated materials to be reproducible at some future date, their dissociability strength must exceed a certain critical value, namely, the threshold of availability. The most important cause of the unavailability of meaningfully learned materials, therefore, is a decrease in dissociability strength below this threshold of availability. Whether or not dissociability strength is sufficient to exceed threshold value, however, is also, in part, a function of the method used in measuring retention.

Recognition and recall, for example, make quite different demands on the degree of dissociability of a given item that is necessary for exceeding the threshold of availability. In recognition, the originally learned material is presented along with other plausible alternative variants and the subject need only selectively identify it; in the case of recall, on the other hand, the subject must *spontaneously* or on demand reproduce the substance of the original material. Obviously, therefore, recognition can lead to successful reproduction at a much lower level of dissociability strength than can recall. Items "on the tip of one's tongue" that cannot be recalled spontaneously can be both recalled with the aid of a hint (e.g., providing the first letter of the correct answer) and recognized correctly on a multiple-choice test. Subjects can even predict recognition successes and failures for items they cannot recall (Hart, 1965). In addition to this differential in dissociability strength between recognition and recall, another explanation of the difference in reproducibility is that the threshold of availability is higher for recall than for recognition when dissociability strength is held constant.

Thus, still another independent, although secondary, source of variability in the availability of subsumed materials inheres in fluctuations of the *threshold of availability itself.* Hence, a particular item of knowledge may manifest more than sufficient dissociability strength to exceed the threshold of availability. Similarly, a particular item of knowledge may manifest more than sufficient dissociability strength to exceed the *typically* prevailing threshold value, but may still be unavailable because of some *temporary* elevation of the threshold of availability. The most common reasons for such a transient elevation of threshold value are:

1. "Initial learning shock,"
2. The competition of alternative or conflicting memories, and
3. Negative attitudinal bias or motivation *not* to remember (repression).

Removal of these threshold-raising or retrieval-inhibiting factors (that is, disinhibition) naturally results in an apparent facilitation of memory. The most extreme example of disinhibition occurs during hypnosis, when, because of increased suggestibility, drastic restriction of the learner's field of awareness occurs, reducing the competing effects of alternative ideational systems in memory to a bare minimum (Rosenthal, 1944). The same result can be produced to a lesser extent by a reduction of repression.

Reminiscence (the Ballard-William phenomenon) refers to an apparent *increment* in the retention of meaningfully learned material over a period of two or more days without any intervening practice.[2] Since retention cannot possibly exceed original learning under these conditions, this phenomenon is probably reflective of spontaneous recovery from the threshold-elevating effects of "initial learning shock." It is postulated, in other words, that both a certain amount of resistance to learning and generalized cognitive confusion occur when unfamiliar new ideas are first introduced into cognitive structure, that this confusion and resistance are gradually dissipated as the new ideas become more familiar and less threatening, and that the existence of the initial resistance and confusion and their gradual dissipation are paralleled, respectively, by a corresponding initial elevation and a subsequent lowering of the threshold of availability. This interpretation is strengthened by the fact that reminiscence occurs only when the material is partially learned or not overlearned and when practice trials are massed, that is, when maximum opportunity for immediate confusion and later clarification exists.

The fact that reminiscence has been convincingly demonstrated only in elementary school children (Sharpe, 1952) and declines (Sharpe, 1952) or is not exhibited at all (Williams, 1926) in older subjects suggests that initial "learning shock" tends to decrease with increasing age as cognitive structure becomes more stable and better organized.

CAUSES OF FORGETTING RELATIVE TO PHASES OF MEANINGFUL LEARNING AND RETENTION

The various causes of forgetting may be integratively summarized by categorizing them both with respect to the processes or mechanisms primarily involved in each category, and also with respect to the particular phase of the meaningful learning and retention sequence in which the designated cause is primarily operative. Each phase, thus, contributes in distinctive and observable ways to discrepancies between what is actually learned or experienced, on the one hand, and the memories of same that are not retained or reproducible in part or in whole and, thus, are indicative of what is conventionally regarded as forgetting, on the other.

Temporally, three distinct functional and overlapping phases may be distinguished during meaningful reception learning and retention. Each phase gives rise in terms of its corresponding process to characteristic kinds of forgetting. During the first phase, meaningful learning, new meanings are acquired as a result of logical and potentially meaningful ideas in the instructional material being related to and interacting with relevant ideational material (anchoring ideas) in cognitive structure, thereby generating idiosyncratic meanings with a given degree of dissociability strength, each linked in storage to its corresponding anchoring idea. The latter outcome, of course, depends also on the effects of cognitive, motivational, and affective variables influencing meaningful retention positively or negatively during this interval.

Much of the particularity of obliterative assimilation, if taken to the ultimate end-point of the assimilative process of total forgetting, reduces the newly-learned meanings to the more general, non-particularized, and unqualified content characterizing the ideas that subsume or assimilate them. The most important factors influencing the resulting degree of obliterative assimilation or loss of dissociability strength, in the first and second phases of meaningful learning and retention, are the cognitive variables (the availability, stability, clarity, and discriminability of the relevant anchoring ideas). Practice, task, affective, and motivational factors also help determine the latter outcomes, especially during the third and final phase of the meaningful learning and retention process.

The third and final phase of the meaningful learning and retention sequence and process involves the retrieval and reproduction of those newly acquired and retained meanings that, as explained above, either exceed the threshold value of availability or fail to do so and, hence, are said to be forgotten. The same cognitive and affective factors, mostly negative, that raise or lower the threshold of availability also alter the actual process of reconstructing and reformulating the surviving (retained) or unforgotten items into a more generalized and unparticularized summary statement that is appropriate of the demands of the current recall situation (Bartlett, 1932).

Table 3 summarizes, particularizes, briefly identifies, and explains the various sources or causes of forgetting discussed in this as well as in prior and subsequent chapters.

TABLE 3. Causes of Forgetting

I. In Meaningful Learning Phase

1. Absence of necessary cognitive conditions for meaningful learning: lack of logical meaningfulness of the instructional material; rote (instead of meaningful) learning set; lack of relevant anchoring ideas in the learner's cognitive structure.
2. Obliterative assimilation: making memories less specific and particular than they were originally as a result of assimilation of the latter content by the import of the prevailing generalities.
3. Very potent, seemingly plausible, and well-established, relevant misconceptions in cognitive structure that can assimilate to itself its objectively more valid and veridical counterpart ideas in the learning passage, thereby detracting from their veridicality.
4. Selective cultural and idiosyncratic frames of reference and attitudinal biases. These exert their influence maximally by setting an erroneous or ethnocentric initial direction that often tends to be followed undeviatingly thereafter.
5. An elevated threshold of availability for particular items in the learning passage that often generate anxiety or guilt feelings as in instances of repression.
6. Vague, diffuse, ambiguous, imprecise, or confused aspects of the learning material the meanings of which are unclear or obscure.
7. Inadequate affective support and/or motivational energization: deficient deliberate or explicit intent to learn (incidental learning); insufficient mobilization and focusing of attention and effort; insufficient ego involvement and interest in acquiring knowledge generally, and also specifically with respect to the particular subject matter of the instructional passage.
8. Meaningful learning, retention, and forgetting are maximally facilitated or inhibited by certain designated properties of the relevant anchoring ideas (i.e., cognitive structure variables) shortly after the latter ideas interact with their counterparts in the instructional material. These variables include the availability of suitably relevant, specific, and particularized anchoring ideas that are clear, stable, and discriminable from other related and confusably similar ideas both in the instructional passage and in related ideas in cognitive structure.
9. A sufficient number of repetitions, practice trials, or rehearsals has not been performed to stabilize dissociability strength and an adequate level of stability.
10. Degenerative, toxic, and traumatic changes in those cerebral nerve cells and/or fibers of specific neurological tracts responsible for the retention and storage of experiential events and learned information, as in Alzheimer's Disease.
11. Deficient aspirational needs and self-critical attitudes in the learner for acquiring clear, precise, stable, and veridical ideas and knowledge from the sources available to him.
12. Deficient verbal learning, retention, and intellectual ability to learn, comprehend, and transfer verbal concepts and propositions.

TABLE 3. Causes of Forgetting (continued)

II. In Meaningful Retention and Reproduction Phases

1. In accordance with our previously noted observation that most of the processes accounting for forgetting in the course of meaningful learning and retention can also be found in all three phases of the various mechanisms or processes underlying the acquisition, retention, and consolidation of knowledge. Nine of the separately listed and identified twelve causes of forgetting in the meaningful learning phase (Table 3) are also operative in the retention and reproduction phases—with two notable exceptions in the causes of forgetting, the effects of which influence the first phase but not the subsequent two. The two exceptions are the effects of (1) inadequate mobilization and focusing of effort and attention and (2) insufficient ego involvement, interest, and self-critical attitudes with respect both to acquiring and retaining knowledge.
2. Under strong motivation an individual may "remember" that another person, formerly close to him or her, but now alienated, is guilty of certain disreputable, dishonorable, or heinous acts. The latter malevolencies are borrowed from books, newspapers, magazines, movies, TV, etc., and are simply inserted into his store of memories of that person. To accommodate all of the insertions, the time scale may be stretched in the appropriate paces and several actual events that took place at different times in the maligned person's life may be "remembered" as happening simultaneously or successively.

Furnishing learners with additional contextual information, e.g., biographical data about the characters involved in an historical event enhances rather than depresses memory of the event despite the increased burden this additional context imposes on memory (Boon & Davies, 1993), as long as this additional context is appropriate to the event.

This finding about the addition of context to a memory task is reminiscent of the difficulty of recognizing one's butcher when he is seated in a box at the opera, as compared to the ease of doing so when he is working in a meat market. Memories of similar or related events that actually occur at different times also tend to fuse in retention and to be erroneously remembered as occurring simultaneously or successively. Similarly, because intentions are usually executed or implemented, those that are not also tend often to be erroneously remembered as if they were actually carried out as originally intended.

In general it can be safely predicted that any substantive overlap in content between background knowledge in cognitive structure and instructional material (presented as explicitly and coherently as possible) enhances the retention and reproduction of such material. This is obviously the case because background knowledge typically provides relevant anchoring ideas for the initial incorporation of and interation with the logically meaningful ideas of the instructional material, which interaction results in the emergence of new meanings.

Motivated Insertion of Selective Pseudomemories

Generally speaking, in anecdotal instances where a marked objectively verified discrepancy exists between an actual past event and the same allegedly remembered autobiographical event, the event in question is typically remembered as culturally more common, conventional, traditional, socially acceptable, and biased in favor of the remembering individual than is actually the case—except in those relatively rare cases in which the latter individual is strongly motivated to perceive one of his opponents in a highly negative, dishonorable, immoral, or even criminal light. For example, an alleged event—e.g., forcible incestuous rape of a daughter by her father—irrespective of whether it actually occurred in fact, may be repressed for many years because of its traumatic emotional implications and the resulting potent, self-protective needs *not* to remember, mediated by marked elevation of its threshold of availability.

In the current fashionable cultural climate, for example, that promotes public acceptance at face value of the validity of these alleged long-repressed memories, they may then surface many years later with the assistance of a psychotherapist's prompting and veiled suggestions that the patient's "opponent," perhaps her father, is really guilty of the repressed and forcibly incestuous acts already known to have happened in some other families. The alleged repressed sexual memories are then magnified in frequency and age of onset and distorted by the selective insertion of forcible rape and of various other examples of sexual assault. These fictional insertions are typically culled from dreamed versions of lurid stories originating in sensational newspapers, sex magazines, movies, and television, and also in psychiatric case histories from medical journals. All of these alleged events are then "remembered" with the therapist's prompting as having actually, vividly, and traumatically happened to her personally, in reality, even if it is definitely demonstrated to her later that her recollections were physically and temporally impossible and, therefore, had no basis in reality. This drastic shift from complete repression of incestuous sexual abuse, involving rigid self-protection against the emotionally traumatic implications of this sexual misconduct, to seeking punishment and revenge against the now hated antagonist represents a motivational full circle from a need for complete self-protective repression to a need for complete revelation.

Repression and Hypnosis

It is empirically well-established, both experimentally and clinically, that the recall of ordinarily available memories may be inhibited (repressed) by factors such as negative attitudinal bias (McKillop, 1952). This phenomenon is more or less equivalent to the clinical Freudian mechanism of *repression* or the unavailability (unretrievability) of retained memories (ordinarily retrievable or above threshold value) due to the selective raising of particular clinical thresholds of unavailability. The underlying motive for the repression of the memory of an idea or an event is typically a potent self-protective need or desire *not* to remember a particular self-disparaging act, a sense of guilt, or an anxiety-producing intention, act, idea, or event.

Contrary to Freud's formulation of the concept of repression, however, only the time-limited raising of the particular thresholds of availability of the latter memories in question are credibly demonstrated—not the alleged rigid banishment of these latter memories to a hypothetical, topographical, isolated, and generally inaccessible unconscious.

Hypnosis is a good example of the opposite condition of repression, enhancing memories of repressed self-disparaging or self-threatening acts, ideas, and events. This condition, opposite in process to what purportedly takes place in repression, is brought about by a *lowering* of the relevant thresholds of availability of those existing memories in an individual's store of same, that have always been viable but at a level substantially below this threshold, or to have been particularly subjected to repression after first originating as uninhibited memories. In fact, at one time, more in the past (but still found in the present), hypnosis was used therapeutically to retrieve unretrievable patient memories that were believed to have been previously repressed in the past and to have remained so thereafter.

The capability of hypnosis in effecting this latter change in the threshold value of availability, thereby making particular memories retrievable, is usually attributed (1) to a suggestible subject's positive response to the hypnotist's suggestion that he, the subject (under the direction and volition of the former), is thoroughly capable of retrieving the sought after and temporarily unavailable material and; (2) to the extreme mobilization and focusing of effort and attention, that is, to the complete exclusion of all existing and possible competing ideation.

Proactive and Retroactive Interference

The position is taken throughout this and previous chapters, in contrasting meaningful and rote learning processes, that since rote learning material is not logically meaningful and, thus, cannot be substantively (nonarbitrarily) related to or interact with relevant anchoring ideas in cognitive situations, it can at best be related on a nonmeaningful, fragmentary basis to unitary symbols or letter components of words and phrases in cognitive structure. Such verbal, symbolic relationships, of course, are completely isolated from, and naturally cannot contribute to, any existing body of knowledge.

It is largely for this reason, and also because newly acquired meanings are linked to, and stored with, their anchoring ideas, and, hence, share vicariously in the latter's high resistance to obliterative assimilation that interpolated rote learning material does not exert much proactive or retroactive interference in a *meaningful* learning and retention task, whereas both forms of interference are undoubtedly much more involved causally in the forgetting of a rote learning and retention task.

Nevertheless it seems likely that the effects of this type of interference were partly overstated for didactic reasons in stressing the contrast between the basic process differences of rote and meaningful learning and retention, respectively. In effect, this was offered as an explanation of the relative insusceptibility of meaningful retention to rote or meaningful interference. Actually, this explanation applies more to the usual or typical than to the atypical retrieval situation.

Hence, it is entirely conceivable that extremely pronounced, similar, conflicting, contradictory, or emotion-laden memories, generated shortly before or after meaningful learning could result in temporary blocking of the retrieval of the memory in question. This blocking, and its subsequent lifting shortly afterwards, thus, allowing "tip of the tongue" memories to be finally retrieved, can be most plausibly explained as a consequence of temporary elevation of the threshold of availability.

In more explicit and summary terms, another significant reason for the large interference effects, proactively or retroactively (in the case of *rote* as contrasted with meaningful learning) is the fact that because of the rote nature of the material, only fragmentary, discrete, unitary, and component relatability of this interpolated material to comparable symbols in cognitive structure is possible. Nevertheless they still cannot be summarily ignored and dismissed as irrelevant to the current learning task. In the case of meaningful learning, on the other hand, the meaningfulness of the interpolated material enables the learner to make an instantaneous judgment of its relevance to the learning task; and if he judges it to be irrelevant, he can then summarily ignore it, thus precluding most interfering effects.

Recall versus Recognition

A more typical everyday manifestation of the unretrievability of certain memories, because of the selective operation of the threshold of availability, is the familiar experience of being unable to *recall* on demand either an episodic memory or a proper noun that was learned as part of instructional material, but at the same time being quite able to recognize it when it is presented among a number of possible and plausible alternatives (as in a multiple-choice examination). A credible explanatory hypothesis here that was also considered above is that the threshold of availability for the recall of a memory of given dissociability strength is generally sufficiently higher for recall than for recognition as to make a functional difference in ability to retrieve it.

Selective Bias and Distortion in Meaningful Learning and Retention

The logical and veridical meanings inherent in instructional materials are often subjectively distorted in memory because every individual evidently possesses in his cognitive structure both idiosyncratic and cultural frames of reference for evaluating people and events. Additionally, he possesses both idiosyncratic and cultural biases to which new learning material is related and with which it interacts (along with more objective ideas in cognitive structure) in generating new meanings. Thus, the resulting new meanings that emerge idiosyncratically from the meaningful learning and retention processes described above are a function of (1) the particular obliterative assimilations that occur and (2) the selective emphases, distortions, biases, omissions, dismissals, discounting, and reversals suggested both by particular objective, as well as subjective, logical meanings present either in the instructional material or in idiosyncratic cognitive structure.

When the instructional material is more objective in content and has fewer upsetting affective implications, individual differences in emergent new meanings tend to be more a reflection of idiosyncratic experience, identifications, vocation, and education than of the learner's internalized array of personal attitudes and biases.

In addition to the selective raising of their thresholds of availability, retained meanings themselves may also be altered in part in the very process of being reconstructed in accordance with the social requirements of the current reproductive situation (e.g., the expectations of the particular people who happen to be involved).

The initial phase of meaningful learning (i.e., the introductory presentation of the instructional passage to the learner, with its eventual corresponding emergence of initial new meanings) is probably the most significant phase in terms of determining a learner's later and lingering memory of its purported original substantive content, especially if it has implicit or explicit affective references and implications (Bartlett, 1932). The selective initial choice of one particular dominant and interpretive set of meanings by a given learner from among several possible sets, obviously points the direction (through a process of serial sensitization) that the subject's results on future learning and retention trials will take.

Bartlett (1932) attributes this initial subjective interpretive reaction of the learner both to the affect-laden narrative material and to a form of selective *perception* reflecting the subject's own cultural frame of reference (instead of the alien fictional character's in the narrative passage).

Actually, however, the selective emergence of meaning in the latter meaningful learning situation resembles much more strongly a *cognitive* rather than a *perceptual* process. Perception as a process involves an almost immediate or instantaneous apprehension of the meaning or significance of an object, event, idea, etc., without any intervention by relatively complex and time-consuming mental operations. Typically, however, once cognition is well-established in a particular learning situation and takes place almost immediately or instantaneously, one can assuredly say that it has been superseded by perception. Before this latter time, the process aspects of cognition include the determination of the most relevant subsumers (anchoring ideas) in cognitive structure; the nature of the latter's interaction with its counterpart ideas in the instructional material; and the attitudinal and affective reaction to the emergent new meanings. Usually, after several repetitions, these component aspects of cognition become telescoped, and the learner apprehends immediately (perceptually rather than cognitively) what the word, phrase, sentence, or paragraph means simply because he had learned its meaning once before (but not long enough ago to have forgotten it) and does not have to learn it again when encountering it in the future.

In considering the three general mechanisms described above, accounting for the selectively better retention of meaningfully than rotely learned material, and for the subjective "slanting" of meanings by the learner's idiosyncratic and cultural attitudinal bias, it is evident that the relative weight of current *idiosyncratic* cognitive, affective, and motivational factors in determining the substantive (denotative), connotative, and attitudinal content of newly-acquired meanings is often much greater than that of the objective thrust of the logical component meanings inherent in the instructional material.

Neurological Causes and Decay

It is undoubtedly irrefutable that in order for individuals both to have some awareness and record (permanent or semi-permanent) of the results of their past experience and of their prior involvement in formal and informal learning endeavors, some corresponding representational or correlated neural changes of an enduring or quasi-enduring nature must occur in those nerve calls and/or fibers in the localized areas of the cerebrum functionally associated with symbolic (verbal) learning and memory. That this must be the case is demonstrated objectively both by the amnesia preceding and following concussion, as well as by traumatic brain injury, and even more strikingly by the gradual loss of total memory due to progressive pathological degeneration of nerve cells, as in Alzheimer's Disease, occurring especially in senescent individuals.

These well-known facts have in a sense unintentionally stimulated a revival of the former widely accepted "decay" theory of forgetting that attributed at least some forgetting to spontaneous "decay" of the neuroanatomical and neurophysiological representation of memories, somewhat vaguely referred to as "traces."

What supposedly undergoes spontaneous "fading" or "decay" in the absence of practice or overlearning, according to this theory, is attributable merely to the passage of time itself. Generally, however, in psychological states, as in most homeostatic physiological states of the body, neither total loss nor cessation of function (decay), on the one hand, nor antecedent stages in progressing gradually toward decay (fading), on the other, occur spontaneously. Such physiological states are typically equilibria maintained by opposing forces that vary in relative potency and also tend to fluctuate over time. In obliterative assimilation of an emergent new meaning relative to its anchoring idea, for example, the dissociability strength of the newly acquired meaning may decline gradually for various reasons; but one would hardly call this "spontaneous fading." Similarly, if and when this meaning is eventually forgotten it is much less a case of decay than of declining dissociability strength gradually being overcome by obliterative assimilation (fading) until it reaches the zero point (decay). It is, in other words, less a case of a weakened psychological state fading spontaneously out of the picture by itself than of an opposing psychological state becoming relatively stronger at the expense of its weaker antagonist until it is no longer in contention to express itself at all.

The decay theory, in my opinion, lacks ordinary credibility, theoretical parsimony, and empirical verification, as well as fails to counter the more persuasive arguments of opposing theorists. In contrast to the decay theory, for example, it requires no new unsubstantiated or radical assumptions, such as the spontaneous disintegration (decay) of the structural or functional basis of a memory trace with the mere passage of time *per se* in order to account for total forgetting of a memory through (1) gradual, progressive, and cumulative obliterative assimilation of the particularities, qualifying conditions, and specifics of a new learning passage by the generalities contained in its relevant anchoring idea(s) or (2) similar gradual, progressive, and cumulative loss of dissociability strength due to obliterative assimilation caused by factors other than the assimilative (generalities) tendencies of anchoring ideas for the subordinate ideas they subsume (e.g., in the case of misconceptions; vague, diffuse, and ambiguous learning material; cultural frames of reference; idiosyncratic attitudinal bias). Various experimental tests by Brown (1958) of the decay theory of immediate memory yielded, on the whole, equivocal and inconclusive findings.

This gradual loss of dissociability strength leads to forgetting simply because insufficient functional capacity to dissociate is present in a given memory trace for exceeding the prevailing threshold of availability. Except in toxic, degenerative, and traumatic pathological cases of memory impairment, however, neuroanatomical damage to the substrate of memory is not involved at all.

Overt and demonstrable psychological states and phenomena obviously exist at the highest level of human phenomenology (e.g., memory). Nevertheless, psychological states such as memory still depend functionally on the substrate integrity (intactness) of two memory-correlated microbiological regions of the cerebrum, both of which are localized and specialized in function: first, on the anatomical and physiological properties of neurons considered as neural tissue and, thus, as neurally distinct structurally and functionally from all other cells of the body; and, second, on those nonneural properties of these latter neural cells which they share with all other bodily cells.

According to modern non-reductionistic viewpoints in the philosophy of science, one should ordinarily seek complete explanations of psychological phenomena that are pursued solely at a psychological level of analysis. We have, therefore, endeavored above to explain meaningful forgetting completely in terms of several different likely psychological processes or mechanisms—by obliterative assimilation at the level of the relevant anchoring ideas; by gross loss of dissociability strength due to the assimilative presence of potent misconceptions in cognitive structure; by vague, diffuse, and ambiguous learning material; by cultural frames of reference; by idiosyncratic attitudinal bias; and by elevated thresholds of availability. It is true, of course, that such non-psychological causes of meaningful forgetting as concussion and traumatic, degenerative, and toxic damage or pathology to localized and specialized cerebral areas were listed above as non-psychological causes of forgetting. In the first place, however, these latter causes are not the usual reasons why people forget; and the underlying mechanisms are not the typical processes involved in inducing the very common psychological phenomenon of human forgetting. This was primarily discussed in another context in which it was demonstrated that the very concept of a learned and remembered idea implies some correlated semi-lasting substrate change in the brain—a change that could be disrupted by neurological pathology and become thereby an atypical cause of forgetting.

The fact that disruption of the neural substrate underlying such psychological functions as memory can also thoroughly disrupt all other psychological functions that depend on its intactness for its normal functioning has led many psychologists to believe that neural substrate factors normally regulate, control, and explain the psychological states and processes that depend on the integrity of this substrate. A more defensible conclusion at this point would, therefore, be that normal psychological functioning requires a normally functioning neural substrate.

MEANINGFUL VERSUS ROTE LEARNING PROCESSES

Meaningfully and rotely learned materials are learned and retained in qualitatively different ways because potentially meaningful learning tasks, unlike rote learning tasks, are, by definition, relatable and anchorable to relevant established ideas in cognitive structure. They can be related to existing ideas in cognitive structure in ways making possible the understanding of various kinds of significant (e.g., derivative, correlative, subordinate, superordinate, and combinatorial) ideational relationships.

Most new ideational materials that pupils encounter in a school setting are nonarbitrarily and nonverbatimly relatable to a previously learned background of meaningful ideas and information. In fact, the curriculum is, and should be, deliberately organized in this fashion to provide for the untraumatic introduction of new facts, concepts, and propositions into each subject-matter area as children progress in age. Rotely learned materials, on the other hand, are discrete and relatively isolated entities that are relatable to components of relevant cognitive structure in only an arbitrary, verbatim fashion, not permitting the establishment of any of the different kinds of relationships considered above.

This crucial difference between rote and meaningful learning has important implications for the kind of learning and retention processes underlying each category. Since rotely learned materials do not interact with cognitive structure in a substantive (nonarbitrary, nonverbatim) fashion, they are learned and retained on a purely associative basis; and their retention is influenced primarily by the interfering effects of *similar* or conflicting rote materials learned *immediately* before or after the learning task. Learning and retention outcomes in the case of meaningful learning, on the other hand, are influenced primarily by the properties of those relevant and cumulatively established ideational systems in cognitive structure with which the primary learning task interacts and which determine its dissociability strength. Compared to this latter kind of extended interaction, concurrent interfering effects have relatively little influence on and explanatory value for meaningful learning.

Meaningful Learning Processes

Nonverbatim and nonarbitrary incorporation of a potentially meaningful learning task into relevant portions of cognitive structure so that a new meaning emerges implies that the newly acquired meaning becomes an integral part of a particular and interrelated ideational system. The possibility of this type of relatability to and incorporability into cognitive structure has two principal consequences for learning and retention processes. First, learning and retention are no longer dependent on the rather frail human capacity for retaining arbitrary and verbatim associations as discrete and isolated entities in their own right (a memory span of 7±2). As a result, the temporal span of meaningful retention is greatly extended. Second, the newly learned material becomes subject to the organizational principles governing the learning and retention of the macro and micro systems by which it is assimilated and incorporated. First, the very acts of assimilation and incorporation require appropriate (relevant) placement within a hierarchically organized system of knowledge. Later, after incorporation occurs, the new material initially retains its substantive identity by virtue of being dissociable from its anchoring ideas, but then gradually loses its identifiability as it becomes reduced to and undissociable from these latter ideas (obliterative assimilation).

In this meaningful type of learning-retention process the formation and strengthening of arbitrary associative bonds between discrete, verbatim elements, isolated in a substantive and organizational sense from established ideational systems, play only a very limited role. Unfortunately, most of the research in psychology laboratories in the past involved rote or arbitrary and verbatim learning; and unwarranted extrapolations of the findings were then made to classroom learning.

Meaningful learning, dependent as it is on the idiosyncratic cognitive structure of particular individuals, does not lend itself easily to simple laboratory studies. Nevertheless it remains the predominant mode of school and academic learning. The important mechanisms involved in this process are:

1. Achievement of appropriate relational anchorage within a relevant ideational system.
2. Retention reflecting resistance to the progressively increasing inroads of obliterative assimilation or loss of dissociability and characterizing the organization and long-term memorial integrity of meaningfully learned materials in cognitive structure.

Rote learning tasks can be incorporated into cognitive structure only in the form of arbitrary associations, that is, as discrete, self-contained entities organizationally isolated for all practical purposes, from the learner's established ideational systems. The requirement that these arbitrary associations be constituted on a verbatim rather than substantive basis (since anything less than complete verbatim fidelity is valueless in the case of purely arbitrary associations) further magnifies the discreteness and isolated nature of rotely incorporated entities.

One important implication of the discrete and isolated incorporation of rote learning tasks within cognitive structure is that, quite unlike the situation in meaningful learning, long-term anchorage to established ideational systems is not attained. Hence, since the human mind, unlike a computer, is not efficiently designed for long-term, verbatim storage of large quantities of arbitrary associations, the retention span for rote learnings is relatively brief. The much steeper gradient of forgetting in the case of rote as compared to meaningful learning requires that we examine the rote retention process and the factors that influence it within its highly abbreviated time span, delay beyond this very brief period of time leaves us with nothing to study because by then all is forgotten. The time span of retention is a matter of hours for nonsense syllables (Ebbinghaus, 1913) and days for poetry (Boreas, 1930).

A second important implication of the arbitrary, verbatim incorporation of learning material within cognitive structure is that *association* necessarily constitutes the basic learning-retention mechanism, and the laws of association constitute, by definition, the basic explanatory principles governing rote learning and retention. The major goals of rote learning and retention, therefore, are to increase and maintain associative strength—not to achieve appropriate anchorage within cognitive structure to preserve dissociability strength, or to acquire meaning and knowledge. Such variables as contiguity, frequency, and reinforcement are accordingly important and crucial for rote learning; and retention and forgetting are influenced primarily by concurrent interference (of both internal and external origin), on the basis of intra- and intertask similarity, response competition, and stimulus and response generalization.

EVIDENCE OF MEANINGFUL LEARNING

It is surprisingly not always easy to demonstrate that meaningful learning has occurred. Genuine understanding implies the possession of clear, precise, differentiated, and transferable meanings. But if one attempts to test for such knowledge by asking students to state the criterial attributes or the essential elements of a principle, one may simply elicit rotely memorized verbalizations. At the very least, therefore, tests of comprehension must be phrased in different language and must be presented in a somewhat different context than the originally encountered learning material. Perhaps the simplest way of doing this is to require students to differentiate between related (similar) but not identical ideas or to choose the identifying elements of a concept or proposition from a list containing those of related concepts and propositions as well (multiple-choice tests).

Independent problem solving is often the only feasible way of testing whether students *really* comprehend meaningfully the ideas they are able to memorize and verbalize so easily. But here we have to be careful not to fall into a trap. We may warrantedly say, for example, that problem solving is a valid, practical method of measuring the meaningful comprehension of ideas. However, this is *not* the same as saying that the learner who is unable to solve a representative set of problems based on a given group of instructional material *necessarily* does not understand, but has merely rotely memorized, the principles exemplified by these problems. Successful problem solving demands many *other* abilities and qualities—such as reasoning power, perseverance, flexibility, venturesomeness, improvisation, problem sensitivity, and tactical astuteness—in *addition* to comprehension of the underlying principles. Hence failure to solve the problems in question may reflect deficiencies in these latter factors rather than lack of genuine understanding of the learning passage. At the very worst it may reflect a lower order of understanding than that manifested by ability to apply the principles successfully to related problem solving. Conversely, demonstrated ability to solve problems based on adequate comprehension of a meaningfully learned instructional passage similarly does not necessarily indicate that true understanding of the previously learned instructional passage exists. This is the case because successful application of principles from a learning passage to the transfer task may simply reflect trial-and-error learning or lucky chance on random trials and no understanding or appreciation of the applicability of the learning passage to the solution of the class of problems in question.

Another more feasible method of testing for the occurrence of meaningful learning does not involve this latter difficulty of interpretation: The learner is presented with a new, sequentially dependent learning passage that cannot possibly be mastered in the absence of genuine understanding of the prior learning task. Relearning of the *same* learning passage is then a feasible variant of the same approach: Some degree of original learning can be assumed if relearning results in appreciable improvement of performance.

In seeking evidence of meaningful learning, therefore, whether through verbal questioning, sequentially dependent learning, or problem-solving tasks, the possibility of rote memorization should always be borne in mind. Long experience in taking examinations makes students adept at memorizing not only key propositions and formulas, but also causes, examples, reasons, explanations, and ways of recognizing and solving "type problems." The danger of rote simulation of meaningful comprehension may be best avoided by asking questions and posing problems that are both novel and unfamiliar in form and require maximal transformation of existing knowledge.

THE SUPERIORITY OF MEANINGFUL OVER ROTE LEARNING AND RETENTION

Several lines of evidence point to the conclusion that meaningful learning and retention are more effective in terms of what is learned and remembered than their rote counterparts. First, Briggs and Reed (1943) demonstrated that it is much easier meaningfully to learn and remember the substance of potentially meaningful material than it is to memorize an equivalent quantity of connected discourse in rote, verbatim fashion.

Second, material that can be learned meaningfully (poetry, prose, and observations of pictorial matter) is learned much more rapidly than are arbitrary series of digits or nonsense syllables (Reed, 1938). The same difference holds true for gradations of meaningful learning: Simple narrative material is learned more quickly and is remembered better than are more complex philosophical ideas that are difficult to understand (Reed, 1938). An increase in the amount of material to be learned also adds relatively less learning time to meaningful than to rote learning tasks (Cofer, 1941).

A third type of experimental evidence is derived from studies demonstrating that various problem-solving tasks (card tricks, match-stick problems) are retained longer and are more transferable when subjects learn underlying principles rather than merely rotely memorized solutions (Hilgard, Irvine, & Whipple, 1953).

A related line of evidence showing that "substance" items are learned (Cofer, 1941) and retained (Edwards & English, 1939; English, Welborn, & Kilian, 1934; Newman, 1939) more effectively than are "verbatim" items is more inferential than direct. Presumably, although verbatim items can also be learned meaningfully, they are more likely to be memorized rotely than are concepts and generalizations.

In this connection, an ingeniously designed study by Newman (1939) comparing retention during periods of sleep and waking throws much light on the relative retention spans and respective forgetting processes of rotely and meaningfully learned materials. In Newman's study the unessential details of a narrative were remembered much better after a period of sleep than after a period of normal daily activity, whereas there was no corresponding difference in the case of substance items. A warranted inference here is that immediate retroactive interference, which is obviously greater during daily activity than during sleep, is an important factor in rote memory, but it does not significantly affect the retention of meaningfully learned materials.

It has also been shown that ideas in a prose passage that are rated as more meaningful or comprehensible (Johnson, 1973), that are more familiar (and, hence, presumably more firmly established in cognitive structure (Annis & Davis, 1972), and that are also more salient or superordinate in the structure of a paragraph, (Mayer & McConkie, 1973) or of a discipline, tend to be remembered better, particularly on a long-term basis.

Many classroom studies support the findings of this last-mentioned experimental approach. In general, they show that principles, generalizations, and applications of principles studied in such courses as biology, chemistry, geometry, and physics are remembered much better over periods of months and even years than are more factual items such as symbols, formulas, and terminology (Eikenberry, 1923; Frutchey, 1937; Kastrinos, 1965; R. W. Tyler, 1930).

A second type of classroom evidence demonstrates that knowledge of number facts (addition, subtraction, multiplication, and division) learned with understanding is retained more effectively and is more transferable than when learned in mechanical, rote fashion (Brownell & Moser, 1949; Thiele, 1938). Newson and Gaite (1971) found that students recalled more after one week from reading a short passage (300 words) than a long passage (2500 words) of science fiction. The short passage was written from information retained by students one week after reading the long passage.

Both types of evidence (experimental and classroom) encourage one to believe that the discouraging picture of rapid forgetting of the vast majority of subject-matter learnings, that certainly characterizes most students today, is not necessarily inevitable. Much of this loss is reflective of rote learning, of poorly organized and programmed subject matter, of correctable ambiguity and confusion in the presentation of ideas, and of inadequate pacing and review of material (cramming). If subject matter were adequately organized and programmed, if relevant ideas were available in cognitive structure, if material were presented lucidly and incisively, if misconceptions were corrected promptly, and if suitably motivated students learned meaningfully and paid attention to such considerations as optimal review and pacing, there is good reason to believe that they would retain over a good portion of a lifetime much of the important ideas they learned in school. At the very least one would expect them to be able to relearn, in short order and with relatively little effort, most of what they had forgotten. In subsequent chapters we shall examine the important cognitive structure variables that have most effect on the longevity of meaningfully learned subject matter.

Many different kinds of explanations have been offered for the superiority of meaningful over rote learning and retention. One explanation identifies meaningful learning with the learning of meaningful material and advances all of the arguments referred to above in explaining why meaningfulness facilitates rote verbal learning. Our definition of meaningful learning, however, implies that it is a characteristic *process* in which meaning is a *product* or outcome of learning rather than primarily an attribute of the content of what is to be learned. It is this process rather than the meaningfulness of the content[3] that is learned which characterizes meaningful learning. Thus, the same reasons that explain why *more* meaningful materials can be *rotely* learned and retained more readily than *less* meaningful materials do not necessarily explain why meaningful learning and retention outcomes are superior to those of their rote counterparts.

Gestalt theorists (e.g., Katona, 1940; Koffka, 1935), on the other hand, equate insight and the understanding of relationships with the establishment of stable "structural" traces, that are contrasted, in turn, with the relatively "rigid" and unstable discrete traces established by rotely memorized materials. This explanation, however, really begs the question because it accounts for the superiority of meaningful learning processes simply by endowing the neural representation of these processes with superior potency. In effect, then, it is claimed that meaningful learning processes yield superior learning outcomes because they give rise to more stable traces. This, obviously, adds little to our understanding because the real problem is to understand why such processes allegedly "result in more stable traces."

It should also be noted that, although rote learning is typically more difficult than meaningful learning in most circumstances, it may actually be, or seem, easier for the individual who lacks the necessary and relevant ideational background for meaningful learning of a particular learning task. In addition, to the anxiety-ridden person who lacks confidence in his ability to understand difficult and unfamiliar new propositions, and, hence, feels threatened by such a learning task, rote learning often *appears* easier than meaningful learning.

MEANINGFUL VERSUS ROTE RETENTION

Does the superiority of meaningful over rote retention reflect an actual difference in the efficacy of the respective *retention* processes, or does this superiority merely reflect the greater efficacy of meaningful over rote *learning*? Obviously, if meaningfully *learned* material is mastered better to begin with, more assimilated meanings would be available at any subsequent time when retention is tested—even if rote and meaningful retention *processes* themselves were equally efficacious. In the case of *rote* learning of materials varying in degree of meaningfulness, it has been demonstrated that degree of *learning* is the only important variable. When more and less meaningful materials are learned to the same criterion of mastery (by allowing a greater number of trials for the less meaningful material), they do not differ in retention outcomes (Postman & Rau, 1957; Underwood & Richardson, 1956).

If, however, our theory retarding the existence of fundamental differences (including relative effectiveness) between rote and meaningful *retention* processes were correct, we would *not* expect that if rotely and meaningfully learned materials were mastered equally well, they would also be remembered with equal effectiveness. According to assimilation theory, the same variables influencing the outcome of meaningful learning, and the same factors accounting for the superiority of meaningful over rote learning processes, *continue* to operate during the retention interval and to affect retention outcomes. Hence, even if rotely and meaningfully learned materials were learned to the same criterion of mastery, the superiority of the meaningful retention process would be reflected in higher retention scores. Studies by Kastrinos (1965) and Kuhn (1967) show that meaningfully learned concepts and propositions may be retained for a period of years and that they may continue to facilitate the meaningful learning of new instructional materials.

OTHER THEORIES OF INFORMATION PROCESSING AND OTHER THEORIES OF FORGETTING

Forgetting and Retroactive and Proactive Interferences

A basic premise of the assimilation theory of meaningful verbal learning is the proposition that retention and forgetting constitute later phases in cognitive functioning of the *same* interactional learning process between new learning materials and existing relevant ideas in the learner's structure of knowledge (Ausubel, 1960, 1963). By virtue of this interactional process new concept, representational, or propositional meanings come into being.

During the retention interval the newly emergent meanings remain functionally linked to the anchoring ideas but are dissociable at first from them; whereas later in the retention interval the dissociability strength of the newly learned meanings typically falls below the critical thresholds of recall and recognition. When this happens these meanings become no longer available to the learner as separately identifiable entities; because of obliterative subsumption forgetting has occurred. The same variables that influence meaningful learning in the first place, thus, continue to influence retention and forgetting in the same way afterwards, except that there are other variables such as motivation, repression, and hypnosis that influence retention by affecting the threshold of availability (without influencing in any way the dissociability strength of retained ideas in cognitive structure).

As part of this hypothesis about the nature of retention and forgetting, it was also postulated that the functional incorporation of newly learned meanings into a hierarchical system of relevant anchoring ideas in cognitive structure would partially protect these meanings from the proactive, concurrent, and retroactive interfering effects of similar but conflicting materials. Thus, it was predicted that the retroactive and proactive interference encountered in rote verbal learning and retention would be largely inoperative in meaningful prose learning.[4] This prediction was verified with respect to retroactive interference by Ausubel, Robbins, and Blake (1957) as well as by many earlier and later studies. In fact, in one study (Ausubel, Stager, & Gaite, 1968), the interpolation of conflicting material actually *facilitated* the retention of the original material, presumably by increasing its clarity and discriminability and by prompting its rehearsal.

In the conclusion of the Myrow and Anderson (1972) study is the following startling but revealing admission about the true psychological significance of their research methodology (and findings):

> Observers of the classroom may wonder how frequently in "the real world," forgetting analogous to RI (retroactive interference) actually occurs. How often does it happen that the preconditions to RI—similar stimuli paired with different responses—coincidentally appear in ordinary classroom activity? We seldom teach students different answers to the same question. If RI is generated in prose only when the materials are so closely similar, we must question the efficacy of the interference model as an inclusive explanation of forgetting in the classroom.[5] The atomistic approach that was required to make good the analogy between paired-associate retroactive interference and prose retroactive interference seems at once necessary and potentially misleading.

Gestalt Theory

According to Gestalt theory (Koffka, 1935), forgetting is brought about by two principal mechanisms each of which has relatively little in common with the other. The first mechanism, *assimilation,* is conceptualized as a process whereby memory traces are obliterated or replaced by similar traces in cognitive structure that are relatively more stable.[6] Although this phenomenon is superficially similar to the assimilative process described above in that it seems to imply *interaction* between related ideas rather than the substitution of new and more stable stimulus or response members in a previously learned stimulus-response pair, it is actually more consistent with the assumptions of the interference theory of forgetting. The behavioristic mechanisms of response competition and stimulus or response generalization could quite adequately account for the occurrence of Gestalt assimilation.

The second and more distinctively Gestalt mechanism of forgetting is conceptualized by Gestalt theorists as a process of *autonomous disintegration* within memory traces.[7] In the case of unstructured or poorly organized material (for example, where figure and ground are poorly differentiated), unstable, "chaotic" traces are formed which rapidly undergo a type of "spontaneous decay."[8] In other instances, however, "dynamic stresses" derived from original perceptions persist in the trace; they are gradually resolved by such progressive changes as leveling and sharpening or in the direction of "closure," "symmetry," and "good form." Both this aspect of Gestalt theory and our assimilation theory of forgetting differ, therefore, from the interference theory in regarding the processes underlying forgetting as occurring gradually and continuously rather than only during those times when the stimulus or response members of an association are exercised or in contact.

The Gestalt theory, however, is less parsimonious since it ignores the rule of previously learned and more stable, relevant ideas both in the learning process and in determining the degree and direction of forgetting. It postulates instead the following:

1. New ideas do not interact with relevant established ideas in cognitive structure but, rather, are incorporated as independent traces.
2. These separate traces spontaneously undergo change in the direction of "more perfect" or "less stressful form."
3. Also, as suggested above, the hypothesis that "poorly organized" materials are forgotten quickly, because they form "chaotic traces" which undergo rapid "spontaneous decay," really begs the question.

Assimilation theory, therefore, differs from Gestalt theory in the two following principal ways:

1. It attributes *all* forgetting to interaction between the learning material and existing, relevant cognitive structure and denies that "autonomous disintegration of traces" occurs as a result of the resolution of perceptually derived intratrace tensions. Asymmetrical figures, for example, would sometimes be remembered as more symmetrical than originally perceived ("leveling"), not because of any autonomous changes within the traces but because they are subsumed by and eventually reduced to a memorial residue of familiar, more stable, and symmetrical geometrical concepts in cognitive structure.
2. It conceives of assimilation (loss of original identifiability or decreased dissociability of newly learned materials) as a *progressively occurring* phenomenon rather than as an all-or-none type of replacement in which availability is lost completely and instantaneously. The obliterative or reductionistic aspect of assimilation is also regarded as only the principal *mechanism* accounting for forgetting; the net effect of the anchoring process itself *facilitates* retention.

Bartlett's Theory of Memory

Assimilation theory also has elements in common with Bartlett's (1932) views of cognitive functioning generally and of remembering in particular. Bartlett (1932) conceptualizes a *schema* as an organizing and orienting attitude or affect resulting from the abstraction and articulation of past experience. Although Bartlett is somewhat vague with respect to both its nature and mode of operation, he conceives of it as structurally and functionally comparable to that of an anchoring idea except that it is attitudinal rather than substantive in nature.

In general, however, Bartlett's position on retention differs in two fundamental respects from assimilation theory. First, the schema itself is largely attitudinal, connotative, and affective in nature rather than basically cognitive and denotative; in this sense, of course, it is similar to the connotative aspects of meaning. This difference probably reflects, in part, the fact that Bartlett's learning tasks consist of stories, pictures, and figures instead of the more impersonal material contained in subject-matter content. Second, Bartlett is primarily concerned with the interpretive and reproductive phases of meaningful learning and retention and devotes hardly any attention whatsoever to the retention interval itself and to its underlying processes.

Thus, in accounting for the difference between presented and remembered content, Bartlett emphasizes both (1) the influence of idiosyncratic and culturally based schemata on the original *perception* of the material and (2) a process of "imaginative reconstruction" at the time of recall, as a result of which particular content is selected, invented, and reorganized in accordance with the nature and requirements of the current reproductive situation. Assimilation theory, on the other hand, attributes most forgetting to spontaneous interactional process [between presentation and reproduction (recall) of the learning task], involving anchoring ideas and assimilated content. Thus, although the individual, in remembering, undoubtedly selects from what is available in memory and also invents some new material suitable for the occasion, he is actually also *reproducing,* for the most part, materials that have undergone memorial reduction, in addition to *reconstructing* the retained residue of original meanings.

According to Bartlett, the first opportunity for schemata to influence memory occurs when they interact with the incoming stimulus content of the instructional task. The learner attempts to make the content of the learning task meaningful in terms of a relevant schema in cognitive structure as well as contextually consonant with it. Hence, schemata significantly determine the initial interpretation of the message, which, in turn, persistently influences the nature of what is retained.

Contrary to Bartlett's contention, however, this interpretative process that results in the emergence of meaning is *cognitive* rather than *perceptual* in nature. Newly acquired meanings are not reflective of a perceptual process that yields an immediate content of awareness; rather, they are products of a more complex cognitive process of assimilation. Meanings are idiosyncratic, therefore, not so much because a particular individual's attitudinal schema selectively influences the *perception* of learning material but because such material is nonarbitrarily and nonverbatimly related to the idiosyncratic relevant content of anchoring ideas in cognitive structure (a cognitive process) in selective fashion.

Bartlett largely ignores the retention phase of the learning-retention sequence during which acquired meanings are retained. He states, rather, that the schema's principal impact on memory occurs during the *reproductive* phase. At this time the subject differentially selects those elements that are both most consistent with his own attitudes, interests, and cultural milieu and also most appropriate in terms of the requirements of the current situation. To this he adds some invented detail (to fill in gaps and to enhance coherence, meaningfulness, and "fit") and combines and reformulates both kinds of elements into a new, self-consistent whole. The reconstructed product, therefore, when compared to the original learning material, manifests such tendencies as simplification, condensation, rationalization, conventionalization, and importation. Dawes (1966), McKillop (1952), Paul (1959), and Taft (1954) report similar findings in the recall of value-laden narrative material.

The weakness of Bartlett's position, therefore, does not inhere so much in postulating the existence of idiosyncratic schemata or imaginative reconstruction, but rather in the fact (1) that many of the memorial changes he attributes to such reconstruction actually reflect changes in availability due to assimilation and (2) that the effect of idiosyncratic advance sets are cognitive rather than perceptual in nature.

Post-Bartlett Varieties of Schemata Theory

Related to Bartlett's notion of schemata is a slightly modified form of his original schemata concept that purports to be theoretically more explicit and parsimonious, experimentally more rigorous, as well as more relatable to the kinds of learning that occur in the classroom (e.g., R. C. Anderson, 1977). Actual experiments generated from this new "schemata" approach (Pichert & Anderson, 1977), however, bear very little relation to the acquisition and retention of new subject matter or, for that matter, of new meanings. In effect they merely demonstrate the relatively trivial everyday truism that when the same items are embedded in a familiar context (or narrative prose passage) they are better recalled than when they are embedded in a less familiar context. For example, one's butcher is more readily recognized as such in the familiar meat market context than in the strange context of a box at the opera. This is obviously the case because the more congruous "meat market" schema is operative in the first case and the less congruous "opera" schema in the second, even though the same butcher appears in both scenarios.

Both in the latter simple example and in "schemata" experiments where the same objects are presented in the same order in familiar or unfamiliar contexts (i.e., embedded in likely or unlikely narrative prose passages), it is a self-evident commonplace, hardly requiring experimental verification, that one will spontaneously recall more objects in the likely than in the unlikely context. In both instances one is *not* learning *new* meanings (i.e., concepts, concept words, propositions), as in the acquisition of *new* subject-matter knowledge, but is simply recalling better *already* meaningful object (concept) names that are presented in a more congruous context.

The facilitative orienting effects of congruence of context on *rote* learning and retention must, of course, be differentiated from the substantive facilitating (ideational scaffolding) effects of relevant context on meaningful learning (comprehension) and retention (e.g., Bransford & Johnson, 1972; Sherman, 1976) as well as from the substantive facilitating (ideational scaffolding) effects of advance organizers that increase the learner's awareness of relevant subsumers in his existing cognitive structure.

Psychoanalytic Theory of Forgetting

Psychoanalytic theory maintains that *all* forgetting is motivated; in other words, that it is invariably a product of repression. Ideas or impulses that would generate anxiety if permitted to enter consciousness are said to be repressed into the unconscious and are, thus, consciously forgotten.

The chief difficulty with this theory, of course, is that it accounts at best for a relatively rare type of forgetting. Only a very small percentage of the ideas that are forgotten are in any sense potentially productive of anxiety; and in these instances it is more parsimonious to hypothesize that their threshold of availability is temporarily elevated rather than that they are banished into a reified topographical area of the mind. It is also true that many anxiety-producing ideas remain painfully and obsessively in the forefront of consciousness rather than undergoing repression.

Cybernetic and Computer Models of Cognitive Functioning

One of the most flourishing of the more eclectic theoretical positions in recent years has been a variant of the cybernetic or information theory approach based on a computer model of cognitive organization and functioning. The general flavor of this approach is behavioristic in the sense that it deals somewhat mechanistically with input-output relations; but in place of an associative or conditioning model of cognitive processes, it substitutes a more substantive view of the nature of information as well as the cybernetic principle of a control system that is both (1) sensitive to feedback indicative of behavioral error or discrepancy between existing and desired states of affairs, and (2) differentially responds to such feedback in ways that correct the existing error or discrepancy.

The particular computer model of human thinking proposed by Newell, Shaw, and Simon (1958), for example, involves a receptor mechanism capable of interpreting coded information plus a control system consisting of a large store of memories, a variety of processes for operating on the information in these memories, and rules for combining the processes into complex strategies or programs which, in turn, can be selectively activated by the input information. It is true that this type of cognitive model has recently had considerable appeal for certain learning theorists (e.g., Berlyne, 1962; Gagné, 1977; Miller, Galanter, and Pribram, 1960) who were formerly identified with the neobehavioristic school of thought. In fact, Miller, Galanter, and Pribram have even proposed a new cybernetic or discrepancy-testing unit of analysis (TOTE) to replace the S-R paradigm. The difficulty with placing the computer model approach on the neobehavioristic-cognitive continuum, however, is that its advocates fail to make explicit their stand with respect to the conscious versus the purely automatic status of information and information-storing and -processing. Either position is theoretically compatible with the cybernetic point of view.

The theoretical and heuristic value of the computer model view depends, of course, on the tenability of the *particular* theories of information processing proposed by theorists of this persuasion to account for human cognitive functioning. Computer programs certainly seem capable of generating many of the same kinds of cognitive operations, such as generalizing, abstracting, categorizing, logical decision making, that are performed by humans; the crucial question, however, is whether the programs generating these operations in computers are genuinely comparable to the processes underlying the analogous operations in humans, that is, conform to the same information-processing model.

For example, one would anticipate basic differences in underlying processes depending on whether the model in question assumes a capability of storing and interrelating vast quantities of discrete units of information that are simultaneously or successively presented (as is true of most computers), or merely a capability of remembering and manipulating only a few discrete units at a time (7±2), simultaneously or successively (as is true of human beings). In the latter instance one might anticipate such compensatory mechanisms as "chunking," the learning of generic codes, and the cataloguing of facts, concepts, and propositions under more inclusive subsumers.

Differences in process would also presumably arise depending on whether the model assumes the possession of a fallible or infallible memory; stability over time or developmental change in information-processing methods and capacities; and rigid adherence to designated (programmed) problem-solving sequences or a capacity for imaginative improvisation, creative inspiration, and independent thinking.

As Hovland points out, however, the computer can also be used in a theoretically neutral fashion as merely a *simulator* of any hypothetical human cognitive processes rather than as a cybernetic model exemplifying a *particular* kind of information-processing theory. It is theoretically possible to program a computer in accordance with the assumptions of *any* theory of cognition or in accordance with the known or hypothesized properties of human cognitive functioning, although the fidelity of the simulation might be open to question in certain instances. One could then use the computer either to test the predictions made by different theoretical models or to obtain much additional information about cognitive functioning in particular circumstances that are too complex to permit prediction or experimental investigation.

Cognitive theorists, on the other hand (e.g., Ausubel, 1962, 1963), maintain that meaningful verbal learning rather than chunking is the primary human mechanism for acquiring and storing the vast quantity of ideas and information represented in any body of knowledge. Meaningful verbal learning, as suggested already, involves the acquisition of new meanings from potentially meaningful material under the auspices of a meaningful learning set. This distinctively human capacity is dependent, of course, upon such cognitive capabilities as symbolic representation, abstraction, categorization, and generalization. It is the possession of these latter human capacities that makes possible the acquisition of generic concepts and propositions, and, hence, the subsumptive emergence and retention in cognitive structure of those subordinate, correlative, superordinate, and combinatorial meanings comprising the bulk of knowledge.

Associative and Semantic Network Theories of Information Processing

In recent years it has been fashionable to refer to and to categorize certain theories of learning under the umbrella term of "information processing." The obvious difficulty with this latter term is that *all* conceptions of learning and retention and of their underlying psychological processes are forms of information processing. Thus, the term has little or no differential value in distinguishing among the different kinds and theories of learning and retention.

More recent varieties of information-processing models have been offered by J. R. Anderson (1976), R. C. Anderson (1977), Gagné (1977), Kintsch (1974), Lindsay and Norman (1977), Neisser (1970), Norman (1968), and Rummelhart and Tulving (1972). These theorists place great weight on pattern recognition (really a perceptual rather than a cognitive process) and the distinction between long-term and short-term memory. The latter distinction *per se,* in our view, has little explanatory value for subject-matter learning because it does not differentiate intrinsically in process terms between rote and meaningful learning and retention or between reception and discovery learning. Each of these latter types of memory also imply either a short- or long-term temporal phase.

The designation of memory as either short- or long-term actually refers more to the *time frame* in which qualitatively different types of memory (e.g., rote or meaningful) occur, i.e., to the relative time interval in which each type takes place, rather than to contrasting critical differences in process characterizing the different major categories of memory. Although learning, memory, and cognitive psychologists tend to use the short- and long-term designations as if they had transcending theoretical or explanatory value with respect to process and/or outcome differences for the different types of memory, it is quite apparent that this current usage constitutes misleading use of these largely temporal terms.

However, in one correlative sense, rote and meaningful learning and retention, on the one hand, and short- and long-term memory, on the other, can be significantly and veridically related to each other. In order for long-term memory to exist as such, unpracticed, it must usually be meaningful rather than rote and reflect a more complex, time-consuming underlying process of interaction between an idea in the learning material and an anchoring idea in cognitive structure. Short-term memory, on the other hand, typically involves a simpler, more rapid learning process with no possibility of emergent, substantive meaning or of linkage to an anchoring idea; the underlying process, therefore, is usually rote.

Lindsay and Norman (1977) delineate three different distinctive temporal aspects of memory:

> One aspect is primarily important for the proper operation of perceptual processing, including the mechanisms of pattern recognition. Thus we appear to have a memory system that maintains a detailed image (for a few tenths of a second) of the sensory information that has arrived at a particular sense organ. This information system is called *sensory information storage.* A second aspect of memory maintains information for a few seconds, perhaps a few minutes. This is the *short-term memory system.* But short-term memory is not like sensory information storage, for now the information is already encoded, already categorized by pattern recognition mechanisms. Short-term memory is also the stage where we maintain information that we need temporarily for a few minutes or that we are trying to organize and store permanently. The third aspect of memory is *long-term memory system.* Here is where permanent records of our experiences are maintained. This memory has essentially unlimited capacity (Lindsay & Norman, 1977).

In the first place, this latter aspect of the formulation of information processing and its representation in memory is essentially a sequential account of what happens at a descriptive or nominalistic level that elucidates the chronological limits and temporal sequences of memory but really begs the question of the underlying process or phenomenological differences involved in the different kinds of memory. Of course, the latter descriptive account necessarily associates short- and long-term temporal intervals with the corresponding complexity of the learning and memory processes involved in each temporal category. Complex and long-term processes obviously require more time for their operation than their simpler counterparts. However, it does not in any way differentiate theoretically between rote and meaningful memory, between reception and discovery learning, or between the underlying process differences in these different types of learning and memory or in their respective conditions of learning. It is true, of course, that it requires less effort and repetition to retain long-term *meaningful* than long-term *rote* meanings, and that more long-term memories (because of their very nature and process of acquisition and retention) belong in the former than in the latter category. Thus, the distinction between rote and meaningful memory also apparently has much more explanatory value for the distinction between short- and long-term memory than vice versa. Information-processing theorists are, thus, largely confounding cause and effect.

Second, these theorists place excessive weight on such essentially irrelevant perceptual phenomena as pattern recognition in explaining cognitive phenomena and fail to distinguish discriminably between perception and cognition.

Third, according to this point of view (J. R. Anderson, 1976; Kintsch, 1974; Lindsay & Norman, 1977), the meanings of concepts and propositions are acquired as a result of being associated with propositions of which they are a part. The tree-like relationships thus formed between the component words of a proposition and existing propositions in cognitive structure supposedly constitute the associative or semantic matrix from which a concept derives its meaning in learning and maintains it in memory.

Examination of such "trees," however, indicates that the relationships they exemplify are much more syntactic and associative than semantic in nature and that the same word can be related to a given proposition in many different semantic ways. As we remarked in discussing the assimilation theory of learning or knowledge acquisition, concepts and propositions acquire their meanings and are stored hierarchically (not linearly) in memory by being related in *particular* semantic (not associative or syntactic) ways to *particular* ideas in a hierarchically organized cognitive structure with stable and explicit meanings; and the process of retaining them is not one of maintaining an essentially *syntactic* or associative relationship to a propositional network, but rather one of maintaining their dissociability from the more general and inclusive meanings of the established ideas in cognitive structure that assimilate them *semantically*. This latter view has the additional advantage of considering the acquisition and retention of meanings as two progressive stages in the same assimilative process.

Fourth, the present writer perceives little explanatory value in differentiating (1) between "nodes" representing ideas in memory and "links" representing the relationship between them or (2) between the "propositional" knowledge (represented by nodes and links) and the "productions" representing "procedural" knowledge (J. R. Anderson, 1976). Unitary generic ideas (concepts) and propositional ideas (composed of relationships between concepts augmented by syntactically generated meanings) *all* conform to the same sets of processes and conditions governing the acquisition and retention of meanings; and since *both* concepts and propositions exhibit relational properties, the distinction between nodes and links seems superfluous and misleading for both reasons. "Procedural" knowledge, in addition, is qualitatively no different in terms of the conditions and processes of acquisition and retention than substantive knowledge except for its different epistemological functions. The use of such metaphorical neobehavioristic jargon, therefore, not only fails to explain the hierarchical organization of cognitive structure, but also adds nothing, in our opinion, to the explanation of the processes involved in learning, retention, forgetting, transfer, and problem-solving. It is essentially neobehavioristic doctrine clothed in mechanistic terminology and addressed to cognitive phenomena.

Finally, to postulate that all nodes, links, and productions, once established in memory, leave "ineradicable traces" that are at least potentially meaningful (J. R. Anderson, 1976) is an unparsimonious, unsubstantiated assumption at variance both with common sense and everyday experience. Forgetting cannot simply be attributed to transitory interferences (e.g., competing linkages) inhibiting retrieval or to excessively few and weak pathways established between nodes and recently presented information. It must, rather, be ascribed to inadequate or ambiguous initial learning (attributable, at least in part, to detrimental cognitive structure properties), to lack of review, and most of all, both to progressive loss of dissociability strength in the absence of review and to the continuing occurrence of obliterative assimilation.

As a basis for encoding in meaningful learning, the particularity and lack of generality and inclusiveness associated with concrete images necessarily precludes their use as subsumers or anchoring ideas in most cases. A developmental exception to this evaluative judgment exists in the early representational learning of young children when images of objects and events typically serve as the referents in existing cognitive structure to which words (names) are related as representational equivalents. Somewhat later in meaningful learning from text, pictures and graphic diagrams, evoking images, also facilitate learning and retention by furnishing substantive and contextual cues that enhance concept and propositional comprehension and retention.

Of course, verbal anchoring ideas need not necessarily be stated in propositional (sentence) form. Schematic models and diagrams, flow charts, etc., often indicate the relationship between ideas more effectively and succinctly than sentences and paragraphs. They can thus serve as advance organizers in many instances, especially for learners who find it easier to "take in" at a glance an explanatory model than to read successive sentences and paragraphs. To refer, however, to such models that indicate the interrelationships existing within a system of ideas as producing their effects through "imagery" is misleading since these models typically consist of *higher-order abstractions* with arrows indicating cause-effect relations, sequence, and direction of influence. In elementary school children, however, who typically need concrete props to learn relationships between abstractions, Arnold and Brooks (1976) found that pictorial organizers, depicting the interrelationships between the elements in a prose passage, were more effective than verbal organizers at the fifth grade level.

NOTES

[1]It will be convenient henceforth (as we have already done) to refer to the established relevant idea *A* in cognitive structure (to which the new potentially meaningful idea *a* is related) as the "anchoring idea." Strictly speaking, however, the actual anchoring idea (after subsumption) is *A'*—not *A;* but this distinction can be ignored for all practical purposes since *A'* and *A* are typically not very different from each other. It *is* important to bear in mind, however, that it is not *a* that is anchored to *A*, but rather *a'* (the modified potential meaning of *a*).

It should also be noted that the term "assimilation" has been used here in the narrow sense of the term to apply to the potential meaning's loss of its original identity, to the linkage of the emergent new meaning with its anchoring idea for storage purposes, and also to the later reduction process. It would additionally be legitimate to include the earlier aspects of the meaningful learning process (in which the new idea is related to, and interacts with, its relevant established idea in cognitive structure to yield a new meaning) as part of the assimilation process in the broader sense of the term. This broader usage is not only consistent with what is usually meant by assimilation, but is also consistent with the fact that the linkage of the new modified meaning with its anchoring idea during the storage (retention) interval necessarily implies that the potentially meaningful idea in the meaningful learning process is *first related* to, and *interacts* with, that established idea to yield the initial emergent version of its psychological meaning to the learner.

[2]Short-term reminiscence, manifested two to six minutes after learning (the Ward-Hovland phenomenon) will not be considered here since it is concerned exclusively with rote memorization.

[3]It was also indicated earlier in several contexts that in meaningful learning the instructional materials are not *already* meaningful but only *potentially* meaningful. The very object of meaningful learning is to convert potential meaning into actual (psychological) meaning. *Both* rotely and meaningfully learned tasks contain already meaningful components, but in the first instance the task *as a whole* is not potentially meaningful, whereas in the second instance it is. The presence of the already meaningful components, therefore, is, at most, an *indirect* factor accounting for the superior learning (rote or meaningful) that occurs when the latter components are included in the task. It cannot possibly account for the superiority of meaningful over rote learning with respect to the learning task as a whole. The more important reason for the superiority of meaningful over rote learning obviously inheres in the fact that in meaningful learning the task as a whole is potentially meaningful and, therefore, can be nonarbitrarily and nonverbatimly related to cognitive structure.

That meaningful learning primarily refers to a distinctive *process* of learning rather than to the meaningfulness of the presented content is further highlighted by the fact that both the meaningful learning process and its outcome can be rote—even when the learning task as a whole is potentially meaningful—if the learner does not exhibit a meaningful learning set.

[4]Royer, Sefkow, and Kropf (1977) demonstrated that less retroactive interference occurs when prose materials are relatable to anchoring ideas in cognitive structure.

[5]In all kinds and causes of forgetting (except for that caused by raising the threshold of availability alone), that is, with dissociability strength held constant, as, for example, in the case of misconceptions, the common mediating factor between the occurrence of the precipitating cause of the forgetting and the actual phenomenological forgetting itself is a large cumulative loss in the dissociability strength of the items that are forgotten. In these latter instances (unlike the case in repression), the threshold of availability presumably remains relatively constant.

[6]Variability in these cognitive structure factors occurs naturally in the course of meaningful learning and retention. Greatly increased variability in these factors, however, can be contrived, especially in research and pedagogic situations, by manipulating them one at a time in an advance organizer experimental design.

[7]Destruction by disease or trauma of the neurological substrate of (1) the memories of past conscious experiences and of (2) the psychological processes underlying meaningful learning and retention necessarily precludes the future psychological occurrence of the latter experiences and processes. It does not necessarily prove, however, that this substrate *ordinarily* regulates and controls and could also explain their functioning at a substrate level. In order for personal experience and the results of learning to be retained—even for a short time—these differentiated conscious events must obviously induce some semi-lasting correlative neurological (not substrate) changes in the brain; but these changes could conceivably be correlated only in a representational or code-like sense with the overt psychological changes rather than in a functional or regulatory sense with explanatory capacity.

[8]The reason for this exception is that no functional channel exists through which positive affective and motivational factors can lower thresholds of availability of the memory items in question. Negative affective or motivational factors, however, can raise thresholds of availability, thereby decreasing the reproducibility or elicitability of memory for the items involved.

REFERENCES

Anderson, J. R. *Language, memory, and thought.* Hillsdale, N.J.: Lawrence Erlbaum, 1976.

Anderson, R. C. The notion of schemata and the educational enterprise. In R. C. Anderson, L. J. Spiro, & W. E. Montague (Eds.), *Schooling and the acquisition of knowledge.* Hillsdale, N.J.: Lawrence Erlbaum & Associates, 1977.

Anderson, R. C., & Myrow, D. C. Retroactive inhibition of connected discourses. *Journal of Educational Psychology Monograph,* 1971, *62,* 81–94.

Arnold, D. J., & Brooks, P. H. Influence of contextual organizing material on children's listening comprehension. *Journal of Educational Psychology,* 1976, *68,* 711–716.

Ashcraft, M. H. *Human memory and cognition* (2nd ed.). New York: Harper Collins College Publishers, 1994.

Aulls, M. W. Expository paragraph properties that influence literal recall. *Journal of Reading Behavior,* 1975, *7,* 391–400.

Ausubel, D. P. *The psychology of meaningful verbal learning.* New York: Grune & Stratton, 1963.

Ausubel, D. P. The use of advance organizers in the learning and retention of meaningful verbal material. *Journal of Educational Psychology,* 1960, *51,* 267–272.

Ausubel, D. P., Robbins, L. C., & Blake, E. Retroactive inhibition and facilitation in the learning of school materials. *Journal of Educational Psychology,* 1957, *48,* 334–343.

Ausubel, D. P., Stager, M., & Gaite, A. J. H. Retroactive facilitation in meaningful verbal learning. *Journal of Educational Psychology,* 1968, *59,* 250–255.

Berlyne, D. E. *Structure and direction in thinking.* New York: Wiley, 1962.

Bransford, J. D., & Johnson, M. K. Contextual prerequisites for understanding: Some investigations of comprehension and recall. *Journal of Verbal Learning and Verbal Behavior,* 1972, *11,* 717–726.

Briggs, L. J., & Reed, H. B. The curve of retention for substance material. *Journal of Experimental Psychology,* 1943, *32,* 513–517.

Brown, J. A. Some tests of the decay theory of immediate memory. *Quarterly Journal of Experimental Psychology, 10,* 12–21.

Brownell, W. A., & Moser, H. E. Meaningful versus mechanical learning: A study of grade III subtraction. *Duke University Research Studies in Education,* 1949, No. 8.

Carmichael, L. H., Hogan, H. P., & Walter, A. A. An experimental study of the effect of language on visually perceived form. *Journal of Experimental Psychology,* 1932, *5,* 73–86.

Cofer, C. N. A comparison of logical and verbatim learning of prose passages of different length. *American Journal of Psychology,* 1941, *54,* 1–20.

Dawes, R. M. Memory and distortion of meaningful written material. *British Journal of Educational Psychology,* 1966, *57,* 77–86.

Deese, J. *The structure of associations in language and thought.* Baltimore: Johns Hopkins Press, 1965.

Edwards, A. L., & English, H. B. Reminiscence in relation to differential difficulty. *Journal of Experimental Psychology,* 1939, *25,* 100–108.

Eikenberry, D. H. Permanence of high school learning. *Journal of Educational Psychology,* 1923, *14,* 463–482.

English, H. B., Welborn, E. L., & Kilian, C. D. Studies in substance memorization. *Journal of General Psychology,* 1934, *11,* 233–260.

Frutchey, F. P. Retention in high school chemistry. *Journal of Higher Education,* 1937, *8,* 217–218.

Granit, A. R. A study on the perception of form. *Journal of Experimental Psychology,* 1921, *12,* 223–247.

Greeno, R. K. *Human memory.* Hillsdale, N.J.: Lawrence Erlbaum Associates, 1992.

Hart, J. T., Memory and the feeling-of-knowing experience. *Journal of Educational Psychology,* 1965, *56,* 208–216.

Hildreth, G. E. The difficulty reduction tendency in perception and problem solving. *Journal of Educational Psychology,* 1941, *32,* 305–313.

Hildreth, G. E. The simplification tendency in reproducing designs. *Journal of Genetic Psychology,* 1944, *64,* 327–333.

Hilgard, E. R., Irvine, R. P., & Whipple, J. E. Rote memorization, understanding, and transfer: An extension of Katona's card trick experiments. *Journal of Experimental Psychology,* 1953, *46,* 288–292.

Hirt, E. R., McDonald, H. E., & Erikson, G. A. How do I remember thee? The role of encoding set and delay in reconstructive memory processes. *Journal of Experimental Social Psychology,* 1995, *31,* 379–409.

Johnson, R. E. Meaningfulness and the recall of textual prose. *American Educational Research Journal,* 1973, *10,* 49–58.

Jones, E. E., & De Charms, R. The organizing function of interactional roles in person perception. *Journal of Abnormal & Social Psychology,* 1958, *57,* 155–164.

Kastrinos, W. A study of the retention of biological facts by high-school biology students. *Science Education,* 1965, *49,* 487–491.

Keppel, G., & Underwood, B. J. Proactive inhibition in short-term retention of single items. *Journal of Verbal Learning and Verbal Behavior,* 1962, *1,* 153–161.

Kintsch, W. *Memory and cognition.* New York: Wiley, 1977.

Kintsch, W. Text comprehension, memory, and learning. *American Psychologist,* 1994, *49,* 294–303.

Kintsch, W. *The representation of meaning in memory.* New York: Lawrence Erlbaum Associates, 1974.

Kintsch, W., et al. Comprehension and recall of text as a function of content variables. *Journal of Verbal Learning and Verbal Behavior,* 1975, *14,* 196–214.

Koffka, K. *Principles of Gestalt psychology.* New York: Harcourt, Brace, Jovanovich, 1935.

Lindsay, P. H., & Norman, D. A. *Human information processing.* New York: Academic Press, 1972.

Mayer, B. J. F., & McConkie, G. W. What is recalled after hearing a passage? *Journal of Educational Psychology,* 1973, *65,* 109–117.

Miller, G. A., Galanter, E., & Pribram, K. *Plans and the structure of behavior.* New York: Holt, Rinehart & Winston, 1960.

Myrow, D. C., & Anderson, R. C. Retroactive inhibition of prose as a function of type of test. *Journal of Educational Psychology,* 1972, *63,* 323–328.

McKillop, A. S. *The relationship between the reader's attitude and certain types of reading response.* New York: Teachers College, Columbia University, 1952.

Neisser, U. *Psychology of cognition.* New York: Appleton-Century-Crofts, 1970.

Newell, A., Shaw, J. C., & Simon, H. A. Elements of a theory of human problem solving. *Psychological Review,* 1958, *65,* 151–166.

Newman, E. B. Forgetting of meaningful material during sleep and waking. *American Journal of Psychology,* 1939, *52,* 65–71.

Newson, R. S., & Gaite, A. J. H. Prose learning: Effects of pretesting and reduction of passage length. *Psychological Reports,* 1971, *28,* 123–129.

Norman, D. P. *Memory and attention.* New York: Wiley, 1968.

Paivio, A. *Imagery and verbal processes.* New York: Holt, Rinehart & Winston, 1971.

Paul, I. H. Studies in remembering: The reproduction of connected and extended verbal material. *Psychological Issues,* 1959, *1,* no. 2 (Whole no. 2).

Pichert, J. W., & Anderson, R. C. Taking different perspectives on a story. *Journal of Educational Psychology,* 1977, *69,* 309–315.

Postman, L., & Rau, L. Retention as a function of the method of measurement. *University of California Publications in Psychology,* 1957, *8,* 219–270.

Reed, H. B. Meaning as a factor in learning. *Journal of Educational Psychology,* 1938, *29,* 419–430.

Rosenthal, B. G. Hypnotic recall of material learned under anxiety and non-anxiety producing conditions. *Journal of Experimental Psychology,* 1944, *34,* 368–389.

Royer, J. M., S.R., & Kropf, R. B. Contributions of existing knowledge structure to retroactive inhibition in prose learning. *Contemporary Educational Psychology,* 1977, *2,* 31–36.

Rummelhart, D. E., Lindsay, P. H., & Norman, D. P. A process model for long-term memory. In E. Tulving & W. Donaldson (Eds.), *Organization of memory.* New York: Academic Press, 1972.

Sherman, J. L. Contextual information and prose comprehension. *Journal of Reading Behavior,* 1976, *8,* 369–379.

Sternberg, S. Memory scanning: New findings and current controversies. *Quarterly Journal of Experimental Psychology,* 1975, *27,* 1–32.

Taft, R. Selective recall and memory distortion of favorable and unfavorable material. *Journal of Abnormal & Social Psychology,* 1954, *49,* 23–28.

Thiele, C. L. The contribution of generalization to the learning of addition facts. *Contributions to Education,* No. 763. New York: Teachers College, Columbia University, 1938.

Underwood, B. J., & Richardson, J. The influence of meaningfulness, intralist similarity and serial position in retention. *Journal of Experimental Psychology,* 1956, *52,* 118–126.

Vygotsky, L. S. *Thought and language.* New York: Wiley, 1962.

Wickens, D. D. Characteristics of word encoding. In A. W. Melton & E. Martin (Eds.), *Coding processes in human memory.* New York: Winston, 1972.

Wickens, D. D., Born, D. G., & Allen, C. K. Proactive inhibition and item similarity in short-term memory. *Journal of Verbal Learning and Verbal Behavior, 2,* 440–445.

CHAPTER 6

THE EFFECTS OF COGNITIVE STRUCTURE VARIABLES ON THE ACQUISITION, RETENTION, AND TRANSFERABILITY OF KNOWLEDGE

In previous chapters we have considered the nature, conditions, and underlying properties of meaningful verbal reception learning and retention. We have also concluded that various specifiable properties of existing cognitive structure are the most important single class of factors influencing the acquisition, retention, and transferability of knowledge. Now we are ready to operationalize these cognitive structure variables, to cite and consider available research evidence regarding their effects on subject-matter learning and retention, and to suggest how they may be optimally manipulated and applied to instructional practices so as to maximize students' acquisition and retention of knowledge.

In this chapter it will also be convenient to consider, among other issues, the effects of language on the transferability of knowledge. Both for theoretical purposes of discovering how human beings acquire and retain large bodies of knowledge, and for the practical ends of enhancing instructional practices, it is simply not sufficient to stress the importance for meaningful learning and retention of relevant antecedent knowledge that is represented and stored in existing cognitive structure. Before fruitful experimentation and verification can be attempted it is necessary to specify, conceptualize, and explicitly operationalize the most significant and manipulable variables (attributes) of the learner's existing body of knowledge that influence new learning and retention. Contrary to E. Gagné's (1978) assertion, these variables have all been operationalized already conceptually, as well as procedurally, the testing instruments (instructional prose passages) and experimental procedures primarily relying on and manifesting, in most instances, self-evident content validity.

Since existing cognitive structure exhibits, by definition, the residual impact of all prior learning and retention, it invariably involves the problem of transfer when new learning occurs.[1] To be objectively demonstrable, however, a specific cognitive structure variable must be designated and measured, as well as its effect on new learning and retention tasks, in comparison with that of a control group. In this connection, R. M. Gagné (1977) distinguishes between *lateral* and *vertical* transfer that is partly analogous to the distinction between general and long-term versus specific and short-term transfer presented in Chapter 2. In the first instance (lateral transfer), existing learning capabilities are applied somewhat indirectly, and in a general sense, to the understanding of subject-matter content and the solution of related problems in the same field of knowledge or to the understanding of subject-matter material and problem-solving in other disciplines. This (lateral transfer) involves the generalizability of the residue of one set of existing learnings both to the comprehension and problem solution of tangentially or metaphorically related problems in a somewhat different but related area of knowledge or problem-solving experience.

Vertical transfer, on the other hand, applies to the situation where the mastery of a rather specific set of "subordinate capabilities" is prerequisite to the acquisition of higher-order capabilities within a rather limited subarea of knowledge (Gagné, 1977). In our terms, vertical transfer would be present whenever the availability of relevant superordinate ideas in cognitive structure enhances the learning of subordinate ideas in the instructional material (subsumption), and more particularly in reception than in discovery learning and in substantive knowledge than in problem-solving capabilities.

In contrast to *developmental* readiness that depends on discontinuous age-level increases in developmental level of cognitive functioning, the kind of readiness we shall consider here may be termed "subject-matter" readiness. It may be defined as those content and organizational properties of existing knowledge in the learner's cognitive structure relative to a given aspect of a discipline or to the discipline as a whole, that influence his or her capability of learning and retaining new components of knowledge in that field with reasonable economy of time and effort. In both instances we are dealing with a type of readiness for new learning. In the latter case, however, the readiness is a function of previously acquired, particular subject-matter knowledge, that is, of its substantive and organizational properties. In the former case, it reflects the learner's *maturity* of intellectual functioning both on an overall basis and in the particular discipline in question. These two sets of factors or kinds of readiness are not unrelated. Each factor both independently influences the acquisition and retention of knowledge and, in addition, influences the other factor.

MEANINGFUL LEARNING AND THE AVAILABILITY OF RELEVANT ANCHORING IDEAS

Whether or not relevant anchoring ideas at an appropriate level of abstraction, generality, and inclusiveness are available in cognitive structure is an obviously important antecedent variable in meaningful learning and retention. In this section we propose to review various short-term studies of meaningful learning, retention, and problem solving in which this variable is implicated. Studies such as these exemplify the transfer paradigm providing that the cognitive structure variable is manipulated during a preliminary or training period so that its effect on a *new* learning task can be ascertained. For example, a study indicating that the overlearning of a given passage results in increased retention would *not* constitute relevant evidence—from the standpoint of transfer—about the influence of cognitive structure on retention; it would merely reflect the influence of degree of practice on retention inasmuch as practice rather than altered cognitive structure is the only *measurable* independent variable that is relevant under these circumstances. On the other hand, evidence that the overlearning of passage *A* by an experimental group (as compared to a control group that does not overlearn passage *A*) leads to superior retention of related passage *B*, would be pertinent evidence of the influence of relevant and consolidated existing ideas in cognitive structure, i.e., of positive transfer.

Availability of relevant ideas in cognitive structure may be ascertained by multiple-choice or essay pre-tests, by Piaget-type clinical interviews, by employing Socratic questioning, and by "cognitive mapping." Consensual ratings by subject-matter experts and teachers may also be used to judge degree and proximateness of existing cognitive relevance for a given learning task.

In addition to their practical usefulness as a pedagogic device, advance organizers can also be used to study programmatically the effects of cognitive structure variables. By systematically manipulating the properties of organizers, it is possible to influence various attributes of cognitive structure (e.g., the availability to the learner of relevant and proximately inclusive subsumers; the clarity, stability, discriminability, cohesiveness, and integrativeness of these subsumers), and then to ascertain the influence of this manipulation on new learning, retention, and problem solving. The occurrence of positive transfer can then be warrantedly inferred (if control subjects, who are exposed to overtly similar introductory materials that do not emphasize a cognitive structure variable) fail to obtain comparable results.

The Nature, Underlying Process, and Effects of Advance Organizers

Advance organizers are pedagogic devices that help implement the principles of progressive differentiation and integrative reconciliation by bridging the gap between what the *learner already* knows and what he *needs* to know if he is to learn and retain new instructional material efficaciously.

Operationally, organizers are defined as relatively brief introductions, differing from overviews and previews, in that the ideas they contain (1) are both more abstract, inclusive, and general than the more detailed learning material they precede, and (2) are relatable to, and take account of, existing relevant ideas already present in cognitive structure. The latter criterion is necessary, of course, if the organizer itself is to be learnable.

Advance organizers operate on the same general principle as already existing antecedent and relevant ideational material in cognitive structure in the sense that the new instructional material to be presented later is sequentially dependent on it (except for the fact that its relevance for both the new learning material and for relevant anchoring ideas in cognitive structure is both more specifically and more explicitly targeted). Summaries and overviews, on the other hand, are ordinarily presented at the same level of abstraction, generality, and inclusiveness as the learning material itself. They simply emphasize the salient point of the material by omitting less important information and largely achieve their effect by repetition and simplification.

The function of the organizer, after it interacts with relevant subsumers in cognition structure, is to provide ideational scaffolding for the stable incorporation and retention of the more detailed and differentiated material that follows in the learning passage as well as to increase discriminability between the latter material and similar or ostensibly conflicting ideas in cognitive structure.[2] For relatively unfamiliar material only an "expository" organizer needs to be used to provide relevant proximate subsumers. These subsumers, which bear a superordinate relationship to the new learning material, primarily furnish ideational anchorage in terms that are already familiar to the learner. For relatively familiar learning material, on the other hand, a "comparative" organizer is used both to integrate new ideas with basically similar ideas in cognitive structure as well as to increase discriminability between new and existing ideas that are essentially different but confusably similar.

The advantage of deliberately constructing a special organizer for each new unit of material is that only in this way can the learner enjoy the advantages of subsumers that both give him a general preview of the more detailed instructional material in *advance* of his actual confrontation with it, as well as provide organizing elements that are inclusive of, and take into account more efficiently relevant ideas in his cognitive structure. Any existing subsumer in the learner's cognitive structure that he could independently employ for this purpose without an organizer typically lacks *particularized* relevance and inclusiveness for the new material and would hardly be available in advance of his initial contact with it. Also, although students might possibly be able to improvise a suitable subsumer for future learning efforts *after* they become familiar with the material, it is unlikely that they would be able to do so as efficiently as a person sophisticated in both subject-matter content and pedagogy, i.e., the skilled teacher or subject-matter methodologist who prepares the organizer. Preorganizers (organizers that precede the learning material), as might be reasonably expected, are uniformly more effective than post-organizers (Mayer, 1977b; Mayer & Brombage, 1978).

The pedagogic value of advance organizers obviously depends, in part, upon how well-organized the learning material itself is. If it already contains built-in organizers and proceeds from regions of lesser to greater differentiation (higher to lower inclusiveness), rather than in the opposite direction of the typical textbook or lecture presentation, much of the potential benefit derivable from advance organizers will not be actualized. Regardless of how well organized the learning material is, however, it seems plausible to expect that learning and retention can still be facilitated for most learners by the use of advance organizers at an appropriate level of inclusiveness. Such organizers are available from the very beginning of the learning task, and their integrative properties are also much more salient than when introduced concurrently with the learning material. To be useful, however, *organizers themselves must obviously be learnable and must be stated in familiar terms.* Such learnability, therefore, should be empirically demonstrable rather than merely assumed.

Organizers are constructed so as to provide general superordinate concepts, propositions, and principles for the subsumption of those ideas in the learning task that are subordinate to these latter more general ideas. Thus, it follows that organizers should have their strongest positive effects on conceptual and propositional ideational units and on transfer problems that require general concepts for their solution (Mayer, 1979), as exemplified by studies of Mayer and Brombage (1978). At the same time it must be realized that for organizers to be most effective they must be formulated at higher rather than lower levels of conceptualization (Mayer, Stiehl, & Greeno, 1975) and that instructional materials must be more highly differentiated than the organizers themselves (Ausubel, 1963). Also if the instructional materials are highly abstract, they contain their own built-in organizers and their learning is not apt to be facilitated by advance organizers.

For similar reasons instructional materials should be unfamiliar, difficult, technical, and unrelated to areas of knowledge where students already have or are likely to use proximately relevant subsumers (Ausubel, 1960, 1963, 1968; Mayer, 1979). Mayer's (1978) finding that advance organizers are more effective when the ideas in textual material are arranged in random rather than in logical order, as well as his finding that students with low scholastic aptitude (who are less likely to possess or be able to construct their own organizers or to perceive the relevance of existing subsumers (Ausubel & Fitzgerald, 1962; Mayer, 1975b; Schulz, 1966) are consistent with the above principle.

In order to conform to the operational considerations considered above, pilot studies of advance organizers should be conducted to establish that the learning material is generally unfamiliar, and that the organizer itself is both learnable and does not directly provide any material that helps the learner answer post-questions (Ausubel, 1960, 1961, 1963, 1968). It goes without saying that a control group exposed to a non-organizer type of introduction of the same length (and superficially resembling the organizer) is essential in the design of organizer experiments.

To fulfill the criterion of the organizer's relatability to cognitive structure, one or more of the procedures noted above for ascertaining the availability of relevant ideas in the learners' cognitive structure should be used. Degree and proximateness of relevance of the ideas in the organizer can be established by using such criteria as agreement among both teachers and subject-matter specialists.

One of the basic premises of the use of advance organizers is that they must be geared to the level of intellectual functioning of the learners in question. Thus at the elementary-school level, the inclusion of concrete-empirical props in organizer content is advocated to make the generalizations in question comprehensible to elementary-school children (Ausubel, 1963).

Lawton and his co-workers at the University of Wisconsin carried this principle one step further in using an organizer approach to preschool education. They believe that preschool children could learn subject-matter material through expository teaching if content organizers were supplemented by "process" organizers, i.e., organizers that explain to these pupils, in general terms, the nature of such cognitive processes as classification, implicit knowledge of which is taken for granted as lying within the information-processing skills of elementary-school children and beyond. To date they have demonstrated that a combination of process and content organizers is significantly superior to content organizers alone or to an approach to preschool education based on Piagetian assumptions.

The use of expository organizers to facilitate the learning and retention of meaningful verbal learning is based on the premise that potentially meaningful instructional material becomes incorporated most readily and stably in cognitive structure insofar as it is subsumable under specifically relevant anchoring ideas. It follows, therefore, that increasing the availability in cognitive structure of specifically relevant subsumers—by introducing therein suitably targeted organizers—should enhance the meaningful learning of such material. This supposition is confirmed, in fact, by much research evidence (e.g., Ausubel, 1960; Ausubel & Fitzgerald, 1961, 1962; Ausubel & Youssef, 1963; Kuhn & Novak, 1971). The facilitating effect of purely expository organizers, however, typically seems to be largely limited to learners who have low verbal ability (Ausubel & Fitzgerald, 1962; Mayer, 1975b) and low analytic ability (Schulz, 1966), and hence presumably less capability for developing an adequate schema of their own for organizing new material in relation to existing cognitive structure.[3] The same availability of a relevant superordinate proposition in cognitive structure also enhances meaningful retention by decreasing the rate at which the original dissociability strength of the material declines (by decelerating the rate of obliterative assimilation) (Ausubel & Fitzgerald, 1961b).

Thus, advance organizers probably facilitate the incorporability and longevity of meaningfully learned material in three different ways. First, they explicitly draw upon and mobilize whatever relevant anchoring concepts are already established in the learner's cognitive structure and make them part of the subsuming entity. Thus, not only is the new, potentially meaningful material rendered more familiar and actually meaningful, but the most relevant ideational antecedents in cognitive structure are also selected and utilized in integrated fashion. Second, by making subsumption under specifically relevant ideas possible (and drawing on other advantages of subsumptive learning), advance organizers at an appropriate level of inclusiveness provide optimal anchorage for the instructional material. This promotes both initial learning and later resistance to obliterative subsumption. Third, the use of advance organizers renders unnecessary much of the rote memorization to which students often resort because they are required to learn the details of an unfamiliar discipline before having available a sufficient number of key anchoring ideas to render these details meaningful. Because of the frequent unavailability of such ideas in cognitive structure to which the details can be nonarbitrarily and substantively related, the material, although logically meaningful, often lacks potential meaningfulness.

The consensus of research opinion regarding the empirical validity of advance organizer findings was expressed by Mayer (1979). In analyzing Barnes and Clawson's 1975 review, and summarizing his own studies on advance organizers in terms of the predictions of assimilation theory, he concluded that "advance organizers when used in appropriate situations and when evaluated adequately, do appear to influence the outcome of learning."

Preconceptions and Misconceptions

Postman's (1954) study of the effect of learned rules of organization on rote learning and retention is an interesting precursor of the use of advance organizers in the meaningful learning of potentially meaningful connected verbal discourse. This investigator found that explicit training in the derivation of figural patterns from code models facilitates the retention of the figural material, that the relative "effectiveness of such preliminary training increases with the retention interval," and that the training reduces the susceptibility of the memory material to retroactive interference. In essence, then, this experiment involved the facilitation of rote (verbatim) retention by meaningful rules of organization: The learning task was relatively arbitrary, verbatim, and unrelatable to cognitive structure, but each component was relatable to an explicitly learned code, which, in this instance, was analogous to a subsuming principle. Reynolds (1966) similarly demonstrated that an organized perceptual structure can facilitate rote verbal learning.

The relevance of the precursory antecedent elements of anchoring ideas in cognitive structure for the new learning material is also an important factor in cognitive functioning. Concepts and rules are more easily acquired if the specific instances from which they are abstracted are frequently rather than rarely associated with their defining (criterial) attributes or exemplars and if subjects have more rather than less relevant information about the nature of these attributes (Nagata, 1976; Underwood and Richardson, 1956).

Relevant and meaningful antecedent context (Bransford & Johnson, 1972) and advance exposure to "key terms" (Jenkins & Bausell, 1976) similarly facilitate the comprehension of connected discourse, particularly when it is vague or ambiguous. The same effect is shown on the perception of such material as measured by subthreshold tachistoscopic exposure time. Not only are superordinate ideas remembered longer and more accurately than subordinate ideas (Kintsch et al., 1974; Meyer & McConkie, 1973), but they are also more effective than coordinate ideas as subsumers (i.e., when used as advance organizers) (Rickards, 1975; Rickards & McCormick, 1976). These findings are, of course, consistent with the fact that the duration of long-term retention of various forms of subject matter varies directly as a function of their level of abstraction, generality, and inclusiveness. Meyer (1975a, b, c, 1976b) and Saugstad (1955) demonstrated that much of the variance in problem solving is accounted for by the availability of relevant knowledge in the learner's cognitive structure.

In the previous section on "Sources of Forgetting," we considered several studies showing how differential advance sets, attitudes, and orientations differentially influence the content of acquired meanings. Although the availability of relevant anchoring ideas in cognitive structure generally facilitates meaningful learning and retention, we have considered the possibility and some evidence indicating that recently prior experience may produce proactive interference and (less frequently) retroactive interference as well, by generating cognitive confusion (e.g., Suppes & Ginsberg, 1963), and through "functional fixedness" and "rigidity" in problem-solving strategy (e.g., Luchins, 1946).

It is apparent, therefore, that not only is the presence in cognitive structure of clear, stable, discriminable, and relevant anchoring ideas the chief facilitating factor in meaningful learning but also that the *absence* of such ideas constitutes the primary limiting or negative influence on new meaningful learning. One such limiting factor is the existence of erroneous but tenacious preconceptions. Unfortunately, however, very little research has been conducted on this crucial problem, despite the fact that the unlearning of preconceptions in certain instances of meaningful learning and retention might very well prove to be the most determinative and manipulable single factor in the acquisition and retention of subject-matter knowledge.

In any case, anyone who has attempted to teach science to children, or to adults for that matter, is painfully aware of the potent role of preconceptions in inhibiting the learning and retention of scientific facts, concepts, and principles. These preconceptions are amazingly tenacious and resistant to extinction because of the influence of such factors as primacy and frequency and because they are typically anchored to highly related, stable, and antecedent preconceptions of an inclusive nature (for example, general, unqualified propositions expressive of a positive rather than inverse relationship; predicated on single rather than multiple causality or on dichotomous rather than continuous variability).

Moreover, resistance to the acceptance of new ideas contrary to prevailing beliefs seems to be characteristic of human learning. Some of the reasons for individual differences in the tenacity of preconceptions probably include those that are related to cognitive style, to such pervasive personality traits as closed-mindedness, and to self-consistent individual differences in generalized aspects of reductionism in cognitive functioning. Pines (1977) has shown that when misconceptions are not uprooted, they may become more elaborated and stable as a result of instruction.

A very common preconception, for example, among elementary-school children is that the outer integument constitutes a kind of sack filled with blood. Prick it at any point and it bleeds. Actually this is not a bizarrely implausible hypothesis. Is it conceivable, therefore, that one can effectively instruct such children about the circulatory system without taking into account and trying to undermine the relative credibility and explanatory power of this preconception as compared with that of a closed system of vessels? Oakes (1945, 1947) has shown that misconceptions exist at all levels of age and education. Thus, a seemingly important precondition for constructing individualized organizers for instructional units in science is to ascertain what the more common preconceptions of learners are by means of appropriate pretests, clinical interviews, or cognitive mapping and then to match suitably tailored organizers with pupils exhibiting corresponding preconceptions.

Long-Term Studies of Cognitive Structure Variables

Despite their self-evident significance for school learning, long-term studies on the effects of cognitive structure variables on subject-matter achievement are extremely sparse. Very little research in this area conforms to the minimally necessary research design (the transfer paradigm) which requires that a single attribute of cognitive structure first be deliberately manipulated, using adequate experimental and/or statistical control procedures, and that this altered cognitive structure attribute then be related to long-term academic achievement outcomes in an extended program of *new* studies in the same field.

Influence of Existing Degree of Knowledge on Academic Achievement

Studies in which degree of existing knowledge of subject matter at one level of educational attainment is related to academic performance at subsequent educational levels conform to the long-term transfer paradigm. Constancy of academic attainment is, of course, partly attributable to constancy of academic aptitude and motivation as well as of external pressures. But especially when these latter factors are controlled, it is reasonable to attribute some of the obtained positive achievement relationship between earlier and later educational levels to the cumulative effects of cognitive structure variables[4] (Ring & Novak, 1971; Swenson, 1957; West & Fensham, 1976) on subsequent learning and retention.

Swenson, for example, reported that, holding academic aptitude constant, students from the upper two-fifths of their graduating classes make significantly higher quality-point averages in college courses than do students from the lower three-fifths. Engle (1957), on the other hand, found that university grades in psychology for students who studied psychology in high school were no higher than the grades of students who did not study psychology in high school. This lack of relationship probably reflected, in part, significant differences in content and emphasis between high school and college psychology courses.

From the standpoint of rational principles of curriculum development, however, introductory courses in a given field of knowledge might normally be expected to establish the kind of antecedent cognitive structure that would facilitate the later assimilation of more advanced and highly differentiated material in the same field of knowledge. It could also be argued, of course, that mastery of high-school psychology has independent goals in its own right that are unrelated to those of college psychology and are not intended as preparation for, or as a means of enhancing, mastery of the latter. Naegele (1974) found that learning time for sequential units in a physics course is more dependent on the adequacy of learning the earlier units in the course than on pretest scores for the physics course itself, thus illustrating the importance of *specifically* relevant cognitive-structure differentiation for the facilitation of subsequent learning.

Improvement of Instruction

Many of the curriculum reform movements attempted to enhance long-term learning and retention by influencing cognitive structure variables. The University of Illinois Committee on School Mathematics (Beberman, 1958), for example, stressed initial self-discovery of generalizations by students, followed by precise, consistent, and unambiguous verbalization of modern mathematical concepts. The Secondary School

Physics Program of the Physical Science Study Committee (Finlay, 1959) placed great emphasis on the more integrative and widely generalizable concepts of modern physics; on inquiry in depth rather than on broad, superficial coverage of the field; on careful, sequential programming of principles; and on conveying to the student something of the spirit and methods of physics as a developing experimental science. In my opinion, it is not unreasonable to infer that implicit in each program was the assumption that whatever ultimate superiority in academic attainment was achieved by following these pedagogic principles, was attributable to cumulative changes in the organizational and substantive properties of cognitive structure.

Achievement test data provided by evaluative studies of such programs, however, offer only presumptive evidence regarding the long-term effects of cognitive structure variables, inasmuch as this type of research does not adequately conform to our transfer paradigm, i.e., the learning of *new* material or later academic performance in the same subject-matter field is not studied as a function of earlier substantive or organizational changes in cognitive structure that can be plausibly attributed to *specifiable* characteristics of the curriculum. Such studies tell us only that *cumulative* achievement at some designated point in time is presumably superior because of the *cumulative* effects of the program as a whole. Furthermore, not only is it impossible in such programs to isolate the effects of the particular independent variables involved, but also only rarely is any effort made to obtain comparable achievement data from control groups or to control for the "Hawthorne effect."[5] Measurement is also a difficult problem because standardized achievement tests cover various traditional subject-matter units deliberately ignored by these new curricula, as well as fail to measure knowledge of the more modern content which the latter emphasize.

All of these difficulties point up the unfeasibility of using curriculum-development research as a source of rigorous experimental evidence bearing on a *single* cognitive structure variable.

Improvement of Critical Thinking

Attempts to enhance critical thinking ability by influencing cognitive structure in particular subject-matter areas have been made by Novak (1958), Abercrombie (1960), and Smith (1960). Novak found that a six-week experience in problem solving in botany did not increase problem-solving ability as measured. Abercrombie tried to improve medical students' ability to reason more effectively by providing them with opportunities for "therapeutic" group discussion in an unstructured, nonauthoritarian atmosphere. Analysis of X-rays was used as the criterion measure for assessing the effects of this training. Abercrombie's findings were generally in the predicted direction but are vulnerable on the grounds of failure to control for the so-called "Hawthorne effect."

The promise of this approach is twofold: First, the attempt to influence critical thinking is based on the simultaneous teaching of the logic of a *particular* subject-matter field along with its content rather than on instruction in *general* principles of logic applicable to all disciplines. Second, by quantifying crucially important but elusive teaching variables, this category system can do much to place long-term classroom studies of cognitive structure variables on a sound experimental basis.

Transfer of General Principles in Problem Solving

Much positive transfer in problem solving and other kinds of learning is attributable to the carryover of general elements of strategy, orientation, and adaptation to particular instances of problem solving. Systematic instruction in approach to a given task has been shown to facilitate both motor learning (Duncan, 1963) and memorization.

THE ROLE OF DISCRIMINABILITY IN MEANINGFUL LEARNING AND RETENTION

The discriminability of new learning material from previously learned concepts in cognitive structure is a major cognitive structure variable in meaningful learning and retention. In the effort to simplify the task of apprehending different aspects of the environment and representing them in cognitive structure, existing anchoring ideas in cognitive structure that resemble analogous ideas in the learning material often tend to be interpreted as identical with, or equivalent to, the latter, despite the fact that objective identity hardly exists in fact. Existing knowledge, in other words, tends to preempt the cognitive field and to superimpose itself somewhat vaguely on similar potential meanings in the instructional material.[6] Under these circumstances the resulting meanings that are learned cannot possibly conform to the objective content of the learning material. In other instances learners may be aware of the fact that the new propositions presented to them differ somehow from established propositions in cognitive structure, but they are unable to specify wherein the difference lies. When either situation arises, ambiguous meanings tend to emerge, permeated by doubt, confusion, and alternative or competing meanings. In either case, however, the newly learned meanings exhibit relatively little initial dissociability strength. Furthermore, if new meanings cannot be readily distinguished from established meanings, they can certainly be adequately represented by the latter for memorial purposes and, thus, tend rapidly to lose their initial dissociability strength or to become obliterated more rapidly than initially discriminable meanings. This is especially true for longer retention periods. Over short retention intervals nondiscriminable material can often be retained on a purely rote basis.

Lack of discriminability between new ideas and previously learned concepts or propositions in cognitive structure may account for *some* negative transfer (proactive interference) in school learning. This is particularly the case when the two sets of ideas are confusably similar, and when the previously learned ideas are neither clear nor well established. Under these latter conditions the learner understandably encounters greater difficulty in learning the new ideas than if he had not been previously exposed to a confusably similar and undiscriminable set of propositions. Suppes and Ginsberg (1962), for example, found evidence of negative transfer when first-graders learned the concept of identity of ordered sets after previously learning the concept of identity of unordered sets.

The discriminability of a new learning task is also in large measure a function of the clarity and stability in cognitive structure of the existing ideas to which it is related. In learning an unfamiliar passage about Buddhism, for example, subjects with greater knowledge of Christianity (the related and relevant subsuming ideas in cognitive structure) make significantly higher scores on the Buddhism test than do subjects with less knowledge of Christianity (Ausubel & Blake, 1958; Ausubel & Fitzgerald, 1961; Ausubel & Youssef, 1963). This significantly positive relationship between Christianity and Buddhism test scores holds up even when the effect of verbal ability is statistically controlled (Ausubel & Fitzgerald, 1961). When a parallelly organized passage about Zen Buddhism is introduced after the Buddhism passage, superior knowledge of the latter passage similarly facilitates the learning of the Zen Buddhism material when verbal ability is held constant (Ausubel & Youssef, 1963). Thus, much of the effect of overlearning—both on retaining a given unit of material and on learning related new material—is probably a reflection of the enhanced discriminability the overlearning induces. This effect can be accomplished by overlearning either the learning material itself or its anchoring ideas in cognitive structure.

When discriminability between new learning material and established ideas in cognitive structure is inadequate because of the instability or ambiguity of prior knowledge, comparative organizers that explicitly delineate similarities and differences between the two sets of ideas can significantly increase discriminability and, hence, facilitate learning and retention (Ausubel & Fitzgerald, 1961). This approach to facilitating learning and retention is probably more effective than overlearning of the new instructional material itself, since overlearning does not strengthen or clarify established concepts in cognitive structure that provide anchorage for long-term retention. When anchoring ideas in cognitive structure are *already* clear and stable, however, organizers understandably do not have a significant facilitating effect (Ausubel & Fitzgerald, 1961). Under the latter circumstances overlearning of the new material is the only feasible way of further enhancing discriminability.

Sometimes in meaningful learning and retention new learning material may be adequately discriminable in fact from existing ideas in cognitive structure, but it may still seem to be in real or seeming contradiction to these latter ideas. When this happens, the learner may peremptorily dismiss the new propositions as invalid, may try to set them apart from previously learned knowledge (compartmentalize or retain them on a rote basis), or, hopefully, may try to reconcile and integrate the two sets of conflicting ideas in relation to a more inclusive subsumer. The function of an advance organizer in this type of learning situation would be to provide just such a subsumer.

Operationally, discriminability is measured most easily by multiple-choice tests or Socratic questioning calling for fine distinctions between related or similar concepts and propositions. It may be manipulated (1) by overlearning either existing ideas in cognitive structure or related learning materials or (2) by comparative organizers that explicitly highlight, at a high level of abstraction, generality, and inclusiveness, similarities and differences between already established ideas and similar, confusable ideas in the learning material.

STABILITY AND CLARITY OF ANCHORING IDEAS

Stability of anchoring ideas refers to the maintenance of their availability over time (longevity) and clarity refers to their degree of explicitness, lucidity, and freedom from vagueness and ambiguity. The stability of either general background knowledge or of more specific anchoring ideas may be ascertained by administering a series of equivalent forms of a pretest, over a specified time interval; and it may itself be manipulated by varying the number of repetitions of such antecedent knowledge to which a group of learners of such antecedent knowledge is exposed and by the confirming and disconfirming of the effects of feedback.

Clarity can be ascertained by obtaining judgmental ratings from knowledgeable individuals of the learner's verbal explanations of various anchoring concepts and propositions. It can also be evaluated from his responses to critical questions in the "clinical interview," on the pretest, or in the course of "cognitive mapping." Clarity can be manipulated in the same way as stability and also by the corrective effects of feedback. As pointed out previously, both stability and clarity are only partial but important determinants of discriminability. Variability in stability or clarity of anchoring ideas is invariably accompanied by corresponding variability in their discriminability.

Little reliable evidence is available regarding the effect of overlearning on the relative stability and clarity (and indirectly on their discriminability) of anchoring ideas in cognitive structure and, hence, on their relative ability to enhance meaningful verbal learning and retention. Ausubel and Fitzgerald (1962) found that degree of relevant knowledge of antecedent learning material is positively related to the learning of a sequentially *dependent* passage; but the number of times that the first passage is read bears no relationship to the learning of an *otherwise* sequentially *dependent* passage if the latter includes all of the essential ideas of the first passage as introductory material (Ausubel & Youssef, 1966).

In other words, the positive transfer effect that increased stability of previously learned material has on the later *learning* of sequentially dependent material is no longer demonstrable if the essential elements of the antecedent material (the elements that make for the sequential dependence) are incorporated as introductory aspects of the second learning task. This, of course, does not imply that the stability of antecedent material in cognitive structure has no positive transfer effect on the *long-term retention* of otherwise sequentially dependent material when a summary of the antecedent material is included in the second task. Thus, the two procedures—overlearning the antecedent material and incorporating a summary of it into the second task—are by no means mutually preclusive, and can be used to complement each other in learning sequentially organized material. The previously cited work of Gagné and Paradise (1961) and of Gagné, Mayer, Garstens, and Paradise (1962) is also relevant in this connection.

Presentation of heterogeneous stimulus material that does not provide sufficient repetition to allow for mastery is not only less effective than homogeneous presentation in learning a principle, but also does not facilitate the learning of a reversal principle during the transfer period (Sassenrath, 1959). According to Bruner, "learning often cannot be translated into a generic form until there has been enough mastery of the specifics of the situation to permit the discovery of lower-order regularities which can then be recombined into higher order, more generic coding systems" (Bruner, 1957).

Reference has already been made to short-term research evidence about the relationship between existing degree of knowledge and the learning of unfamiliar material in the same subject-matter field. Students with a more extensive knowledge of Christianity are better able to learn principles of Buddhism than are students of equal academic aptitude who have less knowledge of Christianity (Ausubel & Fitzgerald, 1961). Similarly, subjects who have more *general* background knowledge in endocrinology learn and retain more unfamiliar material about the endocrinology of pubescence than do a matched control group with less general background knowledge of endocrinology (Ausubel & Fitzgerald, 1962).

In the first instance, where the new learning material (Buddhism) is specifically relatable to existing knowledge (Christianity), the facilitating effect of increased knowledge about Christianity can be attributed both to the availability of more specifically relevant anchoring ideas and to greater discriminability between the two sets of analogous ideas. In the second instance, where the new learning material (endocrinology of pubescence) is not *specifically* relatable to previously learned endocrinological principles, this general background knowledge in endocrinology probably facilitates learning and retention both by providing at least a nonspecific background basis for relating the new material to cognitive structure (combinatorial learning) and by increasing the familiarity of the pubescence material (and hence the learner's confidence in coping with it). The background knowledge here also seems to enhance the effect of an organizer. Similar results were obtained by Kuhn and Novak (1971) in a study involving instruction in "homeostasis" in an elementary biology course.

Perhaps the most important feature of the formerly widely used automated teaching devices, insofar as the facilitation of meaningful learning and retention is concerned, was not the incentive and allegedly drive-reducing (reinforcing) effects of immediate feedback,[7] but rather the extent to which such devices influenced learning by enhancing the stability and clarity of cognitive structure. By deferring the introduction of new learning material until prior material in the learning sequence was consolidated, they maximized the effect of stability of cognitive structure on new learning; and by supplying immediate feedback, these devices ruled out and corrected alternative wrong meanings, misinterpretations, ambiguities, and misconceptions before they had an opportunity to impair the clarity of cognitive structure and thereby inhibit the learning of new material.

Because of the rigorousness with which such variables as degree of consolidation and immediacy of feedback can be controlled, programmed instruction of the non-teaching machine variety can be very useful in studying the effects of the stability and clarity of cognitive structure on sequential learning. With carefully programmed instruction, however, the facilitating effect of advance organizers may not be evidenced, since the entire instructional sequence, as opposed to just an introductory organizer, can serve to augment learning (Gubrud & Novak, 1973; Kahle & Nordland, 1975).

Pedagogic Facilitation of Transfer

What are some of the pedagogic implications both of the foregoing model of the psychological structure of knowledge and of the factors that influence its accretion and organization? The major implication for teaching, perhaps, is that inasmuch as existing cognitive structure reflects the outcome of <u>all</u> previous meaningful learning, control over the veridicality, clarity, longevity in memory, and transferability of a given body of knowledge can be most effectively exercised by attempting to influence the crucial, previously designated cognitive structure variables. This is particularly important in view of the present-day geometrical increase in new knowledge.

In principle, deliberate manipulation of the relevant attributes of cognitive structure for pedagogic purposes should not meet with undue difficulty. As pointed out above, it can be accomplished:

1. *Substantively,* by using for organizational and integrative purposes those unifying concepts and propositions in a given discipline that have the widest explanatory power, inclusiveness, generalizability, and relatability to the detailed subject-matter content of that discipline;
2. *Programmability,* by employing suitable programmatic principles of ordering the sequence of subject matter, constructing its internal logic and organization, maximizing appropriately the positive effects of cognitive structure variables, and arranging practice trials most efficaciously.

Thus, transfer in school learning consists primarily of so shaping the learner's cognitive structure, by manipulating the content and arrangement of his antecedent learning experience in a particular subject-matter area, that subsequent learning and retention are maximally facilitated.

Substantive Factors Influencing Cognitive Structure

The task of identifying the particular organizing and explanatory principles in the various disciplines that manifest the widest generalizability and integrative properties is obviously a formidable and long-range educational project. However, experience with various curriculum reform movements indicates that it yields to sustained and resourceful inquiry, especially when it is possible to enlist the cooperative efforts of outstanding subject-matter specialists, talented teachers, and imaginative educational psychologists. "Correct and illuminating explanations are no more difficult and are often easier to grasp than ones that are partly correct and, therefore, too complicated and too restricted. . . . Making material interesting is in no way incompatible with presenting it soundly; indeed, a correct general explanation is often the most interesting of all" (Bruner, 1960).

The substantive objectives underlying the choice of subject-matter content in the Physical Science Study Committee Secondary School Physics Program are relevant for most disciplines: "(1) to plan a course of study in which the major developments of physics up to the present time are presented in a logical and integrated whole; (2) to present physics as an intellectual pursuit that is part of present-day human activity and achievement" (Finlay, 1959). The primary problem in implementing these objectives is

> . . . how to construct curricula that can be taught by ordinary teachers to ordinary students and that at the same time reflect clearly the basic or underlying principles of various fields of inquiry. The problem is twofold: first, how to have the basic subjects rewritten and their teaching materials revamped in such a way that the pervading and powerful ideas and attitudes relating to them are given a central role; second, how to match the levels of these materials to the capacities of students of different abilities at different grades in school (Bruner, 1960, p. 18).

The rationale of the Physical Science Study Committee for its particular choice of subject matter is clearly defensible in terms of providing a stable and widely transferable basis for the assimilation and integration of knowledge:

> The Committee has chosen to select subject matter and organize it with the intent of providing as broad and powerful a base as possible for further learning—further learning both in and beyond the classroom. Through its materials the Committee seeks to convey those aspects of science which have the deepest meaning, the widest applicability. . . .
>
> The explanatory systems of physics and how they are made have much more forward thrust as educational tools than the individual application and the discrete, unconnected explanation. Thus the PSSC has chosen for its subject matter the big over-arching ideas of physics—those that contribute most to the contemporary physicist's views of the nature of the physical world. . . . The power of the big ideas is in their wide applicability, and in the unity they bring to an understanding of what may appear superficially to be unrelated phenomena. . . . Pedagogically this choice has virtues. . . . Principal among them is the acquisition of criteria by which subject matter can be selected and organized toward the coherence the subject itself strives for (Finlay, 1960).

According to Bruner:

> . . . optimal structure refers to the set of propositions from which a larger body of knowledge can be generated, and it is characteristic that the formulation of such structure depends upon the state of advance in a particular field of knowledge. . . . Since the goodness of a structure depends upon its power for simplifying information, for generating new propositions, and for increasing the manipulability of a body of knowledge, structure must always be related to the status and gifts of the learner. Viewed in this way, the optimal structure of a body of knowledge is not absolute but relative. The major requirement is that no two sets of generating structures for the same field of knowledge be in contradiction (Bruner, 1964b).

Appropriate structure, of course, takes into account the developmental level of the pupil's cognitive functioning and his degree of subject-matter sophistication. Structure that is too elaborate in these terms constitutes more of a handicap than a facilitating device (Binter, 1963; Munro, 1969; Newman, 1957). Similarly, structure that is appropriate for the teacher is not always appropriate for the pupil. Premature acquisition of inappropriate structures may result in "closure" that inhibits the acquisition of more appropriate structures (Smedslund, 1961).

The great expansion in knowledge that is currently taking place demands special care in the selection of the "big ideas." As Ericksen (1967) states:

> . . . teachers at all levels must begin to take more active measures to reduce the curricular lag between what is "nice to know" in contrast to what the present student generation "needs to know." The slow-to-change teacher might unknowingly actually hinder the student's educational efforts to protect himself from informational obsolescence. From the Medical School faculty, for example, I have heard expressions like: "Half of what we teach will be outdated ten years from now,[8] and half of what the physician will need to know in ten years has not yet been discovered (pp. 145-146).

Coordination and integration of subject matter at the different grade levels will also become more important.

> As the high school comes closer to doing the job professors imagine for it, professors will be forced to imagine an appropriate new job for the college. If so, we must first learn that the American educational system is sequential, that changes in one level of education requires changes in others, that the task is shared by all teachers in all schools. We shall find ourselves engaged in re-examination and revision of our own programs, undergraduate and graduate. Starting late, the university must as usual scramble to catch up, to keep up, and finally to get far enough ahead to exercise its function of leadership by example as well as by precept (Diekhoff, 1964, p. 188).

Once the substantive organizational problem (identifying the basic content and organizing concepts in a given discipline) is solved, attention can be directed to the programmatic organizational problems involved in the presentation and sequential arrangement of component units. Here, it is hypothesized, various principles concerned with the efficient programming of content are applicable, irrespective of subject-matter field. These principles naturally include and reflect the influence of the previously listed cognitive structure variables—the availability of relevant anchoring ideas, their stability and clarity, and their discriminability from ideas in the learning material.

OTHER ORGANIZATIONAL WAYS OF FACILITATING TRANSFER

Progressive Differentiation

When subject matter is programmed in accordance with the principle of progressive differentiation, the most general and inclusive ideas of the discipline are presented first and are then progressively differentiated in terms of detail and specificity. This order of presentation presumably corresponds to the natural sequence of acquiring cognitive awareness and sophistication when human beings are spontaneously exposed either to an entirely unfamiliar field of knowledge or to an unfamiliar branch of a familiar body of knowledge. It also corresponds to the postulated way in which this knowledge is represented, organized, and stored in human cognitive structures.[9]

In other words, we are making two assumptions here: (1) It is less difficult for human beings to grasp the differentiated aspects of a previously learned, more inclusive whole than to formulate the inclusive whole from its previously learned differentiated parts; and (2) An individual's organization of the content of a particular subject-matter discipline in his own mind consists of a hierarchical structure in which the most inclusive ideas occupy a position at the apex of the structure and subsume progressively less inclusive and more highly differentiated propositions, concepts, and factual data.

If the human nervous system as a data-processing and -storing mechanism is so constructed that both the acquisition of new knowledge and its organization in cognitive structure conform *naturally* to the principle of progressive differentiation, it seems reasonable to suppose that optimal learning and retention occur when teachers *deliberately* order the organization and sequential arrangement of subject matter along similar lines. A more explicit way of stating the same proposition is to say that new ideas and information are learned and retained most efficiently when more inclusive and specifically relevant ideas are already available in cognitive structure to serve a subsuming role or to furnish ideational anchorage for these new ideas. Organizers, of course, exemplify the principle of progressive differentiation and serve this function in relation to any given topic or subtopic where they are used. In addition, however, it is desirable that both the arrangement of the learning material itself, within each topic or subtopic and the sequencing of the various subtopics and topics in a given course of study, also generally conform to the same principle.

Even though this latter principle seems rather self-evident, it is in fact rarely followed in actual teaching procedures or in the organization of most textbooks. The more typical practice in textbooks is to segregate topically homogeneous materials into separate chapters and subchapters and to order the arrangement of topics and subtopics (and the material within each) solely on the basis of topical relatedness without regard to their relative degree of abstraction, generality, or inclusiveness. This practice is both incompatible with the actual structure of most disciplines and incongruous with the postulated process whereby meaningful learning occurs, with the hierarchical organization of cognitive structure in terms of progressive gradations of inclusiveness from the top downwards, and with the mechanism of accretion through a process of progressive differentiation of an undifferentiated field. Thus, in most instances, students are required to learn the details of new and unfamiliar disciplines before they have acquired an adequate body of relevant explanatory subsumers at an appropriate level of inclusiveness (Ausubel, 1960).

As a result of this inappropriate practice, students and teachers are coerced into treating potentially meaningful materials as if they were rote in character, and students consequently experience unnecessary difficulty and diminished success in both learning and retention. The teaching of mathematics and science, for example, still relies heavily on the rote learning of formulas and procedural steps, on rote recognition of stereotyped "type problems," and on mechanical manipulation of symbols. In the absence of clear and stable ideas which can serve as anchoring points and organizing foci for the incorporation of new, logically meaningful material, students are trapped in a morass of incomprehension and have little choice but rotely to memorize learning tasks for examination purposes.

One outstanding example of a textbook that is organized in accordance with the principle of progressive differentiation is Boyd's (1961) famous *Textbook of Pathology.* In this book Boyd parts company with most traditional treatises on pathology, which typically consist of about twenty chapters, each devoted to describing serially the major kinds of pathological processes occurring within a particular organ or organ system. Boyd, in contrast, reserves serial consideration of the pathology of separate organ systems to the second half of his text and devotes the entire first half to such general organizing and integrative topics as the different categories of pathological processes (e.g., inflammation, allergy, degeneration, neoplasm) and their principal causes and characteristics, the various kinds of etiological agents in disease, types of humoral and tissue resistance to disease, the interaction between genic and environmental factors in the development of pathological processes, and general relationships between pathological lesions and clinical symptoms.

Progressive differentiation of cognitive structure through the programming of subject matter can be accomplished by using a hierarchical series of organizers (in descending order of inclusiveness), each organizer preceding its corresponding unit of detailed, differentiated material, and by sequencing the material within each unit in *descending* order of inclusiveness. In this way not only is an appropriately relevant and inclusive subsumer made available to provide ideational scaffolding for each component unit of differentiated subject matter, but the ideas within each unit as well as the various units in relation to each other are also progressively differentiated—organized in descending order of inclusiveness. The initial organizers, therefore, furnish anchorage at a global level before the learner is confronted with *any* of the new material. Thus, for example, a generalized model of class relationships is first provided as a general subsumer for *all* new classes, subclasses, and species before more limited subsumers are provided for the particular subclasses or species they encompass.

Hence, when undergraduates are first exposed to organizers presenting relevant and appropriately inclusive subsuming principles, they are better able to learn and retain completely unfamiliar ideational material (Ausubel, 1960). Differential analysis in another similar study showed that the facilitating effect of organizers is greatest for those individuals who have relatively poor verbal ability and who, therefore, tend spontaneously to structure such material less effectively (Ausubel & Fitzgerald, 1961). The greater retention by pro-Southern than by pro-Northern students of a controversial passage presenting the Southern point of view on the Civil War can also be explained in terms of the relative availability of appropriate subsuming ideas (Fitzgerald & Ausubel, 1963). The pro-Northern students obviously lack relevant subsumers in their cognitive structures to which the pro-Southern passage can be functionally related. The material, therefore, cannot be clearly and securely anchored to cognitive structure, competes with existing meanings, and is consequently ambiguous and subject to rapid forgetting. The pro-Southern students, on the other hand, possess relevant subsuming concepts; thus, the material can be readily anchored to cognitive structure and is also less ambiguous and subject to forgetting.

Integrative Reconciliation

The principle of integrative reconciliation of cognitive structure, when implemented through appropriate programming of instructional material, can be best described as antithetical in spirit and approach to the usual practice among textbook writers of compartmentalizing and segregating particular ideas or topics solely within their respective chapters or subchapters. Implicit in this latter practice are the assumptions (perhaps logically valid, but certainly psychologically untenable) that pedagogic considerations are adequately served if overlapping topics are handled in self-contained fashion, so that each topic is presented in only *one* of the several possible contexts where consideration is relevant and warranted. Most textbooks additionally assume that all necessary cross-referencing of related ideas can be satisfactorily performed (and customarily is) by students. Hence, little serious effort is made *explicitly* to explore relationships between related ideas, to indicate significant similarities and differences, to reconcile real or apparent inconsistencies, and to combine or integrate similar ideas that are logically relatable to each other.

Some of the undesirable consequences of this compartmentalized approach are (1) that multiple terms are used to represent concepts that are intrinsically equivalent except for contextual reference, thereby generating incalculable cognitive strain and confusion as well as encouraging rote learning; (2) that artificial barriers are erected between intrinsically related topics, obscuring important common features, and thus rendering impossible the acquisition of insights dependent upon recognition of these commonalities; (3) that adequate use is not made of relevant, previously learned ideas as a basis for subsuming and assimilating related new information; and (4) that since significant differences between apparently similar concepts are not made clear and explicit, these concepts are often perceived and retained as identical.

The principle of integrative reconciliation also applies when subject matter is organized along parallel lines, that is, when related materials are presented in serial fashion but there is no *intrinsic* sequential dependence from one topic to the next. Unlike the case in sequentially dependent subject matter, successive learning tasks are inherently independent of each other in the sense that understanding of Part II material does not presuppose understanding of Part I material. Each set of material is logically self-contained and can be adequately learned by itself without any reference to the other; order of presentation is therefore immaterial. This situation, for example, prevails in presenting alternative theoretical positions in ethics, religion, and epistemology; opposing theories of biological evolution; and different approaches to learning and personality theory in the various textbooks in which these topics are respectively relevant.

Nevertheless, although successive learning tasks of parallelly organized material are not intrinsically dependent on each other, much cognitive interaction obviously occurs between them. Earlier learned elements of a parallel sequence serve an orienting and subsuming role in relation to later presented elements. The latter are comprehended and interpreted in terms of existing understandings and paradigms provided by analogous, familiar, previously learned, and already established ideas in cognitive structure. Hence, for learning of the unfamiliar new ideas to take place, they must be adequately discriminable from the established familiar ideas; otherwise the new meanings would be so permeated by ambiguities, misconceptions, and confusions as to be partially or completely nonexistent in their own right.

If, for example, the learner cannot discriminate between new idea *A'* and old idea *A*, *A'* does not *really* exist for him; it is phenomenologically (psychologically) the same as *A*. Furthermore, even if the learner could discriminate between *A* and *A'* at the moment of learning, unless the discrimination were sharp and free from ambiguity and confusion, there would be a tendency over time for *A'* to be reduced to *A* (as the two ideas interact during the retention interval) more rapidly than is typically the case.

In some instances of meaningful learning and retention the principal difficulty is not one of discriminability but of apparent *contradiction* between established ideas in cognitive structure and new propositions in the learning material. Under these conditions the learner may summarily dismiss the new propositions as invalid, may try to compartmentalize them as isolated entities apart from previously learned knowledge, or, hopefully, may attempt integrative reconciliation under a more inclusive subsumer. Compartmentalization may be considered a common defense against anticipated forgetting in many school learning situations. By arbitrarily isolating concepts and information, one prevents confusion, interaction with, and rapid obliterative assimilation by, the more established contradictory ideas in cognitive structure. This, of course, is simply a special case of *rote* learning. Through much overlearning, relatively stable incorporation may be achieved, at least for examination purposes; but the fabric of knowledge learned in this fashion remains unintegrated and full of contradictions and is, therefore, not very viable on a long-term basis.

Ward and Davis (1939) report a study of meaningful retention in which general science was taught to junior high school pupils by means of a textbook that made a special point of reconciling and integrating new ideas with previously learned content. Periodic examinations were also given which tested knowledge of earlier as well as of recently presented material. Under these conditions, students surprisingly retained instructional material as well after sixteen weeks as on tests of immediate retention. Kastrinos (1965) found high retention of biology material for more than a year under similar instructional conditions.

Organizers may also be expressly designed to further learners' application of the principle of integrative reconciliation to their learning tasks. They do this by explicitly indicating in what ways previously learned, related ideas in cognitive structure are either basically similar to, or essentially different from, new ideas and information in the learning task. Hence, for one thing, organizers explicitly draw upon and mobilize all available ideas in cognitive structure that are relevant for and can play a subsuming role in relation to the new learning material. This maneuver effects great economy of learning effort, avoids the isolation of essentially similar ideas in separate, noncommunicable compartments, and discourages the confusing proliferation of multiple terms to represent ostensibly different but essentially equivalent ideas. In addition, organizers increase the discriminability of genuine differences between the new learning materials and seemingly analogous but often conflicting ideas in the learner's cognitive structure. This second way in which organizers purportedly promote integrative reconciliation is predicated on the assumption that if the distinguishing ideational features of the new learning task are not originally salient or readily discriminable from anchoring ideas in cognitive structure, they not only manifest low dissociability strength initially, but also lose it very rapidly because these new ideas can be adequately represented by the more established ones for memorial purposes. It is assumed, in other words, that only discriminable categorical variants of previously learned ideas have long-term retention potentialities.

Thus, if an organizer can first delineate clearly, precisely, and explicitly the principal similarities and differences between the new subordinate or correlative concepts and principles to be learned, on the one hand, and similar established ideas in cognitive structure, on the other, it seems reasonable to make two postulations: (1) The enhanced discriminability of the new anchoring ideas would enable the learner to grasp later the more detailed ideas and information in the learning passage itself with fewer ambiguities, fewer competing meanings, and fewer misconceptions suggested by the established similar ideas in cognitive structure than would otherwise be possible. (2) As these clearer, more discernible, less confused, and highly differentiated new meanings interact with their subsumers (i.e., with analogous, established, and more superordinate or combinatorial meanings during the retention interval), they would also retain their own identity longer. This is the case both because the new material is learned in a clearer, more stable, and more discriminable fashion in the first place, by virtue of the greater discriminability of the new anchoring ideas under which it is subsumed, and because more warrantedly differentiated subsumers are themselves more stable and hence better able to provide continuous secure anchorage. Comparative organizers, for example, have been successfully used in facilitating the meaningful learning and retention of an unfamiliar passage dealing with Buddhism (Ausubel & Fitzgerald, 1961; Ausubel & Youssef, 1963).

Organizers have also been used to facilitate the learning of controversial ideational material contrary to the established beliefs of the learner. The underlying hypothesis of this approach is that selective forgetting under these conditions is not so much a manifestation of selective perception and repression as an indication of the lack of adequate subsumers in cognitive structure for the stable incorporation of such conflicting material. In support of this hypothesis, an experimental group of Illinois high-school students, who studied a comparative ideational organizer prior to learning the Southern point of view about the Civil War, learned and remembered more of this material than did a control group of students who studied a purely descriptive introductory passage (Fitzgerald & Ausubel, 1963).

Sequential Organization

The availability of relevant anchoring ideas in the learner's cognitive structure for use in meaningful verbal learning and retention may obviously be maximized by taking advantage of natural sequential dependencies among the component topical divisions of a discipline—of the fact that the understanding of a given topic often logically presupposes the prior understanding of some antecedently related topic. Typically, the necessary antecedent knowledge is more inclusive and general than the sequentially dependent material, but this is not always true (for example, in superordinate learning). In any case, by arranging the order of topics in a given subject-matter field as far as possible in accordance with these sequential dependencies, the learning of each unit, in turn, not only becomes an achievement in its own right, but also constitutes specifically relevant ideational scaffolding for the next item in the sequence.

In sequential school learning knowledge of earlier appearing material in the sequence plays much the same role as an organizer in relation to later appearing material in the sequence. It constitutes a relevant ideational foundation, and hence a crucial limiting condition, for learning the latter material when the influence of both verbal ability and general background knowledge is held constant (Ausubel & Fitzgerald, 1962; Gubrud & Novak, 1973; Royer & Cable, 1975; West & Fensham, 1976). For maximally effective learning, however, a separate organizer should be provided for each unit of material. Thus, sequential organization of subject matter can be very effective, since each new increment of knowledge serves as an anchoring post for subsequent learning. This presupposes, of course, that the antecedent step is always thoroughly consolidated. Perhaps the chief pedagogic advantage of the once popular, but now all but forgotten, teaching machine lay in its ability to control this crucial variable in sequential learning.

Another advantage of programmed instruction is its careful sequential arrangement and gradation of difficulty, which ensure that each attained increment in learning serves as an appropriate foundation and anchoring post for the learning and retention of subsequent items in the ordered sequence. Adequate programming of materials also presupposes maximum attention to such matters as lucidity, organization, and the explanatory and integrative power of substantive content.

Sequential arrangement of learning tasks relies, in part, on the general facilitating effect of the availability of relevant anchoring ideas in cognitive structure on meaningful learning and retention. For any given topic, however, there is the additional problem of ascertaining what the *particular* most effective sequence is. This involves consideration of logical task analysis, progressive differentiation, developmental level of cognitive functioning, integrative reconciliation, and learning hierarchies.

Further, in superordinate learning it is essential to ensure that both subordinate concepts and propositions and the component conceptual elements of each proposition are previously mastered. Gagné (1977) states the problem very well in the following statement:

> The planning that precedes effective design for learning is a matter of specifying with some care what may be called the *learning structure* of any subject to be acquired. In order to determine what comes before what, the subject must be analyzed in terms of the learning involved in it. The acquisition of knowledge is a process in which every new capability builds on a foundation established by previously learned capabilities. . . . The importance of mapping the sequence of learnings is mainly just this: That it enables one to avoid the mistakes that arise from "skipping" essential steps in the acquisition of knowledge of a [particular] content area (Gagné, 1977).

This latter position, of course, is consonant with Gagné's view that learning generally proceeds from the bottom upwards or from the specific to the general, in contrast to our own view that subject-matter learning principally exemplifies the principles of subsumption and progressive differentiation or from the top downwards.

Consolidation

By insisting on consolidation or mastery of ongoing lessons before new learning material is introduced, one makes sure of continued subject-matter readiness and success in sequentially organized learning. This kind of learning presupposes, of course, that the preceding steps are always clear, stable, and well-organized. If they are not, the learning of all subsequent steps is jeopardized. Thus, new material in the sequence should never be introduced until all previous steps are thoroughly mastered. This principle also applies to those kinds of intratask learning in which each component task (as well as entire bodies of subject matter) tends to be compound in content and to manifest an internal organization of its own. Consolidation, of course, is achieved through confirmation, correction, and clarification, in the course of feedback, and through differential practice and review in the course of repeated exposure, with feedback, to learning material.

Abundant experimental research (Duncan, 1959; Morrisett & Hovland, 1959) has confirmed the proposition that prior learnings are not transferable to new learning tasks until they are first overlearned. Overlearning, in turn, requires an adequate number of adequately spaced repetitions or reviews, sufficient intratask repetitiveness prior to intra- and intertask diversification, and opportunity for differential practice of the more difficult components of a task. Frequent testing and provision of feedback, especially with test items demanding fine discrimination among alternatives varying in degree of correctness, also enhance consolidation by confirming, clarifying, and correcting previous learnings.

In directly sequential tasks, where the learning of Part II materials presupposes full understanding of Part I materials (i.e., where Part II is *sequentially dependent* on Part I), the stability and clarity of the antecedent material crucially affect the learning and retention of the later appearing material (Ausubel & Fitzgerald, 1962; Gubrud & Novak, 1973; Kahle & Nordland, 1975).[10]

The stability and clarity of existing cognitive structure are important both for the depth of anchorage they provide for related new learning tasks as well as for their effects on the discriminability of these new tasks. The discriminability of new learning material, as shown by several of the experiments reported above, is additionally in large measure a function of the clarity and stability of existing concepts in the learner's cognitive structure. Even in the learning of controversial ideas, contrary to prevailing belief (for instance, the learning by Illinois students of the Southern point of view about the Civil War), the more knowledgeable students from the North, namely, those who knew more generally about the Civil War period, are better able to learn and remember the "other side" arguments (Fitzgerald & Ausubel, 1963), presumably because they find them more discriminable from established ideas than do less knowledgeable subjects. Thus, much of the effort of overlearning—both on retaining a given unit of material and on learning related new material—is probably a reflection of the enhanced discriminability that can be induced by increasing the clarity and stability of either the learning material itself or that of its subsumers.

Mastery learning, which has evolved in the past half-century, is perhaps the best example of the principle of consolidation in school learning, particularly in individualized learning settings. Bloom (1974) summarized evidence indicating that interstudent variability in the amount of time required to achieve mastery is greater when measured in terms of elapsed than of actual time. With increased experience in mastery learning, both types of variability tend to decrease.

Much additional research is needed to establish both the most economical degree of consolidation and the most efficient ways of effecting it (e.g., repetition, distribution of practice, feedback, use of organizers, internal logic of the material) that will optimally facilitate the learning and retention of sequentially and parallelly organized subject matter. Such knowledge will obviously have greater pedagogic utility if the effects of these latter variables are tested together with consideration of the pupils' level of cognitive maturity, academic ability, and degree of relevant subject-matter sophistication.

Other Pedagogic Ways of Enhancing Transfer

Some of the principal pedagogic means of facilitating transfer through the manipulation of cognitive structure variables have been presented in prior sections. According to this view, the incorporation of clear, stable, and integrative subsumers in cognitive structure is the most efficacious way of promoting transfer. Although we have been primarily concerned with meaningful reception learning, the same general principle applies as well to meaningful discovery learning. Transferability, in other words, is largely a function of the relevance, meaningfulness, clarity, stability, integrativeness, and explanatory power of the originally learned subsumers that are later doing the transfer. Rote learnings have little transfer value. Generalizations manifest transferability only when they are thoroughly grasped (understood), overlearned (Mandler, 1954), and take into account the pupil's level of cognitive functioning. For elementary school children this usually requires the use of concrete-empirical props.

Transfer, of course, does not take place automatically without deliberate effort to appreciate and practice the opportunities that are present for transfer in a given learning situation. The learner must also perceive the relationship of the training to the criterial task (Ervin, 1960). Geometry, for example, can increase ability to think logically in other subject-matter areas only if awareness of this applicability is *deliberately* induced (Fawcett, 1935; Hartung, 1942). The same is true of the teaching of genetics to reduce superstitious thinking and racial prejudice[11] and of the transferability of Latin to English and second-language learning. In all probability, however, the same investment of time in *direct* study of the target language, as opposed to prior study of Latin, would yield more satisfactory learning results. Merely telling learners that previous learnings might be useful in other situations increases transfer (Dorsey & Hopkins, 1930).

Transferability also depends upon the application of a principle, acquired during original learning, to as many specific contexts as possible (Hull, 1920). Hull showed that familiarity with a concept in a large number of different specific contexts and illustrative forms is more efficacious for generalization than is intensive experience with just a few illustrations, providing, of course, that mastery occurs within each context. Nagati (1976) obtained comparable findings in rule learning. Thus, transfer can be facilitated by providing opportunity for learned principles to operate in as wide a variety of situations as possible, by explicitly emphasizing the similarity between training and criterial tasks, and by presenting the latter tasks continuously or in close succession. In the case of vocational learning, knowledge and skill become more transferable when they are learned originally in realistic and "real-life" situations that are similar to the settings in which final utilization of the training will take place.

Some tasks are so complex, however, that they cannot initially be learned directly as they will be encountered later in a "real-life" situation. The learner must be trained first on a simplified version of the task and then transfer this training to an attempt at mastering the task itself (Baker & Osgood, 1954). For example, in learning a complex tracking task (Lawrence & Goodwin, 1954) or oral comprehension of a foreign language, initial slowing of the auditory component of the learning task is desirable. In some instances the separate components of a very complex performance must be mastered separately before the task as a whole can be attempted with any hope of success (Eckstrand & Wickens, 1954).

The Effects of Verbalization on Transfer

We have already considered the general facilitating role of language in cognitive functioning as well as the mediating function of implicit verbal responses in concept formation. Overing and Travers (1966) found that verbalization of general principles prior to application facilitates problem solving. Building on the earlier work of Ewert and Lambert (1932), Gagné and Smith (1962) also demonstrated the positive effect of verbalization on the discovery of general principles and on their transferability to problem solving, especially in relation to more difficult problems. Their study deals with the verbal-nonverbal dimension of learning rather than with the reception-discovery or rote-meaningful dimensions. It has important implications for pedagogic practice because the findings challenge the widely accepted tenet of Progressive Education that verbal learning is necessarily rote in character and that only nonrepresentational experience is transferable from one problem-solving situation to another. Although it is true that expository teaching and reception learning are typically verbal, discovery learning, as Gagné and Smith (1962) point out, may be either verbal or nonverbal. Their isolation of the verbal-nonverbal variable from the reception-discovery and rote-meaningful variables represents an important methodological advance in the study of problem solving. Thune and Ericksen (1960) report basically similar findings. When their subjects had sufficient concrete experience with the learning task (operating a calculator) generally to understand it, abstract instruction about the mechanism of a calculator was a more efficacious transfer factor than specific operating experience on a single calculator.

Ervin (1960c) also found that verbal instruction in the relevant physical principles underlying a motor task increases transfer to an analogous and more difficult motor performance. This effect, however, does not occur until subjects are able to perceive both the similarity between the two motor tasks and the relationship between verbal principles and performance. Verbal generalization is particularly important for concept attainment in a cognitively sophisticated learner (Heidbreder & Zimmerman, 1955).

THE ROLE OF TRANSFER IN EDUCATION

It is obviously impossible for classroom learning to prepare students to cope with every situation they will face in "real-life" contexts. Further, even if this were possible, the primary goal or function of education still would not be to provide students only with that knowledge that is necessarily applicable to the everyday problems of living. This "social-utility" objective of education has long since been discarded as insufficient and impracticable. In most instances of nonvocational classroom learning, the goal of transfer is considered accomplished if prior learning experience facilitates the learning of subsequent *classroom* learning tasks—even if the knowledge so acquired is neither applicable, nor even applied to, problems outside the classroom. Of course, if the knowledge *is* applicable to the problems of living, so much the better; but this is not the primary objective of transfer in general education.

Another relevant issue here, as indicated earlier, is that inability to apply knowledge in problem-solving situations is not necessarily proof of lack of understanding of the material in question. This is the case because the ability to apply knowledge successfully in problem-solving situations also depends on many other variables completely unrelated to understanding of the underlying principles.

In training students for particular professions, general theoretical principles are taught in the belief that they have considerable transfer value for the solution of practical professional problems.[12] In addition, students are trained in specialized problem-solving skills and methods of inquiry related to their particular professions. How well a particular trainee will be able to utilize his theoretical knowledge in practice, however, is highly related to his ability to apply this knowledge in problem-solving situations. Informal long observation of consistently good and poor problem solvers in the professions suggests that the "application" component of problem-solving ability is less trainable than the "knowledge" component. It may thus be more feasible to enhance problem-solving ability by improving the student's grasp and functional retention of theoretical knowledge than by training him directly in problem-solving skills.

NOTES

[1]This approach does not in any way discount the spontaneous availability of relevant ideas already in cognitive structure (derived from antecedent learning) for the learning of sequentially dependent material. Advance organizers, in fact, are introduced only when such *appropriately* relevant ideas are *not* otherwise present in cognitive structure. Even in the latter case, the organizer makes explicit reference to whatever relevant material already exists.

[2]In preschool education, where the logical or classificatory processes involved in organizing meaningful reception learning are not implicitly known to learners as they are in older pupils, "process" as well as content organizers have been used successfully to enhance learning (Lawton, 1977; Lawton & Wanska, 1977). In learners of all ages, however, explicit awareness of the sequence of epistemological questions in scientific method that must be answered, either in discovery learning or in expository presentation of principles of scientific method, should be helpful. Gowin's (1977) "Vee" is a heuristic device designed to help learners become explicitly aware of the methodological and procedural issues involved in discovering new knowledge.

[3]When the learning task is particularly difficult, however, organizers may differentially benefit high-ability students (Grotelueschen, 1967) and those with more background knowledge (Ausubel & Fitzgerald, 1962) by making it possible for them to learn material that would in any case be beyond the capability of less able and less sophisticated students (Barnes & Clawson, 1975; Grotelueschen & Sjogren, 1968).

[4]In a review of numerous studies Novak, Ring, and Tamir (1971) found that, in general, current achievement level was predicted best by pretests or other background indicators that are closely related to the specific learning tasks comprising current level of achievement.

[5]The "Hawthorne effect" refers to the improvement in criterial task performance induced by some novel but superficial aspects of the treatment given the experimental group (or simply by the fact that this group is singled out for special treatment) rather than by the postulated experimental variable. It can be avoided by using a control group that is given an overtly similar but intrinsically different experimental treatment than that given to the experimental group.

[6]It has been experimentally demonstrated that learners experience considerable difficulty in differentiating cognitively between the meanings of existing ideas in cognitive structure and analogous new ideas that are presented to them in the instructional material (Johnson, Bransford, & Solomon, 1973).

[7]The reinforcement value of feedback, as conceived by Skinner, is discounted by the fact that subjects who make no spontaneous overt response which can be

reinforced (who respond covertly or merely read the correct response), generally learn and retain programmed verbal material just as well as subjects who independently and overtly construct their own responses (Krumboltz, 1961).

[8]This assertion by Ericksen, of course, vastly overstates the case. *Basic* principles in medicine, as in all sciences, generally tend to manifest impressive longevity.

[9]This proposition really restates the principle that subsumptive learning is less difficult than superordinate learning. The argument for using organizers rests on the same principle. It is appreciated, however, that the learning of certain highly general and inclusive propositions requires the synthesis of previously acquired subordinate concepts or propositions (superordinate learning) (Gagné, 1962). The need for periodic superordinate learnings, however, does not negate the proposition that both the psychological organization of knowledge and the optimal organization of subject matter *generally* exemplify the principle of progressive differentiation.

[10]Consolidation (through correction and review) of each successive part of a hierarchically organized task does *not* facilitate the *learning* of later segments of the task when a summary and correction review of the *entire* task are made part of the terminal test on the material (Merrill, 1965). The results of this experiment are therefore consistent with those of Ausubel and Youssef's (1966) study, in which a summary of Part I was presented as an introduction to Part II, thereby making Part II *no longer* sequentially dependent upon Part I.

[11]This does not necessarily imply that a grand heuristic strategy, that can be applied to all disciplines, is discoverable, or that critical-thinking ability can be enhanced by teaching general principles of logic apart from specific subject-matter content. It simply means that in certain instances, specific models or analogies may have relevance for, and heuristic value on, a metaphorical interdisciplinary basis, and that certain substantive or methodological principles have applicability to more than one discipline, provided that their interdisciplinary relevance and implications are made explicit.

[12]The author's choice of medical education to illustrate pedagogic principles of transfer in professional training was partly determined by his own first-hand experience as a medical student, intern, resident, and medical practitioner.

REFERENCES

Anderson, R. E., Spiro, R. J., & Anderson, M. C. Schemata as scaffolding for the representation of information in connected discourse. *American Educational Research Journal,* 1978, *15,* 433–440.

Ausubel, D. P. *Educational psychology: A cognitive view.* New York: Holt, Rinehart & Winston, 1968.

Ausubel, D. P., & Blake, E. Proactive inhibition in the forgetting of verbal school material. *Journal of Educational Research,* 1958, *52,* 145–149.

Ausubel, D. P., & Fitzgerald, D. Organizer, general background, and antecedent learning variables in sequential verbal learning. *Journal of Educational Psychology,* 1962, *53,* 243–249.

Ausubel, D. P., & Fitzgerald, D. The role of discriminability in meaningful verbal learning and retention. *Journal of Educational Psychology,* 1961, *52,* 266–274.

Ausubel, D. P., & Schwartz, G. The effect of a generalizing-particularizing dimension of cognitive style on the retention of prose material. *Journal of General Psychology,* 1977, *87,* 55–58.

Ausubel, D. P., & Youssef, M. The role of discriminability in meaningful parallel learning. *Journal of Educational Psychology,* 1963, *54,* 331–386.

Baker, R. A., & Osgood, S. W. Discrimination transfer along a pitch continuum. *Journal of Experimental Psychology,* 1954, *48,* 241–246.

Barnes, B., & Clauson, E. V. Do advance organizers facilitate learning? *Review of Educational Research,* 1975, *45,* 637–659.

Beberman, M. *An emerging program of secondary school mathematics.* Cambridge, Mass.: Harvard University Press, 1958.

Berkowitz, L. Leveling tendencies on the complexity-simplicity dimension. *Journal of Personality,* 1957, *25,* 743–751.

Binter, A. R. Two ways of teaching percent. *Elementary School Journal,* 1963, *63,* 261–265.

Birch, H. G., & Rabinowitz, H. S. The negative effect of previous experience on productive thinking. *Journal of Experimental Psychology,* 1951, *41,* 121–125.

Bloom, B. S. Time and learning. *American Psychologist,* 1974, *29,* 682–688.

Boyd, W. *A textbook of pathology* (7th ed.). Philadelphia: Lea & Febiger, 1961.

Bransford, J. D., & Johnson, M. K. Contextual prerequisites for understanding: Some investigations of comprehension and recall. *Journal of Verbal Learning & Verbal Behavior,* 1972, *11,* 717–826.

Bruner, J. S. Going beyond the information given. In *Contemporary approaches to cognition.* Cambridge, Mass.: Harvard University Press, 1957.

Bruner, J. S. Some theorems on instruction illustrated with reference to mathematics. In *Theories of learning and instruction,* 63rd Yearbook, Nat'l. Soc. Stud. Educ. Chicago: University of Chicago Press, 1964, Part I, pp. 306–335.

Bruner, J. S. *The process of education.* Cambridge, Mass.: Harvard University Press, 1960.

Cox, J. W. Some experiments on formal training in the acquisition of skill. *Journal of Psychology,* 1933, *24,* 67–87.

Cronbach, L. J. Issues current in educational psychology. *Monographs of the Society for Research in Child Development,* 1965, *30* (Serial No. 99), 109–125.

Detambel, M. H., & Stolurow, L. M. Stimulus sequence and concept learning. *Journal of Experimental Psychology,* 1956, *51,* 34–40.

Dorsey, M. N., & Hopkins, L. T. The influence of attitude upon transfer. *Journal of Educational Psychology,* 1930, *21,* 410–417.

Duncan, C. P. Transfer in motor learning as a function of first-task learning and intra-task similarity. *Journal of Experimental Psychology,* 1953, *45,* 1–11.

Eckstrand, G. W., & Wickens, D. P. Transfer of perceptual set. *Journal of Experimental Psychology,* 1954, *47,* 274–278.

Ericksen, S. C. The zigzag curve of learning. In *Instruction: Some contemporary viewpoints* (L. Siegel, Ed.). San Francisco: Chandler, 1967, pp. 141–180.

Ervin, S. M. Transfer effects of learning a verbal generalization. *Child Development,* 1960, *31,* 537–554.

Fawcett, H. P. Teaching for transfer. *Mathematics Teacher,* 1935, *28,* 465–472.

Finlay, G. C., Secondary school physics: The Physical Science Study Committee. *American Journal of Physics,* 1960, *28,* 574–581.

Fitzgerald, D., & Ausubel, D. P. Cognitive versus affective factors in the learning and retention of controversial material. *Journal of Educational Psychology,* 1963, *54,* 73–84.

Gagné, E. Long-term retention of information following learning from prose. *Review of Educational Research,* 1978, *48,* 629–665.

Gagné, R. M. The acquisition of knowledge. *Psychological Review,* 1962, *69,* 355–365.

Gagné, R. M., & Paradise, N. E. Abilities and learning sets in knowledge acquisition. *Psychological Monographs,* 1961, *75,* No. 14 (Whole No. 518).

Gagné, R. M., & Smith, E. C. A study of the effects of verbalization on problem solving. *Journal of Experimental Psychology,* 1962, *63,* 12–16.

Groteleneschen, A. D., & Sjogren, D. D. Effects of diffferentially structured learning materials and learning tasks on learning and transfer. *American Educational Research Journal,* 1968, *5,* 191–202.

Gubrud, A. R., & Novak, J. D. Learning achievement and the efficiency of learning the concept of vector addition at three different grade levels. *Science Education,* 1973, *57,* 179–191.

Harlow, H. F. The formation of learning sets. *Psychological Review,* 1949, *56,* 51–65.

Hartley, J., & Davies, I. K. Preinstructional strategies: The role of pretests, behavioral objectives, overviews and advance organizers. *Review of Educational Research,* 1976, *46,* 239–265.

Hartung, M. L. Teaching of mathematics in senior high school and junior college. *Review of Educational Research,* 1942, *12,* 425–434.

Heidbreder, E. F., & Zimmerman, E. Problem solving in children and adults. IX. Semantic efficiency and concept attainment. *Journal of Psychology,* 1950, *40,* 320.

Holzman, P. S., & Gardner, R. W. Leveling, sharpening, and memory reorganization. *Journal of Abnormal & Social Psychology,* 1960, *61,* 175–180.

Hull, C. L. Quantitative aspects of the evolution of concepts. *Psychological Monographs,* 1920, *28* (Whole No. 123).

Hyram, G. H. An experiment in developing critical thinking in children. *Journal of Experimental Education,* 1957, *26,* 125–132.

Jenkins, J. R., & Bausile, R. B. Cognitive structure variables in prose learning. *Journal of Reading Behavior,* 1976, *8,* 47–66.

Johnson, M. K., Bransford, J. D., & Solomon, S. K. Memory for test implications of sentences. *Journal of Experimental Psychology,* 1973, *98,* 203–205.

Joyce, B., & Weil, M. *Models of teaching.* Englewood Cliffs, N.J.: Prentice-Hall, 1972.

Kagan, J., Moss, H., & Sigel, I. E. Psychological significance of styles of perception. In J. C. Wright & J. Kagan (Eds.), *Basic cognitive processes in children. Monographs of the Society for Research in Child Development,* 1963, *28,* 73–112.

Kahle, J. B., & Nordland, F. H. The effect of an absence organizer when utilized with carefully sequenced audio-tutorial units. *Journal of Research in Science Teaching,* 1975, *12,* 63–67.

Krumboltz, J. D. Meaningful learning and retention: Practice and reinforcement variables. *Review of Educational Research,* 1961, *31,* 535–546.

Kuhn, D. J., & Novak, J. D. A study of cognitive simptron in the life sciences. *Science Education,* 1971, *53,* 309–320.

Lawrence, D. H., & Goodwin, W. R. Transfer of training behavior in two levels of speed. *USAF Personnel Center Research Bulletin,* 1954, No. AFPTRC TR 54–70.

Lawton, J. T. The development of causal and logical connectives. *British Journal of Educational Psychology,* 1977, *47,* 81–84.

Lawton, J. T., & Wanska, S. K. *An analytical study of the use of advance organizers in facilitating children's learning.* Unpublished manuscript, University of Wisconsin, 1976.

Leggitt, D. Measuring progress in working in ninth-grade civics. *School Review,* 1934, *42,* 676–687.

Leventhal, H., & Singer, D. L. Cognitive complexity, impression formation, and impression change. *Journal of Personality,* 1964, *32,* 210–226.

Mayer, R. E. Can advance organizers influence meaningful learning? *Review of Educational Research,* 1979, *49,* 371–383.

Mayer, R. E., & Brobage. Effects of advance organizers on the pattern of recall protocols. Paper presented at meeting of the Psychonomic Society, 1978.

Mayer, R. E., Streis, C. C., & Greeno, J. G. Acquisition of understanding and skill in relation to subjects' preparation and meaningfulness of instruction. *Journal of Educational Psychology,* 1975, *67,* 331–350.

Merrill, M. D. Correction and review on successive parts in learning a hierarchical task. *Journal of Educational Psychology,* 1965, *56,* 225–234.

Morrisett, L., & Hovland, C. L. A comparison of three kinds of training in human problem solving. *Journal of Experimental Psychology,* 1959, *58,* 52–55.

Munro, B. C. Meaning and learning. *Alberta Journal of Educational Research,* 1959, *5,* 268–281.

Munsinger, H., & Kessen, W. Uncertainty, structure, and preference. *Psychological Monographs,* 1964, *78,* no. 9 (Whole No. 586).

Nataga, H. Effect of number and irregular forms of exemplars on rule acquisition. *Psychologia,* 1976, *19,* 94–101.

Newman, S. E. Student vs. instructor design of an experimental method. *Journal of Educational Psychology,* 1957, *56,* 140–147.

Novak, J. D., Ring, D. G., & Tamir, P. Interpretation of research findings in terms of Ausubel's theory and implications for science education. *Science Education,* 1971, *55,* 483–526.

Overing, R. L. R., & Travers, R. M. W. Effect upon transfer of variations in training conditions. *Journal of Educational Psychology*, 1966, *57*, 179–188.

Paul, I. H. Studies in remembering: The reproduction of connected and extended verbal material. *Psychological Issues*, 1959, *1*, no. 2 (Whole No. 2).

Peeck, J. Effect of prequestions on delayed retention of prose material. *Journal of Educational Psychology*, 1970, *60*, 241–246.

Postman, L. Learned principles of organization in memory. *Psychological Monographs*, 1954, *68* (Whole No. 314).

Rickards, J. A. Processing effects of advance organizers interspersed in text. *Reading Research Quarterly*, 1975, *11*, 599–622.

Rickards, J. A., & McCormick, C. B. Delayed retention of superordinate and coordinate stalemates inserted in text. *Psychological Reports*, 1976, *38*, 210.

Rickards, J. P., & Di Vesta, F. J. Types and frequency of questions in processing textual material. *Journal of Educational Psychology*, 1974, *66*, 354–362.

Ring, D. G., & Novak, J. D. The effects of cognitive structure variables on achievement in college chemistry. *Journal of Research in Science Teaching*, 1971, *8*, 325–333.

Rothkopf, E. Z., & Bibiscos, E. Selective facilitative effects of interspersed questions on learning from written material. *Journal of Educational Psychology*, 1967, *58*, 56–61.

Royer, J., M., & Cable, G. W. Facilitating learning in connected discourse. *Journal of Educational Psychology*, 1975, *12*, 393–397.

Sassenrath, J. M. Learning without awareness and transfer of learning sets. *Journal of Educational Psychology*, 1959, *50*, 205–211.

Siegel, L., & Siegel L. C. Educational set: A determinant of acquisition. *Journal of Educational Psychology*, 1965, *56*, 1–12.

Skelton, R. B. High-school foreign language study and freshman performance. *School and Society*, 1957, *85*, 203–205.

Smith, B. O. Critical thinking. In *Recent research developments and their implications for teacher education*. 13th Yearbook of American Association of College Teachers of Education. Washington, D.C.: The Association, 1960, 84–96.

Smock, C. D. The relationship between "intolerance of ambiguity," generalization, and speed of perceptual closure. *Child Development*, 1957, *28*, 27–36.

Strom, I. M. Research in grammar and usage and its implication for teaching and writing. *Bulletin, School of Education, Indiana University*, 1960, 36.

Suppes, P., & Ginsberg, R. Experimental studies of mathematical concept formation in young children. *Science Education*, 1963, *46*, 230–240.

Swenson, C. H. College performance of students with high and low school marks when academic aptitude is controlled. *Journal of Educational Research*, 1957, *50*, 597–603.

Uhlmann, F. W., & Saltz, E. Retention of anxiety material as a function of cognitive differentiation. *Journal of Personality & Social Psychology*, 1965, *1*, 55–62.

Vannoy, J. S. Generality of cognitive complexity-simplicity as a personality construct. *Journal of Personal & Social Psychology*, 1965, *2*, 385–396.

Ward, A. H., & Davis, R. A. Acquisition and retention of factual information in seventh grade general science during a semester of eighteen weeks. *Journal of Educational Psychology*, 1939, *30*, 116–125.

West, L. H. T., & Fenshaw, P. J. Prior knowledge or advance organizers as effective variables in chemical learning. *Journal of Research in Science Teaching,* 1976, *13,* 297–306.

Wittrock, M. C. Effect of certain sets upon complex verbal learning. *Journal of Educational Psychology,* 1963, *54,* 85–88.

Woodrow, H. The effect of type of training on transference. *Journal of Educational Psychology,* 1927, *18,* 159–172.

CHAPTER 7

PRACTICE AND MOTIVATIONAL FACTORS IN MEANINGFUL LEARNING AND RETENTION

THE ROLE, MEDIATION, AND EFFECTS OF PRACTICE IN MEANINGFUL LEARNING AND RETENTION[1]

The significance of practice and drill in meaningful learning and retention has, in my opinion, been unwarrantedly ignored or downgraded (Gagné, 1962). In many educational circles drill is viewed pejoratively as the hallmark of rote learning. Practice is obviously less important, relatively speaking, in meaningful than in rote learning, because in the latter variety of learning, what is learned cannot be related nonarbitrarily to any ideas in the learner's cognitive structure, and, thus, can only be retained beyond short periods of time by dint of much effortful repetition. Nevertheless, repetition is still a very significant variable that must be reckoned with if we are concerned with long-term meaningful learning and retention, and with transfer to related, sequentially dependent aspects of subject matter.

Although only a single presentation of relatively simple new ideas to a sophisticated learner often suffices to result in long-term retention, more complex ideas generally require a sufficient number of appropriately spaced reviews (overlearning) in order to be retained over longer periods of time and in order to be sufficiently clear and stable to have transfer value for learning related new ideas. Also, because the products of meaningful learning are both intrinsically less difficult than rote learning, and, thus, less vulnerable to rapid forgetting, longer intervals between practice sessions (review rather than practice) are possible.

Repetition enhances learning in essentially two different ways: (1) Shortly after initial learning, before much forgetting occurs, it is able to *consolidate* the learned material most effectively and also to bring about the learning of more subtle nuances and implications that were missed on the first presentation. (2) later, after considerable forgetting occurs, it gives the learner an opportunity to profit from (and, thus, to avoid in later presentations) his awareness of negative factors (such as ambiguity or confusion with similar ideas) responsible for such forgetting. It also enables him or her selectively to focus attention and effort on those components of the learning task that are idiosyncratically most difficult to remember.

In this book, on the grounds of the available empirical evidence, learning is assumed to be an incremental or gradual process (i.e., essentially the increased learning and retention that results after one or more repetitions of a learning trial; face plausibility; the need for multiple practice trials to effect more difficult learning and retention over longer intervals; overlearning; and transfer). These latter outcomes of the effects of repetition are probably largely correct despite the fact, as the nonincremental theorists point out, that the substance of much relatively easy, potentially meaningful material can be grasped after only one reading. The fallacy of the nonincremental position, however, inheres in the unwarranted generalization of the latter outcome of atypical "single-trial" learning to *all* levels of difficulty of the learning material; all lengths of the retention interval; and all degrees of desired precision of retention and of transferability of learning.

Practice is not a cognitive structure variable itself but is one of the principal factors (along with instructional material variables) influencing cognitive structure. The most immediate effect of practice is to increase the stability and clarity, and, hence, the dissociability strength, of the emergent new meanings in cognitive structure that are currently being learned. In turn, the increments and decrements in the stability and clarity of the new meanings (and the correlated changes in their dissociability strength) accompanying their initial learning, intertrial forgetting, and later learning, facilitate the learner's assimilation of the instructional material by related ideas in his cognitive structure during subsequent trials. The changes in cognitive structure wrought by assimilation during the first trial (namely, the establishment of the new meanings), also "sensitize" the learner to the potential meanings inherent in the material. Additionally, the forgetting that occurs between longer-separated successive repetitions or reviews tends to "immunize" the learner (i.e., enables him to take preventive steps) against further forgetting on subsequent trials. Finally, the consolidation of this new material, as a result of practice, makes available in cognitive structure stable new anchoring ideas for other related learning tasks introduced at a later date.

Practice, therefore, modifies cognitive structure in at least four different ways and thereby enhances meaningful learning and retention:

1. It increases the dissociability strength of the newly learned meanings for a given trial and thereby facilitates their retention.
2. It enhances the learner's meaningful responsiveness to subsequent presentations of the same material ("sensitizing effect").
3. It enables the learner to profit from intertrial forgetting ("immunizing" effect) by becoming aware of negative factors causing it and accordingly by avoiding or counteracting them.
4. It facilitates the learning and retention of related new learning tasks.

Actually, for practice to result in meaningful mastery of material the only really essential conditions are that: (1) the learning task be logically meaningful; (2) the learner exhibit a meaningful learning set and possess the necessary anchoring ideas; and (3) the number, distribution, sequence, and organization of practice trials conform to empirically established principles of efficient learning and retention. The uncontrived or unstructured quality of practice is an unessential condition of effective meaningful learning. Moreover, it often leads to no meaningful mastery whatsoever. This is the case because incidental practice is typically haphazard in terms of frequency and distribution of trials. Last, the spontaneous, unstructured organization of learning experiences is more frequently than not inconsistent with established criteria of effective programming in meaningful learning and retention.

Research evidence demonstrates invariably and unequivocally that frequency (repetition, practice) of presentation of the instructional material facilitates meaningful learning and retention (Thorndike, 1931) for the reasons specified above. This is the case not only when the identical instructional material is directly and straightforwardly repeated one or more times, but also indirectly (1) when only new contextual material is presented to the learner simultaneously with the learning task itself in lieu of straight repetition and (2) when an overlapping part of the content of the learning passage has been mastered previously and has, thus, become prior knowledge itself, and, therefore, is able to enhance meaningful learning of the instructional material in much the same manner that frequency customarily operates. Another possibility is that repetition facilitates the availability, stability, clarity, and discriminability of the previously learned overlapping content, now serving both as anchoring ideas and as cognitive structure variables (stability, etc.) for the entire learning passage.

The Role and Effects of Frequency in Meaningful versus Rote Learning and Retention

The role and significance of frequency are different for meaningful than for rote learning and retention precisely because rote and meaningful learning processes themselves are so different from one another. Repeated encounters with the same array of stimulation presumably enhance rote learning and retention by increasing the strength of discrete, arbitrary, and verbatim associative linkages, and/or their resistance to the short- and long-term interfering effects of prior and subsequent learning material. The same repetition, on the other hand, presumably enhances meaningful learning and retention by increasing the dissociability strength of internalized instructional materials that have been nonarbitrarily and nonverbatimly incorporated by an existing (anchoring) concept or proposition in cognitive structure. In other words, repetition enhances the emergence of clear and stable meanings and their resistance to forgetting in the course of meaningful learning and retention.

Thus, it is reasonable to assume that sheer repetition would play an even more significant role in the learning and retention (short- or long-term) of discrete and arbitrary associations, largely isolated from, or only arbitrarily related to, cognitive structure, than it would in the learning and longer-term retention of substantive, logically meaningful materials that can be incorporated within that structure (Peterson et al., 1955). In meaningful learning situations, such other factors as the availability of clear and stable anchoring ideas, the discriminability between these anchoring ideas and the learning task, and the internal logic and lucidity (logical meaningfulness) of the learning task also undoubtedly detract somewhat from the role played by repetition because of their preemptive importance as causal factors. Nevertheless, the influence of repetition is still considerable in the establishment and consolidation of meanings and in the enhancement of their resistance to decremental processes. In any case, it cannot be dismissed as basically extrinsic to the process whereby increments in availability are effected.

From the standpoint of frequency, the chief practical implication of the differences between rote and meaningful learning for classroom teaching is that review can, and largely should, take the place of practice. Since meaningful learning occurs relatively quickly, and since the forgetting of meaningfully learned materials takes place relatively slowly, much of the potentially facilitating effects of frequency can be used more profitably for review than for original learning purposes. In terms of what is actually learned and retained, the relatively long interval between the initial learning and the review sessions in meaningful learning is comparable to the short intertrial practice interval in advanced stages of rote learning.

It is apparent, therefore, that two principal issues must be considered in evaluating the role of frequency in learning and retention. First, is repetition typically required both in gradually establishing associative or dissociability strength at or above threshold level in rote and meaningful learning respectively and in sufficiently enhancing such strength so that the span of retention is extended, or is all effective learning and retention actually accomplished in a single trial? Is frequency, in other words, *intrinsically* related to the learning-retention process, or is gradual improvement with repetition merely an artifactual consequence of various factors involved in the investigation, measurement, and representation of learning-retention outcomes? Second, does the frequency affect learning and retention in any *distinctive* way apart from affording repeated opportunities for other variables such as contiguity, drive reduction, and confirmation-clarification to operate in cumulative fashion?

Evidently, frequency per se is neither a necessary nor a sufficient condition for meaningful learning to occur (E. L. Thorndike, 1931, 1932). The substance of much relatively easy, potentially meaningful material can be grasped after one reading. Typically, however, several readings are required for more difficult learning, for overlearning, for delayed retention, and for transfer.

In addition to being essential for typical meaningful learning situations, frequency has a *distinctive* effect of its own on learning and retention that operates in these situations (and cannot simply be reduced to) the opportunity that subsequent trials provide for other effective variables to influence, in cumulative fashion, the process and outcome of learning and retention. That is, in our opinion, frequency does more than merely make possible a summation of the repeated effects of some other variables such as contiguity, reinforcement through drive reduction, or cognitive confirmation and clarification. Frequency does admittedly provide opportunity for the recurrent operation of these other variables, but it also serves as more than just a vehicle for the cumulation of their repeated effects. Further discussion and explication of how the effects of frequency are mediated can also be found in the section below on the timing of review.

Specific Practice Factors

Timing of Reviews

For purposes of meaningful learning and retention, should review be introduced shortly after original learning, when the material is still fresh in mind and relatively little has been forgotten? Or would it be more effective to introduce review after an appreciable amount of material has been forgotten? The research findings, in general, indicate that neither approach is more effective than the other in facilitating meaningful retention of potentially meaningful learning material, thus, suggesting that the respective advantages of early and delayed review counterbalance each other (Sones & Stroud, 1940). The theoretical advantages of *delayed* review are perhaps more self-evident than those of early review. In the first place, after a longer retention interval, when more material is forgotten, the learner is more highly motivated to profit from the opportunity for review. He or she is less likely to regard this opportunity as unnecessary and superfluous, and is, therefore, more disposed to take good advantage of its in terms of effort and attention.

Second, and even more important, *prior forgetting* conceivably has a facilitating ("immunizing") effect on meaningful learning and retention. As a result of both trying and failing to remember material, the learner tends to become aware of negative factors in the learning and retention situation that promote forgetting—that is, of areas of instability, ambiguity, confusion, and lack of discriminability. Thus forearmed, he can take the necessary steps during the relearning session to strengthen particularly weak components of the learning task, to resolve existing confusion and ambiguity, and to increase discriminability between previously learned ideas and related new propositions. Furthermore, it would seem that greater potential benefit could presumably be anticipated from repetition when a larger proportion of the learning task is forgotten, inasmuch as more remains to be relearned under these circumstances.

In what ways can *early* review conceivably counterbalance these evident advantages of delayed review? The most likely possibility is that repetition (review) has a specially potent consolidating effect on recently learned material while it is still appreciably above the threshold of availability. This consolidating effect probably decreases as the new material becomes progressively less available. Obviously, another trial provides additional opportunity for the learner to interact cognitively with the learning material and to relate the potential meanings it embodies to his or her existing structure of knowledge (Ausubel & Youssef, 1966). New actual or experienced meanings are acquired and previously acquired meanings are consolidated. The learner has another opportunity to acquire more subtle potential meanings in the material that were partially or completely missed on the first trial, as well as to consolidate meanings initially established at that time. To be optimally effective, however, the opportunity for such consolidation may very well presuppose a certain minimal level of residual availability, the presence of which is more likely in early than in delayed review.

Another study trial also provides the learner with informational feedback, in the form of textual reference, for testing the correctness of the knowledge retained from the first trial. This testing confirms correct meanings, clarifies ambiguities, corrects misconceptions, and indicates areas of weakness requiring differential concentrated study. The net effect is consolidation of learning. When the learning task is largely forgotten, however, as in delayed review, the "feedback" role of repetition is minimal.

In what other ways may early review be more advantageous than delayed review? It will be remembered that in addition to enhancing meaningful learning and retention in the two aforementioned direct ways, repetition also influences these processes in another indirect way through modification of cognitive structure wrought by earlier trials. Not only do repeated presentations of the learning task strengthen the newly acquired cognitive content, but the latter cognitive content itself also *reciprocally* induces changes in the *perceived* learning task that make it more learnable. That is, initial acquisition of the meanings potentially present in the learning material and their presence in cognitive structure *sensitize* the learner to the potential meanings it contains when encountering it again. The learner had previously derived meanings from the learning material on the first trial by incorporating potential meanings into cognitive structure. Now the new ideas as a whole, not merely the component words, immediately (that is, perceptually) convey *actual* rather than merely *potential* meaning on second reading.

Hence, on the second trial, actual rather than potential meanings interact on a perceptual basis with the residue of those recently acquired meanings in cognitive structure that were established as a consequence of the learner's first encounter with the material. This type of interaction particularly enhances consolidation of the previously established meanings because this time the learner does not have to *grasp* meanings and can concentrate solely on trying to *remember* them. Moreover, establishment of gross meanings on the first trial sensitizes the learner to more refined meanings and subtle distinctions on the second trial. It stands to reason, therefore, that both the consolidation and "sensitizing effects" of repetition are greater earlier than later during the retention interval, when more of the learned meanings are still available to exert sensitizing effects or to be consolidated.

In summary, then, the principal advantage of *early* review would appear to be its superior consolidating, "feedback," and "sensitizing" effects in relation to more highly available material. On the other hand, the principal advantage of *delayed* review probably inheres in the superior relearning of partially forgotten material, both on motivational and cognitive grounds. Thus, since each kind of review has its own distinctive functions and advantages, the two varieties are presumably complementary rather than redundant or mutually exclusive, and can thus be profitably combined.

Distribution of Practice

Generally speaking, the research evidence supports the conclusion that distributed practice facilitates both learning and retention more than massed practice does (Bumstead, 1943; Sones & Stroud, 1940). The most credible explanation in terms of both internal consistency and the research evidence is the forgetting theory that was discussed in detail above to account for how the effects of frequency on meaningful learning and retention are mediated and for the facilitating effect of delayed review on meaningful retention. Additionally, (1) inasmuch as repetition primarily strengthens those components of the learning task that are still unlearned, the forgetting of previously learned components that occurs between trials in a distributed practice schedule enables these forgotten (as well as the yet unlearned) components to profit from this special strengthening effect of later trials; and (2) rest provides an opportunity for the dissipation of the confusion and resistance to learning that characterizes "initial learning shock" and for the forgetting of interfering (strong, competing, alternative) responses or meanings.

In conclusion, it appears that short and widely spaced practice or review sessions that are introduced progressively further apart are best for meaningful learning and retention.

Recitation versus Recapitulation

In reception learning, where the learning task is to internalize presented materials (e.g., facts, principles, arbitrary associations) so that they are available for later reproduction, the learner may either be confronted with numerous study trials or repetitions of the task or may elect or be required to spend varying proportions of the total practice time in attempting to recall (recite) the material in test trials. The relevant research findings support the conclusion that whereas increasing proportions of recitation tend to facilitate *rote* learning and retention (retention more than learning), the facilitating effect of recitation on *meaningful* learning and retention is both less striking and more equivocal (Ausubel, 1966; Bumstead, 1940; Peterson, 1944).

The effectiveness of recitation, particularly for rote material, may be attributed to several factors. First, since the attempt to recall presented material tests whether and to what extent internalization (learning) has taken place, the "feedback" that is provided in the next trial is, therefore, a much more significant factor after recitation than after recapitulation. It indicates explicitly and systematically what the correct associations or meanings are in relation to the internalized learning that has already taken place. Under these circumstances, all of the effects of feedback—as an incentive condition; as cognitive confirmation, correction, clarification, and evaluation of the adequacy of learning; and as reinforcement following reduction of cognitive and ego-enhancing drives—are considerably intensified.

A closely related immediate consequence of feedback in this context is that as a result of discovering which parts of the learning task have not yet been sufficiently mastered, one is better able to focus one's attention and effort selectively on these latter aspects.

Second, the kind of participation involved in recitation, which is more active than rereading, implies greater learning effort. In addition to exerting a general facilitating influence on learning, this participation differentially salvages items at or near threshold strength and leads to more active and meaningful organization of the learned material (use of rhythmic mnemonic devices, and conceptual organizers).

Third, the conditions of recitation more nearly resemble the conditions under which the learning will eventually be exercised than do those of recapitulation.

The markedly reduced effectiveness of recitation with respect to *meaningful* learning and retention is not difficult to understand. To begin with, the logical sequential structure of connected meaningful discourse makes *implicit* recitation possible during the same trial; that is, in the course of rereading, subjects typically tend to anticipate the remembered facts and propositions that follow logically from the material they are current perusing. In the case of potentially meaningful material, also, where the achievement of understanding is both a reward and an incentive in its own right, less effort is required for learning, and the incentive and ego-enhancement values of feedback are less important. Explicit testing is similarly less necessary for the confirmation, correction, clarification, and evaluation effects of feedback in view of the fact that the internal logic of the material partly provides its own feedback. It enables subjects to appreciate whether they have grasped meanings correctly and, in any case, implicitly to test their understandings against the next presentation of the material. Finally, meaningful learning tasks benefit less from the organizing effects of recitation since they possess an inherent organization of their own. Nevertheless, recitation can still facilitate meaningful learning—even when conducted early in the course of learning.

Task Homogeneity

Proponents of "activity" programs have tended to favor task heterogeneity in practice. That is, they sought, in part, to escape the opprobrium associated with drill by stressing diversity both in the types of learning tasks and in the examples of each type that are presented to the learner.

Relative degree of task homogeneity is often an important practical consideration in the learning of skills and inductively acquired concepts and principles. The issue is whether such learnings can be acquired most efficiently as a result of intensive practice with just a few exemplars or as a result of less intensive practice with a large variety of exemplars. We have already concluded in an earlier chapter that, other factors being equal, the defining attributes of a given concept are learned most readily when the concept is encountered in many diverse contexts. Such experience obviously lessens the particularity and enhances the generality of abstract knowledge and transferable skills.

It is important to qualify this conclusion, however, by indicating that if this multicontextual experience is acquired at the expense of not attaining adequate mastery of the particular component tasks that comprise it, its overall effect on learning is detrimental. In learning general concepts, principles, and skills inductively, experience with a particular exemplar has a positive transfer effect on other exemplars *only* if it is adequately consolidated. Similarly, it is only by mastering several exemplars in the same fashion that the total experience can be successfully utilized in formulating a transferable generalization. Thus, transfer in "learning set" problems requires mastery *within* a given type of problem as well as experience with many variants of this problem type. Also, if the supportive empirical instances of a concept or a proposition are too heterogeneous in content or sequence of presentation, learning is impeded.

It seems, therefore, that efficient learning of transferable skills and knowledge demands a proper balance between the overlearning of particular intratask instances, on the one hand, and adequate exposure to intra- and intertask diversity, on the other (Ausubel, 1968; Kuntz & Hovland, 1956). These two conditions of practice are complementary and mutually supportive rather than antithetical or mutually preclusive. It is quite probable, however, that their optimal proportions vary in different learning tasks. Many cases of disability in particular academic skills can undoubtedly be attributed to overemphasis on the importance of diversified experience in unstructured learning situations, with consequent insufficiency of practice and failure to attain mastery of the component habit exemplars from which the skill in question is derived. Hence, we should not lose sight of the fact that the acquisition of general skills is dependent upon the prior consolidation of more particular habit exemplars and that these skills are, therefore, not efficiently or satisfactorily established unless learners practice the underlying exemplars sufficiently to master them thoroughly. Generally speaking, educators have tended to stress the importance of extensity as opposed to intensity in learning. Actually, if a choice must be made, it is preferable to know a few things well than to have a passing acquaintance with many. A small quantity of consolidated knowledge is both useful and transferable; a large quantity of diffuse and unstable knowledge is utterly useless.

Another obvious advantage of multicontextual learning, if it does not interfere with intratask mastery, is that it prevents boredom and enhances the exploratory drive. This is particularly true in the case of more intelligent learners; less intertask variability is required to sustain the interest of duller pupils.

Learning Set

The term "learning set" refers to current disposition to learn or perform in a particular way (Harlow, 1940). Hence, in its broader meaning it also includes the learner's disposition to learn in a rote or meaningful fashion. Meaningful learning set, as one of the major prerequisites for meaningful learning, is obviously an important general condition of practice, but it has already been discussed in another context.

In the present context, therefore, we shall consider learning set only insofar as it reflects the influence of *recently prior* learning experience or activity. This aspect of learning set reflects both general methodological sophistication in approaching a given learning task or attacking a particular type of problem ("learning to learn") and an appropriate performance attitude or momentary state of readiness for engaging in a particular kind of activity ("warm-up" effect). Both of these components of learning set obviously contribute to positive transfer.

Irrespective of the kind of learning involved, practice on one task tends to facilitate the learning of another similar task, provided that there is no conflictful overlapping of content between them. Learning set is, therefore, a significant general condition of practice to bear in mind in ordering the distribution and sequencing of practice as well as the optimal degree of intertrial task homogeneity.

It is important on theoretical grounds not to confound the learning-to-learn and warm-up aspects of learning set. The former consists of relatively stable *cognitive* acquisitions, concerned with the strategy of learning, that are derived from past learning experience. These acquisitions influence the actual content and direction of ongoing learning activity. The latter consists of transitory readiness factors involved in the momentary focusing of attention, mobilization of effort, and overcoming of initial inertia that are associated with "being properly set" to perform a given task. Warm-up effects, naturally, are rather rapidly dissipated, accounting at most for part of the intertask improvement in learning that occurs during the course of a single day's practice. Longer-term improvement (from one day to another) must be accounted for solely in terms of learning-to-learn effects.

In programming potentially meaningful material, it is obviously important to preserve sufficient commonality between successive learning tasks to take advantage of both the learning-to-learn and warm-up components of learning set. At the same time, however, enough heterogeneity of intertask content should be introduced to prevent the mechanical perseveration of a given learning set and to discourage rigidity of approach and the development of a rote learning attitude. The need for multiple warm-up periods is one of the chief disadvantages of distributed practice. It renders such distribution unfeasible in certain tasks requiring considerable sustained effort.

Transfer versus Direct Practice in Sequential Learning

Repetition is important not only for the mastery of the current or ongoing learning task but also for the learning of new, sequentially dependent tasks that presuppose such mastery or consolidation of the current task. This, of course, is an example of positive transfer. The relative value of transfer and direct practice has already been considered in another context. One might anticipate in the case of sequentially dependent learning material that the learning of such material would be significantly influenced by the extent of retention of relevant antecedent material. The availability of such relevant material—particularly if it were clear and stable—would provide a more secure basis for new learning than if this material were not available at all or were not clear and stable. Since repetition of the earlier background material tends to increase its stability and clarity, it should enhance the learning and retention of sequentially dependent material.

The facilitating effect of repetition (consolidation) of background material on the learning of subsequently presented material apparently seems to operate only when the latter material is sequentially dependent on the prior background material. Thus, in classroom learning tasks it is important to distinguish between (1) sequentially related materials that are sequentially *dependent* on prior learnings and (2) sequentially related materials that are sequentially *independent* of such learnings. When we say that materials are sequentially related, we merely imply that, in terms of the logic of subject-matter organization, it is more reasonable for one set of materials to precede another than vice versa.

Sequential *dependence,* however, also implies that the learning of the later material actually presupposes knowledge of the earlier material and is impossible without it. In sequentially *independent* situations, on the other hand, knowledge of the earlier material is not required for learning the later material. The latter set of materials is self-contained and can be learned adequately by itself without any reference to the previous set. Such sequential independence is frequently brought about in sequentially related lessons by including in the second lesson a synopsis or review of all of the material from the first lesson that is absolutely essential for the understanding of the second.

Prompting and Guidance

The learner's responses during the course of practice may be completely unaided, on the one hand, or receive the benefit of varying degrees of external assistance, on the other. The nature and significance of such assistance obviously differ greatly depending on whether reception or discovery learning is involved. In a discovery learning situation, assistance takes the form of guidance—providing cues that detract from the learner's opportunity for autonomous discovery. Hence, guidance refers to and affects the reception-discovery dimension of learning. The provision of complete guidance is tantamount to presenting the learner with the essential content of the learning task (reception learning), whereas the absence of any guidance whatsoever requires completely autonomous discovery. The degree of guidance furnished in most instances of discovery learning typically falls between these two extremes.

In a reception learning situation, external assistance takes the form of *prompting* during the test trials. This assistance does not affect the autonomy of discovery, since the content of the learning task is wholly presented in any case. It does influence the autonomy of reproduction, however. The learner is assisted, in whole or in part, to reproduce previously presented material that as yet has not been internalized above the threshold of availability. If the entire and explicit substance of the information demanded by the test item is furnished, the stimulus support can be regarded as a *prompt.* If the stimulus support is less complete and explicit during the test trial, it can be considered a *cue.*

Prompting is more necessary and effective in the earlier stages of reception learning because at this time the learner has not yet internalized sufficient material to receive much practice benefit from unaided recitation (Briggs, 1961). Furthermore, the provision of prompts at this early point of practice can prevent guesswork and the learning of errors (incorrect competing responses) and, thus, obviate the necessity for costly unlearning. For such reasons, prompting is more efficacious than confirmation (feedback) for relatively short periods of practice in reception learning.

During the later stages of practice, however, these considerations are obviously less relevant. In addition, it is important that the conditions of practice gradually begin to approximate the desired (unprompted) endpoint of the learning product. Hence, as the quantity of correct learning increases, reduction of both the completeness and explicitness of the prompts and their replacement by confirmation are advantageous for further learning. On theoretical grounds, it also seems plausible that prompting could be profitably dispensed with earlier in the case of meaningful than of rote reception learning because of the more rapid rate of acquisition and the different role played by competing responses.

A review of short-term studies of the role of guidance in meaningful discovery learning leads to the conclusion that guided or semiautonomous discovery is more efficacious for learning, retention, and transfer than is either completely autonomous discovery or the provision of complete guidance in meaningful but contrived and relatively isolated and novel laboratory tasks. Guidance under these circumstances apparently sensitizes the learner to the salient aspects of the problem, orients him to the goal, and promotes economy of learning by preventing misdirected effort.

Some opportunity for autonomous discovery is obviously necessary in those instances where the object of learning is not merely the acquisition of knowledge but also the development of skill in formulating general principles and in applying them to particular problem situations. Verbally presented principles, it is true, are transferable to such situations even if they are not self-discovered. However, the ability to solve a particular class of problems efficiently also presupposes experience in coping with the distinctive features of that class of problems in hypothesis formulation and testing, in the strategy of application, in identifying fruitful approaches that minimize costly risk and unnecessary cognitive strain, in using systematic and economic methods of inquiry, and in maintaining a flexible and meaningful learning set.

In conclusion, it should be appreciated, in the first place, that problem solving and laboratory exercises are not inherently or necessarily meaningful and may lead to little or no meaningful learning and retention if the students' learning set is simply rotely to memorize "type" problems or techniques of manipulating symbols. This is particularly true if the student has an inadequate background in, or appreciation of, the methodological principles illustrated by specific laboratory procedures. It should also be realized, finally, that just as "doing" does not necessarily lead to understanding, understanding does not necessarily imply ability successfully to solve problems involving meaningful appreciation of the principles in question. Factors other than understanding are also implicated in the outcome of problem-solving activities.

Second, what is typically called the "discovery method" is really a contrived type of discovery that is a far cry from the truly autonomous discovery activities of the research scholar or scientist. Pure discovery techniques could lead only to utter chaos and a waste of time in the classroom, inasmuch as immature students generally lack sufficient subject-matter sophistication both to formulate workable problems and to devise appropriate and relevant research methods. Before students can "discover" generalizations reasonably efficiently, problems must be structured by them in such a way as to make ultimate discovery almost inevitable.

Third, numerous short-term studies have demonstrated that guided discovery is more efficacious for learning, retention, and transfer than is either completely autonomous discovery or the provision of complete guidance. However, these findings do not necessarily indicate that guided discovery is more effective for teaching *subject-matter content* than is simple didactic exposition. For one thing, the solving by a naive subject of a few novel problems in a laboratory setting is hardly comparable to the learning of a large body of sequentially organized material.

Much also depends on the relative time/cost of the two approaches, on the learner's cognitive maturity and degree of subject-matter sophistication, on the nature of the learning task (descriptive information, representational equivalents, or principles that are discoverable by stating and testing hypotheses), and on whether the objective of the learning experience is to acquire knowledge, enhance problem-solving ability, or obtain insight into scientific method.

Some General Conditions of Practice in Meaningful Learning and Retention

Knowledge of Results (Feedback)

On theoretical grounds, knowledge of results (or feedback) would appear to be an extremely important practice variable. Nevertheless, because of serious gaps and inadequacies in the available research evidence, we possess very little unequivocal information either about its actual effects on learning or about its mechanism of action.

Some knowledge of results is apparently essential for learning in particular types of perceptual-motor tasks where a variable or indeterminate response must be given to a constantly presented stimulus (Hershberger, 1964; Thorndike, 1931, 1932). Where the learner must simply comprehend and internalize the material presented, feedback facilitates learning and retention but is not indispensable for either outcome (Thorndike, 1931).

An equally important issue, assuming that feedback is indispensable for some kinds of learning and has a facilitating influence on others, concerns the mechanism whereby this facilitation is effected. Neobehavioristically oriented theorists attribute the effects of feedback to the gratification of drive reduction and to the reinforcement of the correct response that follow from confirmation of the correctness or success of the latter choice. It is self-evidently more parsimonious, i.e., involves fewer unprovable assumptions, however, to believe that knowledge of results also has other mostly cognitive effects on meaningful learning and retention. The cognitive aspects of feedback confirm appropriate meanings and associations, correct errors, clarify misconceptions, and indicate the relative adequacy with which different portions of the learning task have been mastered. Thus, as a result of the feedback received, the subject's confidence in the validity of his learning products is increased and his learnings are consolidated. The learner is also better able selectively to concentrate on those aspects of the task requiring further refinement.

On both motivational and cognitive grounds, feedback probably also has less facilitating effect on meaningful than on rote learning. Since the achievement of understanding is a reward in its own right and requires less brute effort than rote learning, it is less necessary in meaningful learning to invoke the energizing assistance of extrinsic motives and incentives. Selective reinforcement of successful responses through drive reduction (gratification) is similarly less necessary for learning, even if it were possible, when logical considerations are applicable to the content of the learning task than when a purely arbitrary and verbatim connection must be established. The internal logic of the learning material also makes possible some implicit confirmation, correction, clarification, and evaluation of the learning product, even in the absence of any explicit provision of feedback.

Effects of Intention on Meaningful Learning and Retention

Although individuals can acquire much miscellaneous information incidentally, deliberate effort is required for the efficient learning of most types of academic subject matter. Many experiments also show that deliberate learning in response to explicit instructions is both more effective and more precise and specific than is unintentional or implicitly instructed learning. It has been tempting for many theorists to invoke the widely-accepted energizing and expediting effects of motivation in explaining these findings. Psychological analysis of intention, however, suggests that it is much closer as a process to a mental set than it is to motivation. Intentions in a very real sense are motivational precursors of mental sets that actually mediate their effects both with respect to the intended actions, and eventually with respect to memory itself, by facilitating meaningful learning. Expectancy acts very much like intention in facilitating meaningful memory, but it only does so for those items consistent with itself (Hirt et al., 1995).

Since intention is mediated at least in part by the increased mobilization and focusing of attention (in addition to the operation of mental sets), a certain minimal degree of attention is necessary for meaningful learning to occur following explicit intention to learn and remember meaningfully. In instances of implicit and incidental learning where this minimum is barely met, therefore, learning and retention do take place (but only minimally), inasmuch as the actual amount of attention essential for learning to occur is really quite minute. The common occurrence of apparently learning without attention is more likely an instance of "unconscious" incidental learning occurring with minimally required attention but no awareness (Ashcraft, 1994).

In contrast, however, to the set to place the relevant muscles in readiness in a certain order (as in "warm-up" effects) or to utilize a particular learning strategy (derived from a "learning to learn" sequence) for solving a given class of problems, the set underlying most learning intentions primarily involves a deliberate focusing and mobilization of attention and effort to perform a particular activity (or not to neglect performing it). Among students, for example, the activity in question, that very frequently could constitute the object of their intentions, is the learning and retention of some portion of academic material, either presented by the teacher in the classroom or studied alone at home or in school. Without executing this or similar explicit intention, it is evident that precious little would be learned.

In the sense delineated above, therefore, one could justifiably consider intention a general cognitive condition of practice comparable to feedback or to degree of naturalness or structuredness of learning activities. It should be noted, however, that like other noncognitive variables (e.g., motivations and drives), the focusing and mobilization of attention and effort can only influence the learning process, not retention. Once new meanings emerge and are linked to relevant anchoring ideas in cognitive structure, there is no possible way in which these latter variables could come into contact with and affect the retention process.

Natural versus Structured Practice Settings

By "natural" learning conditions in this context is meant any one or all of the following relatively unstructured pedagogic principles that by and large have been advocated by "progressive education" schools and "progressive educators" in this country, more so in the past than at the present time:

1. Unstructured and uncontrived learning situations
2. Direct kinds of experience, in a concrete, manipulative sense
3. Unintentional or nondeliberate learning effort
4. Learning by autonomous, unguided discovery
5. Exposure to diversified rather than repetitive experience

How desirable is it that practice take place in natural (real-life, uncontrived) settings? It is true, of course (providing that all other relevant factors are equal), that learning is enhanced when the conditions of practice closely resemble the conditions under which the skill or knowledge in question will eventually be used. Such learning is also less likely to be monotonous and enjoys the benefit of higher levels of interest and motivation. Wholly natural settings, however, rarely provide the practice conditions that are either necessary or optimal for efficient learning.

Generally, it is only during the latter stages of learning, *after* component aspects of the learning task have already been identified and mastered in structured practice sessions, that naturalistic "dress rehearsals" become feasible. In the first place, uncontrived learning experiences typically fail to include a sufficient number of properly spaced practice trials as well as adequate opportunity for differential repetition of particularly difficult components. Second, unstructured practice does not receive the benefit of skilled pedagogic selection, presentation, and organization of material; of careful sequencing, pacing, and gradation of difficulty; and of optimal balancing of intratask repetition, intratask variability, and intertask variability. Third, most learning effort is enhanced by deliberate intention to learn according to almost all research findings.

The important teaching principle of initial simplification of difficult learning tasks for unsophisticated pupils also runs counter to the doctrine of natural or unstructured learning. Exposing unsophisticated learners to all of the complexities of natural, "unarranged" data in the laboratory or of subtle distinctions and qualifications in expository teaching is the surest way of confusing and overwhelming them. The use of artificial "crutches," gradation of difficulty, and slowing down the rate of presentation are common forms of simplification in classroom learning.

Many features of "activity" programs were based on the self-evident proposition that the elementary-school child perceives the world in relatively concrete and intuitive terms. The child requires considerable direct experience with many concrete instances of a given set of relationships before he or she can acquire genuinely meaningful concepts and generalizations. Thus, an attempt was made to teach factual information and intellectual skills through the medium of direct, manipulative experience in natural settings rather than through verbal exposition and drill.

In older pupils, however, as John Dewey himself recognized, once a sufficient number of basic abstract concepts are acquired, new concepts are primarily derived from other verbal abstractions rather than from direct experience, and new propositions are comprehended without any direct reference to or manipulation of concrete props. In the secondary school, therefore, it may be desirable to reverse both the sequential relationship and relative proportion between abstract concepts and concrete data. Thus, there is good reason for believing that much of the time presently spent in busywork laboratory exercises in the sciences could be more advantageously employed in formulating more precise definitions, differentiating explicitly between related concepts, generalizing from hypothetical situations, and so forth.

MOTIVATIONAL FACTORS IN MEANINGFUL LEARNING AND RETENTION[2]

Is Motivation Necessary for Learning?

The weight of the evidence indicates that although motivation is a highly significant factor in and greatly facilitates meaningful learning, it is by no means an indispensable condition, especially for limited and short-term learning. However, it is absolutely essential for the sustained and long-term type of learning involved in mastering a given subject-matter discipline or vocational curriculum. Its effects are largely mediated through such intervening variables as the intensification, focusing, and mobilization of attention and effort; increased frustration tolerance and ability to postpone the need for immediate gratification of hedonistic drives; and heightened persistence and resoluteness.

Considerable research suggests that much learning is apparently neither energized by motivation nor reinforced by drive satisfaction (reduction). Classical or Pavlovian conditioning, for example, merely depends on temporal contiguity of the conditioned and unconditioned stimuli. Some learning, as pointed out above, also occurs incidentally without any explicit intention to learn. Apart from classical conditioning, however, motivation is probably more dispensable for meaningful reception learning (particularly on an unorganized, short-term basis) than it is for any other kind of learning. Because such learning requires relatively little effort, it is less necessary to rely on existing drives and motives within the learner, on incentive conditions, and on extrinsic rewards than is the case, for example, in rote learning or problem solving. But to assert that meaningful learning (particularly of a fragmentary and short-term nature) can occur in the absence of motivation does not, of course, deny the fact that motivation can significantly facilitate learning whenever it is present and operative.

The causal relationship between motivation and learning is typically reciprocal rather than unidirectional. Both for this reason and because motivation is not an indispensable condition of learning, it is unnecessary to postpone learning activities until appropriate interests and motivations have been developed. Frequently, the best way of teaching unmotivated students is to ignore their lack of motivation for the time being and to concentrate on teaching them cognitively as effectively as possible. Some degree of learning will ensue in any case, despite the lack of motivation; and from the initial satisfaction of learning, these students will develop retroactively the motivation to learn more. In some circumstances, therefore, the most appropriate way of arousing motivation to learn is to focus on the cognitive rather than on the motivational aspects of learning and to rely on the motivation that is developed retroactively from successful educational achievement to energize further learning.

Even though *particular* instances of learning may be largely unmotivated, however, it is undoubtedly true that subject matter as a whole must still be related to felt needs if appreciable degrees of *long-term* meaningful learning are to occur. Inability to see any need for a subject is the reason students mention most frequently for losing interest in high-school studies and dropping out.

Where motivation is clearly operative in human learning, it is misleading to extrapolate the familiar paradigm of homeostatic drive reduction that is characteristically used to explain animal learning. Such drives are quickly satiated and, when accompanied by intense affect, disrupt learning. Hence, hunger, thirst, pain, and the like rarely motivate human learning. And although material rewards are often effective, intrinsic (task-oriented) and ego-enhancing motives increasingly tend to dominate the motivational picture with advancing age. Material rewards also tend to become less ends in themselves than symbols of earned or attributed status and, hence, sources of self-esteem.

An optimal level of motivation or ego involvement (neither too high nor too low) apparently exists for complex kinds of learning. Impelling drive states may conceivably disrupt meaningful generic learning—both by overemphasizing the particularity of newly learned concepts and by limiting the learner's ability to apply previously learned principles to newly learned tasks. Stated in terms of an hypothesized physiological basis for motivation, a moderate amount of activation or arousal seems to have an optimal effect on learning.

One of the theoretical biases that should be made explicit here at the very outset is the assumption that both the role and relative importance of different kinds of motivations (for example, cognitive, homeostatic, material, ego-enhancing, aversive, and affiliative) vary depending on the type of learning involved and on the species membership and developmental status of the learner. Hence, it could be anticipated that the role and relative importance of these various kinds of motivations in classroom learning would be quite different than in short-term and fragmentary varieties of rote, instrumental, motor, and discovery learning.

THE MEDIATION OF MOTIVATIONAL EFFECTS IN MEANINGFUL LEARNING AND RETENTION

How do motivational factors actually influence meaningful learning and retention, and how does this influence differ from that of the cognitive variables we have considered previously? In the first place, *cognitive variables influence directly the very conditions determining the interaction between new learning material and existing relevant ideas in cognitive structure.* Hence, they also influence the emergence of new meanings and the maintenance of their separate identity and availability during the retention interval (through the maintenance of the dissociability strength of the new meanings).

Second, *the effects of cognitive variables are also mediated through the same mechanisms in both learning and retention.* That is, these variables determine the precision, stability, clarity, and discriminability of emerging new meanings during learning by influencing the cognitive interactional process in the particular aforementioned ways. This same influence of cognitive variables on dissociability strength both: (1) can be exerted during the retention period as well as during learning, and (2) continues to operate cumulatively during the retention interval, thereby determining the relative degree of availability of newly learned meanings (Ausubel, 1968).

Typically, however, *motivational variables are not directly involved in the cognitive interactional process.* They energize and expedite this process during learning by enhancing effort, attention, and immediate readiness for learning. Thus, they elevate dissociability strength *catalytically* and nonspecifically (rather than through direct and differential involvement in the interactional process determining the acquisition and retention of new meanings).

Furthermore, *the effects of motivational variables on learning and retention, respectively, unlike the mediation of their cognitive counterparts in these two processes, are not mediated through the same mechanisms.* After learning is completed, motivational variables cannot independently affect dissociability strength (that is, apart from their effects on learning itself). Therefore, they can only influence retention, apart from learning, during the reproductive phase of memory by elevating thresholds of availability and by shaping the qualitative aspects of imaginative reconstruction. We can conclude, therefore, that motivational factors affect meaningful learning and retention in ways that are *qualitatively* different from the comparable effects of relevant cognitive variables.

Motivational variables, in other words, are not directly or intrinsically involved in the cognitive interactional process or in the determination of dissociability strength. For the most part they merely impinge indirectly on this process and influence dissociability strength in a nonspecific facilitating or energizing (catalytic) fashion. For example, through such motivational effects as mobilization of effort and concentration of attention, more repetitions of the material can be completed within the stipulated learning time, and each repetition is conducted more efficiently. The net result is an indirect, nonspecific, overall increase in dissociability strength for the learning process so energized (Ausubel, 1968).

It is also reasonable to assume that the effects of cognitive variables on meaningful learning continue along similar lines during retention and are mediated by the same mechanisms. Whatever these effects on the interactional process are, they are simply extended temporally from learning to retention. Thus, the rate at which dissociability strength declines during retention reflects the continuing influence of these same *cognitive* variables on the interactional process during the retention interval. However, once the learning sessions have been completed and the cognitive interactional products have been formed, a channel of communication no longer remains open for the energizing and expediting aspects of *motivation* to influence dissociability strength, even in a catalytic or nonspecific sense. Hence, if motivational factors are to affect retention independently of their effects on learning, a new mechanism is required to mediate this influence—a mechanism that does not operate during the retention interval but only during the reproductive stage of memory. At this point motivational variables continue to affect retention outcomes—that is, independently of their prior effects on learning—but only insofar as they impinge on the threshold of availability and on the *reproductive* aspects of memory.

Thus, both theoretical considerations and the weight of the available evidence suggest that motivational factors influence meaningful retention selectively by inhibiting (raising), rather than facilitating (lowering), particular thresholds of recognition and recall. Positive ego involvement and favorable attitudinal bias, in other words, do not increase retention by lowering thresholds of memorial elicitation. Rather, strong motivation to forget and certain kinds of negative attitudinal bias (for example, in ego-threatening or anxiety-producing situations) may selectively promote forgetting by raising thresholds of availability (repression).

Thus, unlike the situation in learning, the selective influence of motivational variables on meaningful *retention* is inhibitory rather than facilitating (catalytic). Moreover, the influence of these variables is also mediated solely through a change in thresholds of memorial elicitation, without any change whatsoever in dissociability strength itself. Although the latter remains constant, recall or recognition is nevertheless rendered momentarily more difficult because of the selective elevation of particular thresholds of availability.

It appears likely, therefore, that motivational factors influence retention—by raising thresholds of availability—only in those relatively rare instances where retrieval of particular information would be ego-threatening or productive of anxiety. One example is the repression of memories that would, if recalled, give rise to feelings of anxiety, guilt, hostility, or self-disparagement. These kinds of forgetting, however, would not occur very frequently in typical classroom learning situations.

The primary and direct effect of motivational variables on meaningful retention, when they do operate, therefore, is to elevate thresholds of availability (or to make the memories in question less available in relation to their intrinsic dissociability strength). It is theoretically conceivable, however, that motivation (a strong incentive to recall) could also indirectly *lower* thresholds of availability by counteracting or disinhibiting certain inhibitory factors (distraction, inattention, inertia, disinclination toward effort) that temporarily raise such thresholds.

We have already observed how various inhibitory conditions such as initial "learning shock" and the competition of alternative memories tend to dissipate spontaneously, and how hypnosis can reduce the inhibitory effect both of competing memories and of motives and attitudes promoting repression—as, for example, in the case of anxiety-producing material. It still has to be empirically determined whether strong motivation or positive ego-involvement could similarly facilitate retention by disinhibiting temporarily elevated thresholds of availability.

Finally, motivational variables are probably also involved in the reconstructive aspects of the reproductive phase of memory—in making a selection from among the available remembered items and in organizing them into a coherent verbal response to meet the demands of a current situation. Strictly speaking, however, the framing of a response in which memories are reported is not part of the retention process *per se.*

Attention

Much of the facilitating effect of motivation is apparently mediated by an increase in attention. Merely directing students' attention to certain aspects of subject matter, irrespective of how this is done, promotes learning. The mediating variable of attention *per se* is largely equivalent to a mental set to place in readiness a given group of lowered thresholds for learning at such time as when the instructional material is presented.

As a mediating variable in undoubted instances of *motivation,* attention is presumably the major general intervening variable through which motivational factors influence meaningful learning. A major cause of everyday forgetting perhaps in most instances of undue loss of ostensibly learned material (including subject matter) is failure to pay proper attention at the time of learning. Generally speaking, what is not attended to is neither learned nor remembered.

Differentiated intentions and mental sets are two of the other more significant intervening variables mediating the effects of motivational factors on meaningful learning. They do this largely through the selective distribution and focusing that is generally regarded as constituting attention phenomenologically.

In addition to serving as a mediating mechanism for the effects of motivation on meaningful learning (similar to the comparable mediational effects of intention described above), attention probably is a *general cognitive condition* essential for the occurrence of most instances of meaningful learning. Although very simple kinds of motor, incidental, conditioned, rote, and instrumental learning can presumably take place without attention, most learning, even the incidental kind, requires a basic minimum of coincident attention. Mental set and intention are probably also mediated, at least in part, by selective attention; and this relationship could also be partially reciprocal, that is, selective attention may, in turn, be partially mediated by differential mental sets.

Simple learning processes may also conceivably occur in the absence of consciousness (awareness) of same; but this does not necessarily imply that learning is taking place entirely without attention. Consciousness (awareness) of self and of one's mental functions (in this case attention) is only one largely unessential and often absent aspect of a state of attention (e.g., in automatic, habitual, and peripheral actions), rather than being, in a sense, coexistensive with it (Ausubel, 1994).

Although, during periods of relaxation, attention may tend to be focused randomly, or almost exclusively, on the most conspicuous stimuli in an individual's environment, i.e., concentrating on vocational, avocational, scholastic, or other purposeful and organized kinds of activity, a pattern of expectancy typically prevails that determines the particular topical selectivity of his attention as mediated by differential mental sets. Other significant determinants of attentional selectivity are relative degree of interest or ego involvement and all types of scanning activities in which the object of all the scanning is to identify and separate into two or more homogeneous categorical aggregations the corresponding individual members of each category.

Selective attention in the latter type of scanning, thus, acts as a multiply-sensitive differential filter that only allows certain classes of items with predetermined criterial characteristics to pass through it and be processed (Broadbent, 1958). Similarly, only if an item's characteristics are consistent with the learner's expectancy does its memory tend to be facilitated (Hirt et al., 1995). Selective attention also helps to determine differentially the learner's choice in a given equivocal case between short- or long-term memory processing; between rote or meaningful learning set; and between trivial or transient information, on the one hand, and significant information or knowledge, on the other.

Besides its mediating role in the facilitative effects of intention on meaningful learning, intention also has a precursory (introductory), orienting, and initiating role in such learning. Intentions can be plausibly viewed as the precursory aspects of mental sets that first orient the learner to the nature and requirements of the learning task and then initiate the operation of the appropriate learning set. Few if any significant items of knowledge are learned and retained on a long-term basis without deliberate intent to learn; and as suggested above, intention, in all likelihood, is also a general cognitive and mandatory condition for meaningful learning because it orients the learner to what he has to do in order to master the instructional material.

Thus, even though attention is typically "neutral" and objective in experiential and meaningful learning and retention situations with respect to what it "allows" to enter the field of consciousness or awareness and then to be subsequently processed as indicated above, nevertheless, this latter process of "selective attention" is the hallmark of various attentional operations such as scanning (Broadbent, 1958), which makes possible certain necessary forms of differential preliminary processing.

COMPONENT DRIVES IN ACHIEVEMENT MOTIVATION

What is generally regarded as achievement motivation in school settings is by no means the reflection of a unitary or homogeneous drive. It has at least three different components. One of these which we shall encounter soon is cognitive drive—the need for acquiring knowledge and solving academic type problems as ends in themselves. This drive certainly underlies the need for academic achievement to the extent that such achievement represents to the learner the attainment of the knowledge he seeks to acquire. It is completely *task-oriented* in the sense that the motive for becoming involved in the task in question (i.e., acquiring a particular segment of knowledge) is intrinsic to the task itself; it is simply the need to know. Hence, the reward (the actual attainment of this knowledge) also inheres completely in the task itself since it is capable of wholly satisfying the underlying motive.

Achievement motivation, contrary to much prior and current thinking in the area, consists (depending on normative personality factors; individual differences in personality development; differential interaction with parents, peers, teachers, and the wider culture; genically determined temperamental traits; and social class, racial, ethnic, and sex membership) of varying proportions of (1) cognitive drive, (2) affiliative drive, and (3) ego-enhancement motivation.

Cognitive Drive

At the human level, cognitive drive (the desire for knowledge as an end in itself) is more important in meaningful than in rote or instrumental learning. It is, at least potentially, the most important kind of motivation in classroom learning. This is so because of its inherent potency and because meaningful learning, unlike these other kinds of human learning, automatically provides its own reward. That is, as in the case of all intrinsic motives, the reward that satisfies the drive inheres in accomplishing the task itself. In addition, motivation may facilitate learning in ways other than by energizing behavior and by reinforcing the successful variant through drive reduction. It also exerts a purely cognitive effect by highlighting or emphasizing what is to be learned, and by providing confirmatory and corrective feedback. This is evident both in meaningful discovery learning and in meaningful reception learning, where the choice of correct alternatives is rewarded and the choice of incorrect alternatives is not.

Despite the potential centrality of cognitive drive for classroom learning, it is nevertheless true that in our utilitarian, competitive, and achievement-oriented culture, such extrinsic considerations as ego enhancement, anxiety reduction, and career advancement become, with increasing age, progressively more significant sources of motivation for school learning. Beginning with the first four years of school life, ratings of achievement and recognition-seeking behavior tend to remain quite stable. They are reasonably predictive of analogous behavior during adolescence and early adult life. Even material rewards tend to become less ends in themselves than symbols of academic status, achievement, and competitive advantage. Their effects are mediated through the specific needs of the learner.

Eventually, of course, the viability of cognitive drive as an intrinsic, task-oriented type of motivation is impaired as a consequence of the increasing, almost exclusive, association of intellectual interests and activities with ego-enhancing and anxiety-reduction motives. If the desire to learn and understand is almost invariably exercised in the context of competing for grades, obtaining degrees, preparing for a vocation, striving for advancement, and reducing the fear of academic or occupational failure, there is little warrant for believing that much of it survives as a goal in its own right. This trend is reflected in the progressive decline in school interests and intellectual enthusiasm as children move up the academic ladder.

Hence, if we wish to develop the cognitive drive so that it remains viable during the school years and in adult life, it is necessary to move still further away from the educational doctrine of gearing the curriculum to the current concerns and life-adjustment problems of pupils. Nevertheless, it is undoubtedly unrealistic and even undesirable in our culture to eschew entirely the utilitarian, ego-enhancement, and anxiety-reduction motivations for learning. However, we must place increasingly greater emphasis upon the value of knowing and understanding as goals in their own right, quite apart from any practical benefits they may confer.

We should also avoid denigrating subject-matter knowledge. Instead we must discover more efficient methods of fostering the long-term acquisition of meaningful and usable bodies of knowledge, and of developing appropriate intrinsic motivations for such learning.

Ego-Enhancing Drive

A second component of achievement motivation, on the other hand, is not task-oriented at all. It may be termed *ego-enhancing* because it is concerned with achievement as a source of earned status, namely, the kind of status that a young person earns in proportion to his or her achievement or competence level. It is ego-enhancing inasmuch as the degree of achievement determining the individual's earned status simultaneously determines how adequate he or she feels (level of self-esteem), feelings of adequacy in this case always being a direct reflection of relative degree of earned status.

The ego-enhancement component of achievement motivation is therefore directed both toward the attainment of current scholastic achievement or prestige, and also toward the future academic and career goals (later sources of earned status) that depend on this achievement. One of its central ingredients, as we shall see later, is anxiety—fear in response to any anticipated threat of losing earned status and self-esteem that results from threatened failure. Approval from teachers satisfies the ego-enhancement component of achievement motivation by constituting confirmation of achievement or a source of earned status rather than (as in the case of affiliative drive) constituting confirmation of the continued derived status acquired from the superordinate person(s) with whom the learner identifies.

Ego-enhancement motivation reflects the need for the earned status achieved by one's own competence or performance ability. It becomes increasingly important beginning with school age and is the major component of achievement motivation in our culture. It need not necessarily have an ego-aggrandizing flavor. Actually, in many primitive cultures it is "group-oriented."

The emphasis that has been placed on intrinsic motivation for learning should not, however, be interpreted as a denigration of the importance of developing extrinsic motivations. The need for ego enhancement, earned status, recognition through achievement, and the internalization of long-term vocational aspirations are, after all, traditional hallmarks of personality maturation in our culture. Educational aspirations and achievement are both necessary prerequisites for, and steppingstones to, their vocational counterparts. Hence, in addition to encouraging intrinsic motivation for learning, it is also necessary, from the standpoint of personality maturation, to foster ego-enhancement and career advancement motivations for academic achievement. Furthermore, few individuals ever develop enough cognitive drive to master large bodies of subject matter as an end in itself. Long-term ego-enhancement is also necessary.

On the average, ego-enhancement motivation is undoubtedly the strongest motivation available during the active portion of an individual's academic and vocational career. More than any other factor, it accounts for the persistence of high levels of aspiration and task attractiveness both in laboratory and "real-life" settings, despite possible exposure to repeated failure experience.

Carried to an extreme, of course, this type of motivation may generate sufficient anxiety to disrupt learning. It may also lead to highly unrealistic academic and vocational aspirations that are later followed either by catastrophic failure and collapse of self-esteem or by disinvolvement from academic tasks as manifested by unrealistically low levels of aspiration. A related possibility is that excessively high needs for academic achievement may impair students' capacity for perceiving their own limitations, may predispose them to rationalize their failures, and may discourage them from acknowledging that their views are logically or empirically untenable.

Achievement motivation is not linearly related to achievement level. As is the case with potent motivational states generally, very strong achievement motivation may lower the level of performance and achievement, probably because of its frequent association with disruptive neurotic anxiety. Additionally, although individuals with unrealistically high and tenacious aspirations for earned status are undoubtedly more highly motivated to achieve superior academic and vocational success, there is no good reason to believe that their intellectual capacity or scholastic aptitude is correspondingly superior to that of more normally ambitious students.

Still another disadvantage of exaggerated ego-enhancement motivation is that its utilitarian orientation limits its longevity. Thus, students whose academic motivation is principally extrinsic tend to perceive little value in a subject after they pass a related course, or in continuing to learn after they receive their degrees—if such knowledge is unrelated either to future course work or to vocational success. In other words, they no longer evince a desire to learn when they do not have to.

Punishment (nonreward) or threat of failure, however, as expressed by "aversive motivation," has, in my opinion, been unwarrantedly denigrated by American educators and educational psychologists. Within reasonable limits, however, it exerts a demonstrably necessary influence on sustaining long-term education, particularly university and professional education, because of the all-too-human proclivity for procrastination.

One might legitimately even go a step further and assert the unfashionable view that aversive motivation—namely, the threat of those penalties associated with academic failure—is as necessary as is the positive motivation stemming from anticipated rewards for sustaining the long-term academic achievement required for reaching long-term academic and professional goals. Although educators theoretically decry the use of aversive motivation, they implicitly rely on it to keep students studying regularly for their credits, degrees, and diplomas. They do this because they know that cognitive drive and anticipated reward for hard work are not sufficient to overcome both inertia and the typical human proclivity toward procrastination and aversion to sustained, regular, and disciplined work.

Affiliative Drive

The final or *affiliative* component of achievement motivation is neither task-oriented nor primarily ego-enhancing. It is not oriented toward academic achievement as a source of earned status, but rather toward such achievement insofar as it assures them of approval by a superordinate person or group with whom the individual identifies in a dependent sense, and from whose acceptance he or she acquires vicarious or derived status. The latter kind of status is essentially determined not by the individual's own achievement level *per se* but by the continuing intrinsic acceptance by the person(s) with whom he or she identifies; and, hence, one who enjoys such derived status (i.e., a satellizer) is obviously motivated to obtain and retain the approval of this superordinate person(s)—by simply meeting the latter's standards and expectations, including those for academic achievement—since this approval tends to confirm and continue his derived status.

Affiliative drive is, thus, expressive of a pupil's need to do well in school in order to retain the approval (and the continued derived status this signifies) of the superordinate figure (parent, teacher) with whom he identifies in an emotionally dependent sense *(satellization)*. It becomes decreasingly important as the child approaches adolescence.

Varying proportions of the cognitive, ego-enhancement, and affiliative components are normally represented in achievement motivation, depending on such factors as age, sex, culture, social-class membership, ethnic origin, and personality structure. Affiliative drive is most prominent during early childhood. At this time most children largely seek and enjoy a derived status based on dependent identification with, and intrinsic acceptance by, their parents. During this period they typically strive for moderate plus academic achievement as one way of meeting their parents' expectations and, hence, of retaining the approval they desire. Actual or threatened withdrawal of approval for poor performance, therefore, motivates them to work harder to retain or regain this approval. Since teachers are largely regarded as parent surrogates by satellizing pupils, they are related to in similar fashion.

Affiliative drive is, thus, an important source of motivation for the academic achievement of many, perhaps most, children during early childhood. However, children who are not accepted and intrinsically valued by their parents, and who, therefore, cannot enjoy any derived status, are compensatorily motivated to seek an inordinate and often unrealistic degree of earned status through academic achievement. Thus, high levels of achievement motivation in such children typically represent low affiliative drive that is more than compensated for by high ego-enhancement drive.

During late childhood and adolescence, affiliative drive both diminishes in intensity and is redirected from parents toward agemates. Thus, academic competition against the opposite-sex group or other age-grade groups may constitute a powerful motivating factor. Desire for peer approval, however, may also depress academic achievement if such achievement is negatively valued by the peer group. This is a more common occurrence among lower-class and certain culturally disadvantaged minority groups. Middle-class peer groups, as pointed out later, tend to place a high value on academic achievement and expect it from their members.

In most cultures, and particularly in Western civilization, ego-enhancement drive is the dominant component of achievement motivation in adolescence and adult life. This is especially true among males and middle-class groups in our culture.

REWARD AND PUNISHMENT

Rewards influence learning in three general ways. First, by serving as incentives they help set a meaningful problem by relating a specific sequence or organization of component learning activities to a specified, successful goal outcome. Without such goal-relatedness, learning would often tend to be amorphous and undirected. Concomitantly, by providing significant information about the success or failure of responses, rewards provide selective emphasis at critical choice points to desired or correct meanings, thereby facilitating discrimination between relevant and irrelevant cues.

Second, the actual receipt of rewards tends to augment, on a long-term basis, whatever motivations (drives) are originally operative in energizing and directing behavior toward them (the rewards). By satisfying certain needs and drives at any given time, rewards strengthen, on a more permanent basis, those drives that they satisfy at the moment (or temporarily "reduce").

Finally, rewards may increase the relative probability of response recurrence by selectively "sensitizing" to later lowering the thresholds of elicitation of the particular learnings that lead to obtaining the reward and thereby satisfy (or temporarily reduce) the drive in question. This last property of rewards will be considered in greater detail in the discussion of reinforcement in the next section, where the position will be taken that reinforcement occurs only in relation to rotely learned associations and instrumental responses and does not characterize meaningful learning outcomes.

Punishment (in the sense of nonreward or failure to obtain the reward) acts as the reverse of reward in the following ways. First, it also helps structure a problem meaningfully, furnishing direction to activity—and information about progress toward the goal—in terms also of what is to be avoided. Thus, the unsatisfying consequences of an act tend to elicit avoidance, withdrawal, or variation rather than repetition. The individual learns which responses lead to nonreward and, hence, should be avoided. Second, punishment tends to weaken, on a long-term basis, the motivations energizing the behavior that is punished. Finally, punishment may decrease the relative probability of response recurrence, by failing to sensitize to later lowering the thresholds of elicitation of the particular responses that lead to nonreward.

In any case it should be appreciated that the informational aspect of nonreward is less explicit than that of reward. Although it does aid discrimination between correct and incorrect cues through the information it does give as to the consequences of an act, it is less directive and provides less guidance than does reward. It tells the learner only that something else must be done, but does not tell him *what* to do. Reward, on the other hand, clearly indicates that the same response is to be repeated. In this context also, "punishment" simply implies nonreceipt of the stipulated reward because of failure to acquire and retain knowledge derived from presented learning material. In the more usual sense of the term, however, it also involves the introduction of a more active, hurtful, noxious, fearful or anxious, and painful *additional* state of affairs than the mere withholding of the reward that is given to those learners who complete the meaningful learning task or course of studies successfully.

In school and academic learning settings we commonly deal with nonthreatening nonrewards rather than with "true punishment" situations. Nevertheless, to students with appreciable degrees of affiliative and/or ego-enhancing drive who fail to learn and retain their lessons, the aforementioned examples of "true punishment" are inevitably superimposed upon the more typically innocuous nonreward situation. This is the case because failure invariably poses the threat of disapproval in the case of the child who is driven mostly by affiliative drive as well as by the corresponding threat of the loss of current and future self-esteem (and of the related earned status) in the case of the child/adolescent who is primarily motivated by ego-enhancing drives.

Reward and punishment are positive and negative sides of the same motivational coin in school learning. Both are typically involved, in varying degrees, in motivating such learning. It is admittedly more enlightened from the standpoint of mental hygiene for the school to focus on reward rather than on punishment and to minimize rather than emphasize explicit possibilities and threats of failure. On the other hand, it is both unrealistic to deny the existence and effectiveness of punishment as a motivational variable in school learning and unwarranted to deplore it as either immoral or as pedagogically unsound.

We have concluded above that effective extrinsic (nontask-oriented) motivation implies both reward and punishment. Nevertheless the positive role of punishment (as nonreward) in facilitating meaningful learning and retention in school and school-like settings has either been denied or distorted so as to appear outmoded, reactionary, authoritarian, or downright diabolical. Where do these distortions possibly come from that impinge on this issue in terms of relevant cultural ideology?

First, it had been gratuitously assumed that appropriate motivations for learning in school from a mental health standpoint axiomatically had to be either intrinsic in nature (i.e., cognitive drive) or else reflective exclusively of *positive* incentives (e.g., reward).

Second, critics of punishment failed to distinguish between the highly restricted kind of punishment (i.e., nonreward advocated for school learning failure), on the one hand, and its more general meaning in the culture as moral censure or chastisement for unethical or unlawful conduct, and accordingly assumed gratuitously that the second more general meaning was typically intended. The advocates of the nonreward type of punishment, however, not only favored just the first of the two latter forms of punishment, but also not for genuine limitations in learning capacity or attainment but rather for irresponsibility, laziness, culpable neglect of studies, and blatant lack of effort.

Third, these critics similarly failed to appreciate that the real objective of using the punishment of nonreward in the classroom was not *actually* to inflict it on those students who failed but rather to *prevent* such failure in the first place through the effect of the anticipated *threat* of failure (in overcoming laziness, procrastina-tion, etc.).

Caution is obviously indicated in the application of aversive motivation. Used excessively, it may generate a level of anxiety out of all proportion to the actual risk of failure involved in a particular learning task. This may not only disrupt learning but also generalize to other areas. It could induce a negative self-concept (an "emotional block") about entire fields of knowledge, such as mathematics. It could also lead either to ego disinvolvement from a task or to unrealistically high levels of aspiration. The solution, however, is not to outlaw aversive motivation, but to keep it within reasonable bounds, to balance it with cognitive and positive ego-enhancement drives, to make learning more successful for most pupils, and to provide particularly anxious children with counseling.

Drive Reduction and Reinforcement

Although a theoretical possibility exists that the effects of drive reduction could be mediated retroactively through their influence on the thresholds of availability of meaningful learning outcomes—just as in the case of rotely learned items—there is no comparable evidence suggesting that motivational factors can directly *lower* thresholds of availability of meaningfully learned items. Apparently thresholds of availability, in relation to dissociability strength, differ in this crucial respect from corresponding thresholds of availability in relation to associative strength. This is the case in meaningful learning because no mechanisms seem to exist through which the satisfying effects of reducing the cognitive, affiliative, and ego-enhancing components of achievement motivation can reinforce successful (drive-reducing) learning outcomes.

Unlike the *informational* (cognitive) consequences of feedback (confirmation, correction, and enhanced dissociability strength of *previously learned* meanings), the *affectively* satisfying effects of drive reduction are not *intrinsically* related to the factors determining dissociability strength. Hence, they cannot increase it retroactively; they can increase it only *indirectly during* the course of learning by nonspecifically and catalytically enhancing learning outcomes themselves.

This does not mean, however, that reward and punishment do not also facilitate meaningful learning in other ways. Reinforcement, after all, is only one consequence of reward—the aspect that directly increases the elicitability of *rotely* learned responses by sensitizing their thresholds of availability to later lowering when drive states are operative. In the case of meaningful learning, however, reward and punishment have two other more indirect kinds of facilitating effects. In the first place, from a motivational standpoint, awareness of successful learning (satisfaction of cognitive, affiliative, and ego-enhancing drives for acquiring new knowledge) energizes subsequent learning efforts by enhancing learners' self-confidence, by encouraging them to persevere, and by increasing the subjective attractiveness of the learning task. At the same time it motivates individuals to make further use of, that is, to practice, rehearse, and perform what they have already learned. It also encourages them to continue developing and exercising the motives that were satisfied or rewarded, namely, the desire for knowledge both as an end in itself and as a means of enhancing status and self-esteem.

The experience and threat of punishment (nonreward for failure to learn successfully), on the other hand, generate considerable aversive motivation. The learner is, thus, generally motivated to avoid learning failure by paying attention, by displaying suitable effort and perseverance, by delaying the gratification of hedonistic needs, and so forth. In addition, when the learner is informed that a particular, previously learned understanding is incorrect, the threatening implications of this report motivate him or her, to some extent, to avoid or reject it, thereby presumably raising its threshold of availability.

These facilitating effects of aversive motivation undoubtedly more than counterbalance the negative impact of failure experience on the long-term strength of the underlying motivation and on task attractiveness. However, when experience of failure predominates, or when aversive motivation is unsuccessful in averting failure, this is obviously not the case.

Second, reward (awareness of successful learning outcomes) and punishment (awareness of unsuccessful learning outcomes), whether in relation to the intrinsic or extrinsic components of achievement motivation, also have all of the cognitive or *informational* effects of feedback. These latter effects are probably just as important for meaningful learning and retention as are the motivational effects of reward and punishment. By confirming correctly understood meanings and, at the same time, indicating areas of confusion, correcting errors, and clarifying ambiguities and misconceptions, the cognitive aspects of feedback increase the stability, clarity, and discriminability of meaningfully learned ideas (and, thus, enhance their dissociability strength). They also increase the subject's confidence in the correctness of what he understood, and enable him to focus learning efforts selectively on inadequately learned portions of the material. They not only have informational value for subsequent trials of the same learning task, but also have *transfer value* for related new tasks.

NOTES

[1]Most of the material on practice its mediation, effects, and varieties in this chapter has been adapted from D. P. Ausubel, *Educational psychology: A cognitive view* (New York: Holt, Rinehart and Winston, 1968).

[2]Most of the material on the possible necessity of motivation for meaningful learning and retention, on the mediation of motivational factors, on the different kinds of achievement motivation, on reward and punishment, etc., is adapted from D. P. Ausubel, *Educational psychology: A cognitive view* (New York: Holt, Rinehart and Wiston, 1968).

REFERENCES

Ash, P. The relative effectiveness of massed versus spaced film presentations. *Journal of Educational Psychology*, 1950, *41*, 19–30.

Ashcroft, M. H. *Human memory and cognition*. New York: Harper Collins, 1994.

Ausubel, D. P. Early versus delayed review in meaningful learning, *Psychology in the Schools*, 1966, *3*, 195–198.

Ausubel, D. P. *Educational psychology: A cognitive view*. New York: Holt, Rinehart, & Winston, 1968.

Ausubel, D. P. *Ego development and the personality disorders*. New York: Grune & Stratton, 1952.

Ausubel, D. P., & Youssef, M. The effect of consolidation on sequentially related, sequentially independent meaningful learning. *Journal of General Psychology*, 1966, *74*, 355–360.

Briggs, L. J. Prompting and confirmation conditions for the learning tasks employing the subject matter terms. In A. A. Lumsdaine (Ed.), *Student response in programmed instruction*. Washington, D.C.: National Academy of Science—National Research Council, 1961.

Broadbent, D. E. *Perception and communication*. London: Pergamon Press, 1958.

Bumstead, A. P. Distribution of effort in memorizing prose and poetry. *American Journal of Psychology*, 1940, *77*, 669–671.

Gagné, R. M. Military training and principles of learning. *American Psychologist*, 1962, *17*, 83–91.

Harlow, H. E. The formation of learning sets. *Psychological Review*, 1949, *56*, 51–65.

Hershberger, W. Self-evaluational responding and typographical cueing. Techniques for programming self-instructional reading materials. *Journal of Educational Psychology*, 1964, *55*, 288–296.

Hirt, E. R., McDonald, H. E., & Erikson, G. A. How do I remember thee? The role of encoding, set, and delay in reconstructive memory processes. *Journal of Experimental Social Psychology*, 1995, *31*, 379–409.

Kurtz, K. H., & Hovland, C. I. Concept learning with differing sequences of instances. *Journal of Experimental Psychology*, 1956, *4*, 239–243.

Peterson, H. A., et al. Some measurements of the effects of reviews. *Journal of Educational Psychology*, 1935, *26*, 65–72.

Peterson, H. R. Recitation or recall as a factor in the learning of long prose selections. *Journal of Educational Psychology*, 1944, *35*, 220–228.

Sones, A. M., & Stroud, A. B. Review with special reference to temporal position. *Journal of Educational Psychology*, 1940, *31*, 665–676.

Thorndike, E. L. *Human learning*. New York: Century, 1931.

Thorndike, E. L. *The fundamentals of learning*. New York: Teachers College, Columbia University, 1932.

Printed in the United Kingdom
by Lightning Source UK Ltd.
101832UKS00001BC/2

9 780792 365051